Accession n
00939785

KU-302-681

INFORMATION SYSTEMS RESEARCH

...rsity of

CAN

CANCEL

INFORMATION SYSTEMS SERIES

Consulting Editors

D.E. AVISON
BA, MSc, FBCS
*Department of Accounting and
Management Sciences, Southampton University,
Southampton, UK*

G. FITZGERALD
BA, MSc, MBCS
*Oxford Institute of Information Management
Templeton College, Oxford, UK*

This is a brand new series of student texts covering a wide variety of topics relating to information systems. It is designed to fulfil the needs of the growing number of courses on, and interest in, computing and information systems which do not focus purely on the technological aspects, but seek to relate these to business or organizational context.

INFORMATION SYSTEMS SERIES

INFORMATION SYSTEMS RESEARCH

Issues, Methods and Practical Guidelines

Edited by

ROBERT GALLIERS

Warwick Business School,
University of Warwick

CHESTER COLLEGE

ACC. No. 00939785   DEPT.

CLASS No. 004.072 GAL

LIBRARY

ALFRED WALLER LTD

HENLEY-ON-THAMES

This collection © by R.D. Galliers 1992
   Introductions for Parts 1, 2 and 3
   © R.D. Galliers 1992; Chapter 1
   ©F.F. Land 1992; Chapter 2 © R.I.
   Tricker 1990; Chapter 3 © Elsevier
   Science Publishers B. V. 1985; Chapter 4
   © Association for Computing
   Machinery Inc. 1989; Chapter 5 © A.F.
   Farhoomand 1987; Chapter 6
   © Elsevier Science Publishers B. V.
   1991; Chapter 7 © Elsevier Science
   Publishers B. V. 1982; Chapter 8
   © Elsevier Science Publishers B. V.
   1991; Chapter 9 © Sage Publications
   Inc. 1987; Chapter 10 © Sage
   Publications 1987; Chapter 11 © G.P.
   Pervan & D.J. Klass 1992; Chapter 12
   © G.B. Davies 1987

Published by
Alfred Waller Ltd, Publishers
Orchards, Fawley, Henley-on-Thames,
   Oxfordshire RG9 6JF

All rights reserved. No part of this
   publication may be reproduced, stored
   in a retrieval system, or transmitted, in
   any form or by any means, electronic,
   mechanical, photocopying, recording
   or otherwise without the prior
   permission of the publisher.

This collection first published 1992
Reprinted 1994
Set by Best-set Typesetter Ltd.,
   Hong Kong
Printed and bound in Great Britain by
Antony Rowe Ltd, Chippenham,
   Wiltshire

British Library
Cataloguing in Publication Data
Information Systems Research: Issues,
Methods and Practical Guidelines. –
(Information Systems Series)
   I. Galliers, Robert   II. Series
   658.4038

ISBN 1-872474-39-X

Library of Congress
Cataloging in Publication Data
Information systems research: issues,
   methods, and practical guidelines/edited
   by Robert Galliers.
        p.   cm. – (Information systems
series)
   Includes bibliographical references
(p. 251–65) and index.
   1. Management information systems –
Research.   I. Galliers, Robert,
1947–   .   II. Series: Information
systems series (Oxford, England)
T58.6.1515   1992   91-47639
658.4'038'01 107 2 – dc20   CIP

For Claire, Victoria, Nick and Andrew

'Seek after knowledge –
it's your future.'

Contents

Preface

There has been a veritable explosion in the amount of research being undertaken in the field of information systems over the past decade or so. From an off-shoot of computer science, or a somewhat abberant and certainly peripheral element of business and management topics, or of aspects of the social sciences generally, we now have a subject which has grown considerably in importance. We only have to note the number of new journals on the topic to see that this is so. In the last year alone, we have seen the emergence of, for example, *The European Journal of Information Systems*, *The Journal of Information Systems*, *International Information Systems*, and *The Journal of Strategic Information Systems*, to name just four.

More specifically, interest in information systems research has been growing rapidly too. For example, a number of conferences have been held on the specific topic in recent years. The first IFIP WG 8.2 colloquium on the topic was held in 1984 and attracted about 50 participants. The second, in 1990, attracted about four times that number. Similar colloquia have been held in the USA (e.g., at Harvard Business School in 1984 and again in 1989) and elsewhere (e.g., at the National University of Singapore in 1987). Information systems research courses are now given as required elements of postgraduate information systems programmes for example at Curtin University, Western Australia (Galliers 1987a), at the State University of New York and at Hong Kong Polytechnic. In addition the journal *Information Systems Research* was published for the first time in 1990.

Interestingly, though, while interest in the subject of information systems research has been growing rapidly, and while increasing numbers of papers on the topic have been produced, there have only been a very few books in the area published thus far. And while these have made very useful contributions to the subject, they have tended to deal with aspects of the topic only. For example, they have either tended to focus on the Information Systems *issues* (e.g., Boland & Hirschheim 1987) or on appropriate *methods* (e.g., Nissen *et al.* 1991).

Additionally, while there are a number of texts providing very useful, practical advice on undertaking research generally (e.g., Phillips & Pugh 1987) or more specifically in the field of management (e.g., Easterby-Smith *et al.* 1991), nothing of the sort appears to exist for the field of information systems research. And certainly none attempts to combine issues, methods *and* practical guidelines – until now!

This book has been designed to bring together in a single volume, key papers on these aspects of the subject of information systems research. In addition, it begins with a discussion on the subject of information systems itself, arguing that we should be focussing our attention on the ends rather than the means. By this, I mean that our focus has for too long been on technological issues at the expense of what it is we are trying to achieve through the development of information systems. The integration of information systems into the value adding processes of the business, and getting value for money from information technology, are both very much dependent on us taking a much closer look at what is meaningful and informative in the context of our role in organizations and in society generally (*cf.* Galliers 1987b).

The book is divided into three parts. As implied above, Part 1 concerns itself with the subject of information systems. This provides a sound basis for the consideration – in Part 2 – of not only the key information systems topics that require our research attention but also the range of research approaches that appear to provide us with opportunities to produce useful and usable results. Part 2 ends with a consideration of a means by which appropriate choices of research methods can be made in the context of the particular issue being studied.

This leads us neatly into Part 3 which contains some useful practical advice to assist those undertaking information systems research, perhaps for the first time. Topics covered include the development of research proposals and the dos and don'ts of using statistical methods in this field. A list of other useful texts in this field has also been included.

This book is clearly of relevance to all those who are about to embark on information systems research, whether this is to be their first attempt or an on-going activity. Indeed, if we view information systems practice from a professional stance, on-going assessment and review of practice could well be improved as a result of a consideration of the topics contained herein.

While this book is, then, clearly primarily aimed at the information systems research community, it is designed to be read by information systems professionals and aspiring professionals – academics, practitioners and students alike. It will be of considerable use to students embarking on a research project, or even a piece of practical work, and to academics who supervise research projects and research students and who may be in charge of an information systems research course. It will hopefully also provide food for thought for those information systems practitioners who see the need to reflect on their chosen field of employment.

It is also hoped that the book will make a contribution to the wider fields of social science and management/business research generally. For example, the discussion on the limitations of positivism in social scientific inquiry and the sound, practical advice given on, for example, the writing of research proposals and the appropriate use of statistical techniques, contained in Part 3 in particular, is of relevance to those researching in fields quite apart from information systems.

Bob Galliers
University of Warwick
July 1991

Acknowledgements

There are many people I wish to thank for helping in the production of this book. First and foremost I wish to acknowledge the contribution of the authors whose papers make up the volume. These and others who have written on aspects of the subject of information systems research – and social scientific research generally – I acknowledge most warmly.

Significant contributions to my thinking on the topic – and, hence, to the development of this book – have also been made by colleagues and students with whom I have had discussions over the years, most particularly as part of information systems research seminars. These have taken place most significantly here at Warwick, but also at Curtin University in Australia, at the London School of Economics and the University of Salford in England, and at Hong Kong Polytechnic. To all who have contributed, thank you!

I must also mention the tremendous help I have received in putting this book together, most particularly from Francesca Coles, Carol Beacham, Cathi Maryon and Zoë Grimsdale of Warwick Business School, and Ian Drummond and the 'data prep' staff of the University of Warwick Computing Services Centre. Without their help, it would not have been possible.

Both the publishers and I wish also to thank the following for giving us their permission to reprint their papers:

Land F.F. (1992) *The Information Systems Domain*. Unpublished manuscript commissioned for this volume and developed from a London School of Economics student note. Reprinted with permission of the author (*Chapter 1*).

Tricker R.I. (1990) The Management of Organisational Knowledge. *Proceedings: The Impact of Information Technology on Systems Management*. 1990 Conference on Systems Management in Hong Kong. Reprinted with permission of the author (*Chapter 2*).

Hirschheim R.A. (1985) Information Systems Epistemology: An Historical Perspective. In *Research Methods in Information Systems*, (Ed. by E. Mumford *et al.*). Proceedings of the IFIP WG 8.2 Colloquium, Manchester Business School, 1–3 September, 1984. North-Holland, Amsterdam, pp. 13–36 Reprinted with permission (*Chapter 3*).

Banville C. & Landry M. (1989) Can the Field of MIS be Disciplined? *Communications of the ACM*, **32**(1), pp. 48–60. Copyright 1989, Association of Computing Machinery, Inc. Reprinted with permission (*Chapter 4*).

Farhoomand A.F. (1987) Scientific Progress of Management Information Systems. *Data Base*, **18**(3) pp. 48–56. Reprinted with permission of the author (*Chapter 5*).

Watson R.T. & Brancheau J.C. (1991) Key Issues in Information Systems Management: An International Perspective. *Information & Management*, **20**, pp. 213–33 Copyright Elsevier Science Publishers B.V. (North-Holland), reprinted with permission (*Chapter 6*).

Hamilton S. & Ives B. (1982) MIS Research Strategies. *Information & Management*, **5**, pp. 339–47. Copyright Elsevier Science Publishers B.V. (North-Holland), reprinted with permission (*Chapter 7*).

Galliers R.D. (1991) Choosing Appropriate Information Systems Research Methods. In *Information Systems Research: Contemporary Approaches & Emergent Traditions* (Ed. by H-E Nissen et al.). Proceedings of the IFIP TC8/WG 8.2 Working Conference, Copenhagen, Denmark, 14–16 December, 1990. North-Holland, Amsterdam, pp. 327–45. Reprinted with permission (*Chapter 8*).

Locke L.F., Spirduso W.W. & Silverman S.J. 1987. Research Proposals: Function and Content. Taken from Chapter 1 of *Proposals that Work: A Guide for Planning Dissertations and Grant Proposals*, Sage Publications, Newbury Park, California. Copyright 1987, Sage Publications Inc. Reprinted by permission of Sage Publications Inc. (*Chapter 9*).

Locke L.F., Spirduso W.W. & Silverman S.J. (1987) Developing Proposals: Some Common Problems. Taken from Chapters 2, 3 & 5 and Appendix A of *Proposals that Work: A Guide for Planning Dissertations and Grant Proposals*. Sage Publications, Newbury Park, California. Copyright 1987, Sage Publications Inc. Reprinted by permission of Sage Publications Inc. (*Chapter 10*).

Pervan G.P. & Klass D.J. (1991) The Use and Misuse of Statistical Methods in Information Systems Research. Unpublished manuscript commissioned for this volume. Reprinted with permission of the authors (*Chapter 11*).

Davis G.B. (1987) An Individual and Group Strategy for Research in Information Systems. *Proceedings of the Seminar on Current Trends in MIS Research.* Department of Information Systems and Computer Science Technical Report No. TRA8/87, National University of Singapore, pp. 1–19. Reprinted with permission of the author (*Chapter 12*).

Bob Galliers
Warwick Business School
July 1991

Authors' biographies

Claude Banville is Associate Professor at the Université du Québec en Abitibi-Témiscamingue. He is currently teaching in computer science applied to the business administration programme. His research is mainly concerned with the social dimension of MIS, especially with regard to MIS transfers between organizations.

James C. Brancheau is Assistant Professor of Information Systems at the University of Colorado in Boulder. He holds a PhD in MIS from the University of Minnesota and has many years of experience in the information systems field. He has held a wide range of technical, managerial and consultative positions and has published in leading information systems journals such as *MIS Quarterly*, *Information Systems Research* and *Data Base*. Dr Brancheau is currently conducting research on the management of information systems and the diffusion of emerging information technologies.

Gordon B. Davis holds the Honeywell Chair in Management Information Systems, and endowed professorship in the Carlson School of Management at the University of Minnesota. He is a pioneer in management information systems research and education and the author of fifteen texts and numerous articles on management information systems. His book *Management Information Systems: Conceptual Foundations, Structure and Development* has been ranked a classic in the field. He is chairman of Technical Committee 8 (Information Systems) of the International Federation for Information Processing. He has lectured in 25 countries and held visiting faculty appointments in both Europe and Asia.

As part of an involvement in career development for scholars, he is coordinator of the doctoral programme in information and decision sciences at the University of Minnesota and has provided career guidance to a large number of scholars-in-process. He has written a book on managing the doctoral dissertation process *Writing the*

Doctoral Dissertation: A Systematic Approach (1979, with C. Parker). One of his current research interests is management of knowledge work (including effective use of information technology) for improved personal productivity.

Ali F. Farhoomand is Assistant Professor of Decision Sciences and MIS at Concordia University, Canada. His current research interests include information technology and strategic use of information systems.

Bob Galliers is Lucas Professor of Business Systems Engineering at Warwick University Business School. He is Director of Warwick's award-winning master's programme in Business Management Systems, which is designed to broaden business and management awareness among up-and-coming IS/IT professionals, and Associate Chair of the Business School. He was previously Foundation Professor and Head of the School of Information Systems at Curtin University, Perth, Western Australia, where he developed Australia's first master's programme to emphasize the management issues associated with the introduction and utilisation of IT in the organization.

Professor Galliers obtained a bachelor's degree majoring in economics at Harvard University, a master's degree with distinction in Systems at Lancaster University, and a PhD in Information Systems at the London School of Economics, based on his research into information systems planning practice in Britain and Australia. He has consulted in strategic business and information systems planning and in executive information requirements determination on behalf of multi-national corporations and public sector organizations both in Britain and Australia, and has given invited presentations on these topics in many other countries.

He is the author of many books, papers and articles on these topics and on information systems management issues generally. Bob Galliers is editor-in-chief of the *Journal of Strategic Information Systems* and a member of the editorial boards of a number of leading information systems journals.

Scott Hamilton is a senior project manager at COMSERV Corporation, producer of information systems for the manufacturing industry. He was previously an MIS manager and information analyst, and most recently was an instructor at the University of Minnesota's School of Management while completing his PhD in MIS. Scott received a BS in industrial engineering from the University of Wisconsin, and an MBA from Arizona State University. He has published articles in several journals, including the *MIS Quarterly* and *Management Science*, and his research interests include MIS planning and control, system design and implementation, and manufacturing information systems.

Rudy Hirschheim is currently Director of the Information Systems Research Center and Associate Professor of Information Systems in the College of Business Administration at the University of Houston. He has previously been on the faculties of Templeton College, Oxford, and the London School of Economics. He has also worked as a Senior Consultant with the National Computing Centre in Manchester. He holds a BA in Economics from the State University of New York at Buffalo, an MSc in Computer Science and Diploma in Management Studies from the University of Toronto, and a PhD in Information Systems from the University of London. He is the author of a large number of books and papers, particularly in the areas of office automation and information systems research and, with Richard Boland, Consulting Editor of the John Wiley Series in information systems. He also serves on the editorial boards of a number of leading information systems journals.

Blake Ives is an Assistant Professor in the Program in Computer and Information Science at Dartmouth College. He has also served on the faculty at the State University of New York at Binghamton. He received his PhD from the University of Minnesota and holds an MS in computer science from the State University of New York at Albany. His current interests include knowledge utilization, the design of graphic user interfaces, and the management of the computing resource.

Desmond J. Klass is a Senior Lecturer in the School of Information Systems at Curtin University of Technology and Director of the Strategic Planning and Decisions Unit within the Division of Business and Administration which houses the only research and commercial facility for group decision support systems in Australia. His teaching responsibilities are mainly in multivariate statistical analysis and in decision support. His principal area of research is in the support of small group decision making.

Frank Land BSc (Econ) London was, until his recent retirement, Professor of Information Management at the London Business School. He has now returned to the London School of Economics as Visiting Professor. He spent 16 years in the computing industry before taking up an academic career. His research interests include the study of factors leading to successful information systems and the development of appropriate methodologies. He was recently specialist adviser to the Parliamentary Select Committee on Trade and Industry examining UK Information Technology.

Maurice Landry is Professor at the Faculté des Sciences de l'Administration, Université Laval, Ste-Foy, Québec, Canada. He is currently teaching on the MIS programme. His research is mainly concerned with problem construction and problem solving in organizations, especially with regard to MIS development processes.

Larry Locke is Professor and Chairperson of the Department of Professional Preparation in the Schools of Education and Physical Education at the University of Massachusetts. He teaches graduate seminars in retrieval and review of research, research on teaching, and research on teacher development. His most recent publications are concerned with the application of the qualitative paradigm for inquiry into studies in teacher education and physical education.

A graduate of Springfield College (BS and MEd) and Stanford University (PhD), he has served as a teacher and programme administrator at school, college and university levels. The text *Proposals that Work*, from which his chapter is an excerpt, was the product of his experience and that of his coauthors with masters and doctoral students engaged in the preparation of proposals for their theses and dissertations.

Associate Professor **Graham P. Pervan** is the Head of the School of Information Systems at Curtin University of Technology and national Vice President (Education and Courses) of the Australian Society for Operations Research. He teaches research methods to postgraduate and honours students in information systems and computer science and has previously taught many courses in statistics, management science and information systems to undergraduates and post-graduates in the Division of Business Administration at Curtin. He is the author of the book *Quantitative Methods for Business Students* and has published some thirty papers in journals, books and conference proceedings. His research interest areas include group decision support systems (GDSS), executive information systems (EIS) and key issues for information systems managers.

Stephen J. Silverman is Assistant Professor in the Department of Physical and Health Education at the University of Texas at Austin. He is a native of Philadelphia, and holds a bachelor's degree from Temple University, a master's degree from Washington State University and a doctoral degree from the University of Massachusetts at Amherst. Professor Silverman's research focusses on teaching and learning in physical education. He currently teaches classes in research methods and statistics.

Waneen Wyrick Spirduso is Ashbel Smith Professor and Interim Dean of the College of Education at the University of Texas at Austin. She is a native of Austin, and holds bachelor's and doctoral degrees from the University of Texas and a master's degree from the University of North Carolina at Greensboro. Professor Spriduso's research focusses on the effects of ageing on the mechanisms of motor control. She has directed students in the proposal process for over two decades and has received numerous research grants from the federal government.

After study at Oxford and Harvard, Dr **R.I. (Bob) Tricker** became the first Professor of Information Systems in Britain, in 1967 at Warwick University. He subsequently directed the Oxford Management Centre (now Templeton College, Oxford University) throughout the 1970s and founded the Corporate Policy Group, at Nuffield College, Oxford, to study board level direction of companies. Currently Professor of Finance and Accounting at the University of Hong Kong Business School, his research interests are in the fields of corporate strategy and governance and the nature of information in the organizational context. He is on the Editorial Boards of *Information and Management*, *The Managerial Auditing Journal*, *The Journal of Accounting and Public Policy*, *The Pacific Accounting Review*, *The Journal of Strategic Information Systems* and *Accounting, Manage-*

ment and Information Technologies. His publications include *Effective Information Management* (1982 and 1986) and *Management Information and Control Systems* (with R. Boland) (1976 and 1982).

Richard Watson is an Assistant Professor in the Department of Management at the University of Georgia. He studied mathematics and computing at the University of Western Australia where he completed a BSc and Graduate Diploma in Computation. He undertook a Masters of Administration at Monash University in Melbourne, Australia. His PhD in Management Information Systems was awarded by the University of Minnesota. Dr Watson joined the faculty of the University of Georgia in 1989. His current research interests are group decision support systems, executive information systems and information systems management.

Part 1

The Nature of Information Systems

Introduction

Before embarking on our journey into the realms of information systems research, it is as well to pause for a little while and reflect on the very nature of our chosen field of study.

Information systems are a complex topic. The various contributors to Part 1 of this book remind us that it is multi-disciplinary and very much a social, rather than a wholly technical, science (though not a particularly exact science it has to be said!). Foundations for the study of information systems – what Peter Keen (1980), among others, terms 'reference disciplines' – can be found in philosophy and in the organizational and behavioural sciences, as well as in mathematics and the natural sciences, for example.

The importance of Part 1 of this book cannot be overstated. When undertaking information systems research, it is important – and often very useful – to draw on these reference disciplines and to place one's particular research topic in this broader context. In addition, the very nature of information systems has a profound impact on what constitutes appropriate research and what approaches might reasonably be adopted in undertaking this research. This scene-setting section of the book provides much food for thought in relation to both of these considerations.

A key feature of Chapter 1 – by Frank Land – is the point that information systems make sense only in the context of the purpose to which they are being put. This requires us to explore the organizational and societal contexts on the one hand, and the individual context on the other. For example, the organizational structure and culture may well have a considerable impact on the need for a particular information system, while the extent of knowledge of the person using the system, and their particular preferences – in terms of the mode of delivery of information, for example – should all have a considerable impact on the manner in which the system (computerized or otherwise) is designed.

Bob Tricker takes up this theme in Chapter 2, in which he develops the idea that perhaps too much effort in the field of information systems research and practice has been focussed on the means rather than the end. Arguing for much more attention to be paid to what it is we are hoping to achieve through information systems – a more knowledgable organization, that is – he provides a useful summary of the alternative models and paradigms that have been introduced and used in the information systems field over recent years. Not only should the arguments contained in Chapter 2 prove useful for those undertaking information systems research, but the seminal literature he cites will also provide a rich source of material and, certainly, much food for thought.

In addition, there are many useful references to be found in Rudy Hirschheim's paper which forms Chapter 3. More importantly, however, Chapter 3 builds on the arguments provided in Chapters 1 and 2 by overtly moving our focus on to what constitutes valid research in the field of information systems.

Taking an historical perspective, Hirschheim argues for a shift in the research paradigm of information systems towards a 'post-positivist' stance. This would mean doing away with the model of research associated with the physical sciences as the sole acceptable approach to information systems research. He argues that the positivist stance, that knowledge is apodeictic, needs to be replaced by one which is concerned more with belief about knowledge. In other words, research (particularly in a field such as information systems) that produces conclusions that are accepted by the research community as an improvement on our previous level of understanding, (whether these conclusions are incontrovertible or not) is not only acceptable but preferred in our context.

In addition, he raises the issue of methodological pluralism as a necessary outcome of post-positivism. What this means is that in our information systems research we should not assume that there is just one correct research method, but many possible alternatives – a point argued by Kuhn (1970) in relation to the social sciences generally, and taken up in the context of choosing appropriate information systems research methods in Chapter 8.

Part 1 closes with Chapter 4 – by Claude Banville and Maurice Landry. In it, they reinforce Hirschheim's last point, that information systems (MIS to use their term), is a fragmented, essentially pluralistic, field, arguing that it can best be studied and understood by the use of pluralistic models. They question the applicability of Kuhn's (1970) monistic model of scientific development to the field of MIS, given its fragmentary nature. Applying Whitley's (1984a) pluralistic model, they analyse the characteristics of MIS as a discipline with a view to obtaining a better understanding of the ways and means of developing the field still further.

Part 1 concludes with their argument concerning maturation and progress in any scientific field, but particularly with regard to information systems. To paraphrase, maturation is not simply a process towards a conceptually integrated and bureaucratic discipline that represents Kuhn's 'normal science'. And progress not only occurs through the *cumulation* of research knowledge, but also through the *challenging* of that knowledge. We should certainly bear this final thought in mind when considering our continuing research efforts in information systems and our attempts at making progress in this fascinating and challenging field of study.

Chapter 1

The Information Systems Domain

London Business School

Information systems need to be considered not just as artifacts but from the perspective of the people who may wish to use those artifacts to support their activities and decisions in a more informed manner. This chapter builds on this notion to produce a model of an information system that includes the information user and informal sources of data in addition to such formal sources as computer-based information systems. It argues that information systems are essentially social systems of which information technology is but one aspect. It concludes with a warning that information systems designers need to take account of the changing needs of users and that the study of information systems is a multi-disciplinary endeavour.

Researchers in the field of information systems must take account of these issues if the outcome of their research is to have relevance in the real world.

All organizations need information systems in order to function effectively. Every information system – from that which assists the owner of a one-person business or the parish council of a small village, to that which helps a multinational corporation, or supports the administrative offices of a large industrial nation – is made up of a number of components. Some of the components are artifacts: pencil and paper, word processors, computers and communication networks, operating systems and procedure manuals. But all information systems require people to construct, work with, and operate such artifacts. Even a completely automated information system (if it were possible to construct such a thing, as in a fully automated workshop), would still require people to provide back-up and for trouble shooting. In practice, then, information systems rely on people using and interacting with these artifacts.

Any information system can be thought of as comprising an infrastructure and the systems which make use of that infrastructure. The infrastructure consists of a variety of artifacts which include:

- the organizational structure;
- communication channels, ranging from conventional telephone lines and postal services to electronic networks, mobile telephones and faxes;
- facilities such as telephone exchanges and file servers which enable other components of the infrastructure to function;
- apparatus, ranging from office furniture to devices such as mainframe computers, PCs and laser scanners in supermarket checkouts;
- software tools, including spreadsheet systems, compilers, graphics packages and database management systems;
- training, advisory and help facilities provided to support the information systems activities of the user community.

In the past, the requirement to do a particular job led to the introduction of the required infrastructure. Typically the requirement to build a specific system, say an inventory control system, resulted in the acquisition of the necessary infrastructure – communication channels, hardware and software. The trend today is towards the increased use of general purpose enabling infrastructures. The provision of a PC on the desk of a manager is part of an information infrastructure rather than a tool provided to do a specific task.

Information systems vary enormously in the extent to which they rely on formalized, standardized, structured information handling techniques as against informal, often *ad hoc* and subjective techniques (Land & Kennedy-McGregor 1987). All organizations utilize some elements of both types of techniques. But designers of information systems have tended, at best, to ignore or disregard the informal system, and at worst, to try to replace it with the formal system.

Modern information technology, with its apparent need to design to an unambiguous and fixed specification (Horne 1991), has exacerbated the problem, thereby establishing a kind of conflict between the formal and informal systems. More recent technological developments are beginning to restore the balance. Technological infrastructure such as spreadsheets, PCs and electronic mail are providing facilities which can be used in the informal undesigned information system.

A model of an information system (Fig. 1.1) illustrates the relation-

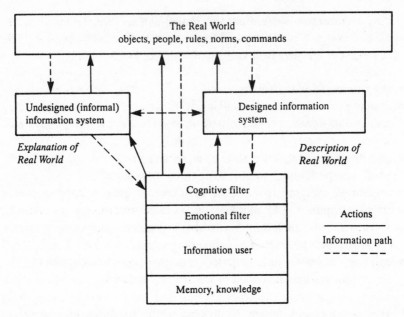

Fig. 1.1 Model of an information system.

ship between the different components of an information system and the formal and informal aspects (Land & Kennedy-McGregor 1987).

Information systems exist in a real world which consists of objects (some concrete, such as machines, stock and buildings; some abstract, such as budgets, accounts and sales forecasts), people (customers, suppliers, managers, clerks, etc.), rules (embodied in legislation, established procedures, rule books and codes of practice), norms (often deeply engrained ways of doing things and modes of thinking and practice), and commands (such as computer programs, standing orders, call off lists, etc.).

A person (shown as an information user in Fig. 1.1) has to perform some task in relation to the real world. The information user may be a manager taking a decision, perhaps a simple decision such as confirming an order for steel bars, or a complex one concerned with some aspect of planning. Or the information user may be a clerk carrying out some task, perhaps recording details of orders received for computer processing.

To carry out a task the person needs information about the real world. This can often be obtained from the real world directly. The manager could walk into the steel store to check how many steel bars are left in stock. Or the manager can use a formal, designed information system. This may consist of a stock ledger card on which a stock control clerk has entered receipts and issues of steel bars. It could alternatively consist of a computer stock control system which the manager can interrogate to discover the level of stock by using a terminal. But the manager can also call up the stock room supervisor and ask how many steel bars are in stock, thus using an informal, undesigned information system.

Most information systems have these three major information sources: the real world itself (which can be inspected); the designed information system – an artifact (which is intended to provide an exact image of the real world); and an informal information system (which sometimes substitutes for the designed system and which is often used to provide qualitative and evaluative information about the real world).

How a person uses information from these three major sources depends on a number of factors. Some of these are generic and some are related to the particular environment or situation in which the information is received. Some of the most important factors are:

(1) *The cognitive style and preference of the person receiving the information* (Norman 1980). Some people have a preference and better understand information in the form of pictures or graphs. Others prefer narrative text. Some prefer information presented in a formal or even symbolic form. Others prefer a more informal, freer style. One school of psychological research (Kilman & Mitroff 1976) distinguishes between those who prefer to take in information in a strictly serial mode and who need to capture each element of a message, and those who prefer to see the 'shape' of a message and are able to grasp its content without the serial sensing of the other type.

What determines a person's cognitive style is not well understood. What is clear is that it differs considerably between different individuals. Each individual receiving a message will perceive the content of the message through a cognitive filter, which may select, amplify, reject, attenuate or distort portions of the message. As a consequence, even quite simple messages may be interpreted differently by different individuals.

Complex messages, such as those involving the description of a complicated sequence of events or the rules embodied in a contract, will almost certainly receive many interpretations. The problem of interpretation is made more difficult by the presence of an 'emotional' filter which further distorts the messages received by the information user (Norman 1980). The emotional filter may equally distort the message returned by the information user to the world outside.

(2) *The knowledge contained in a person's memory*. Again, the working of memory is not well understood and we have, at present, no way of measuring what is in a person's memory, or how that information is accessed, or of discovering what knowledge the person possesses. Nevertheless, it is the association of information received through the senses with knowledge stored in a person's memory, which determines the actions and responses to the received messages. Hence, different individuals may respond differently to similar messages, even if the task they are expected to carry out is the same.

To an extent responses can be trained or conditioned to become more or less predictable. This is the basis of military training. In a sense, this type of training attempts to replace cognitive processes by reflex processes. But such processes cannot cope with situations where information messages are informal or novel. The outcome of the cognitive process which associates sensed data with knowledge stored in the memory is not predictable.

(3) *Language* (Stamper 1974; Winograd & Flores 1987). All information is conveyed to the person in the form of signals or messages. To be meaningful they must be embodied in a code or language. Different languages have different properties with respect to the interpretation of the codes. Natural languages are very rich in the range of information that they can accommodate. On the other hand, they are inherently ambiguous. Formal languages – such as mathematical notation or programming languages – can be very precise, but may lack facilities for coping with a wide range of concepts. A concept such as 'good' cannot be directly expressed by a programming language.

Language, cognitive style and memory operate interdependently. Their operation is often rooted in the individual's culture, education and experience. General models of behaviour, taking into account these three factors, do not at present provide useful guidelines for the design of information systems which are capable of being effectively used by any user. However, an understanding of the importance of these factors suggests that some approaches to the design of systems are to be preferred to others.

(4) *The range of channels used for conveying messages or signals to the user* (Shannon & Weaver 1949; Stamper 1974). Each channel has different attributes. Visual channels are used in a variety of ways. They may be used, for example, to convey precisely coded language in the form of printed or written messages, or quite differently, the more ambiguous messages encoded in the form of body language. Sometimes the formal printed document conveys a certain message, but the body language of the messenger suggests that the written document is not to be trusted. Sound channels too are used to convey a great variety of messages. These can range from spoken language with all its subtleties of expression and 'voice', to precisely coded signals such as the air raid siren or dinner bell, to the uncoded but clear message of a screech of car tyres followed by a bang denoting a traffic accident. All channels are capable of conveying both designed messages and mere 'noise'. The information user has to sift the one from the other.

In addition to the generic factors described above, there are a number of environmental and situational factors which influence the way a person will respond to information and which type of information source they may prefer to use. These will include their understanding and trust in the designed system; the trust they place in the judgement of their peers and subordinates; the time available to respond or take action; the pressure of work; the convenience or inconvenience of looking at the real world; the presence of 'noise' which may distort or attenuate intended messages, and many others.

The amount of discretion available to an individual will depend on their position in the organization. In general, clerks carrying out a routine task specified in a procedure manual will appear to have less discretion in choosing their sources of information and their method of processing than would be the case for a senior manager. But in practice, as the phrase 'working to rule' implies, few actual procedures follow the rule book precisely, and much more use is made of the informal, unspecified system than the laid down procedures suggest.

The above analysis has been couched in terms of an individual information user. In practice, however, most information users operate as a part of one or more groups. Such groups may work in a cooperative manner, sharing information in order to carry out tasks or solve problems. Alternatively, the group may be organized as a hierarchy with strictly allocated tasks and responsibilities. The information system may have been designed to serve the information user as an individual or, in the sense of group decision support systems, to serve a group of information users.

An information system designed to support the work of a group needs to have different characteristics from that designed for an individual user. In recent years, considerable attention has been paid to the problem of designing systems which fit in with the requirements of a group of users each possibly having different ways of 'handling' information. The notion of Group Decision Support Systems (Nunamaker 1990) has generated debate on group dynamics and the role technology plays in that dynamic. One school (Phillips 1989) emphasises the importance of human communication within the group and provides a very unobtrusive technological infrastructure to support the group. Another school sees the technology acting as the facilitator's agent to support and help control the group. The technology is highly visible and seen to be both an integral and important part of the meeting (Aiken *et al.* 1990).

Of course, the information user also participates in the activities of the informal system. The information delivered to the information user may come from inside an organization or it may originate outside the bounds of the organization.

What this analysis indicates is that an information system is a social system, which has embedded in it information technology. The extent to which information technology plays a part is increasing rapidly. But this does not prevent the overall system from being a social system, and it is not possible to design a robust, effective information system incorporating significant amounts of the technology, without treating it as a social system.

It is not enough to design a technical system, and then attempt to make it user-friendly, or to tell the designer to remember to take account of human factors. The informal, undesigned component of the information system will not become less important because of the availability of more sophisticated information technology. The designer of the formal system has to be aware of the contribution made by the other half, and seek to provide links which enable the information user to make the most effective use of all components of the information system. Information technology can now be used to enhance the capability of the informal system as much as the formal system.

The designer needs to be aware that formal, designed information systems undergo a process akin to entropy (Land 1988). They begin to change or evolve the moment they have been implemented. Even the most rigidly defined system will be used by its information users in ways which were neither planned for nor anticipated by its designers. Every designed system begins to have a patina of attributes which stem from the undesigned and informal.

The study of information systems is a multi-disciplinary endeavour. Contributions to the study of information systems come from the natural sciences, mathematics and engineering, from the behavioural sciences and linguistics. Avison (1991) describes the study in terms of a 'position on some kind of multidimensional matrix'. Philosophy and the study of scientific method provide the underpinnings for an understanding of the domain. The field of study designated semiotics (or the theory of signs) provides a valuable framework, in that it is itself multi-disciplinary and helps in an understanding of information at the level of its use in society and within organizations (Liebenau & Backhouse 1990; Stamper 1974). However, there is no single framework which encompasses all the domains of knowledge needed for the study of information systems, and this is a key message which we need to take with us when embarking on information systems research.

Chapter 2

The Management of Organizational Knowledge

R.I. TRICKER

University of Hong Kong Business School

Attempts over two decades to find relevant paradigms and frameworks for information system developments are reviewed. An alternative format based on the concept of organizational knowledge is proposed. Such a framework is more embracing than conventional concepts, treating strategic and organizational issues within the system of development, rather than as part of the information systems environment.

2.1 INTRODUCTION

Twenty years ago one of the examination questions in Oxford University's Master of Philosophy examination in Management Studies read:

'Open systems theory of organization suffers from too much openness and too little theory. Discuss.'

At the time we thought that was rather clever. We expected critical appraisal of both the practical utility and the academic integrity of systems concepts then prevailing.

These ideas had been influenced by the writings of scholars such as Wiener (1948), Boulding (1956), Simon (1960), Beer (1966) and, Bertalanffy (1968). The paradigms of systems theory offered the integration of practices and concepts of the managerial, the organizational and the newly emerging information systems worlds. Some even wrote of the total system, which would unite and unify all levels of an enterprise; others of modelling the dynamics of decisions at the enterprise, the state and even the global level (Forrester 1961).

But the body of knowledge of management information systems

(MIS), as the field was then known, was sparse. An annotated bibliography of MIS published in 1969 (Tricker 1969) could claim to be reasonably comprehensive, yet contained fewer than three hundred references.

Now, decades later, the literature has exploded, and the names have changed. But, as will be argued in this chapter, the paradigms of information and its management remain as ambiguous and ephemeral as ever.

As Boland (1987) has pointed out:

'A problem that has plagued research on information systems since the very beginning . . . is the elusive nature of information itself, and the way we as researchers have failed to address the essence of information in our work.'

2.2 ATTEMPTS AT CODIFICATION

There have been plenty of efforts to identify relevant paradigms, create useful frameworks and build reliable theories.

Contributors of conceptual frameworks and possible paradigms include Banville & Landry (1989) – reproduced as chapter 4 in this volume; Culnan (1986, 1987); Ein-Dor & Segev (1981); Mason & Mitroff (1973); Van Gigch & Pipino (1986), and Nolan & Wetherbe (1980). Others have questioned the taxonomy and the research basis for the study of the subject: Bjørn-Anderson (1985); Culnan & Swanson (1986); Hirschheim (1985b); Lyytinen (1987a); Mumford *et al.* (1985); Whitley (1984).

In their well-known model for information systems research, Ives *et al.* (1980) set information systems in the context of the organizational environment, which is itself set in the context of the external environment. Thus, information systems are presented as being constrained by the organizational environment, interacting with it, but not part of it – as illustrated in Fig. 2.1.

In this model the environment of an information system defines the purposes of, the constraints on, and the resources available for the information system. It does not see the information system as a fundamental part of the organizational model itself, which is the perspective that is advocated later in this chapter.

Lyytinen (1987b), in a seminal paper, identified no less than 26

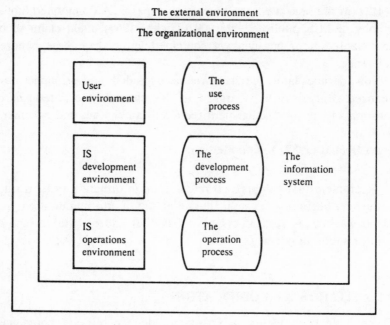

Fig. 2.1 Ives *et al.* model.

alternative theoretical insights into information systems and associated processes. In essence these were as follows:

Models based on advances in information systems operations and system developments

- *Computing environment* approaches focus on the state of the art in information technology, particularly fourth generation languages (Gupta 1982).
- *Support environment* approaches are principally concerned with tools for systems design and development (Wasserman 1980, 1982).
- *Application generators* are part of the support environment, providing specific generic functions (Horowitz *et al.* 1984).

Models based on information systems development processes

- *Life cycle models* presuppose that information systems can be developed along functional lines, being created along a systems life-cycle (Hammer 1981; Keen & Scott-Morton 1978).

- *Prototyping* approaches question the reality of life-cycle ideas in developing complex systems, preferring an adaptive sequence in which requirements and system functions are developed together, learning from experience (Appleton 1983; Jenkins 1983).
- *The PSC model* is a Finnish extension to life-cycle ideas, introducing the pragmatic (P), the semantic (S) and the constructive (C) levels (Iivari 1983).

Models which recognise a learning process in information systems developments

- *An evolutionary approach* sees information systems development as an organizational learning process, evolving over time (Lucas 1981).
- Similarly, the *organizational change* perspective applies an innovative, socio-technical approach to information systems development (Ginzberg 1978; Mumford 1983).

Models emphasising a dialogue process in information systems development

Whereas the learning process models recognise organizational learning and evolution, the dialogue models adopt a political perspective. *Bargaining* methods apply a negotiation approach (Hirschheim *et al.* 1984). *Discourse* approaches feature dialogue between involved parties in information systems developments (Boland 1984, 1987).

Organizational development insights

This body of literature features information systems strategies and their organizational implications (Hirschheim, 1985a, 1985c).

Modelling approaches

Lyytinen (1987b) identifies a set of approaches, broadly referred to as modelling, citing an extensive bibliography, and labelled as:

- information models;
- functional models;
- IS architecture approach;
- information-need approach;
- success factor approach;
- sociotechnical approach;

- evaluation approach;
- contingency models.

Alternative theoretical perspectives

Finally, Lyytinen (1987a) suggests a number of theoretical bodies of knowledge which can provide insights into the information systems process:

- sociotechnical theory;
- class conflict theory;
- inquiry theory;
- sense-making theory;
- soft systems methodology;
- contractual theory;
- language action theory.

2.3 THE FIELD OF INFORMATION SYSTEMS STUDY: AN EVOLUTION OF IDEAS

In the early days of MIS the literature fell into two camps – the intensely practical and the superbly speculative. On the one hand, explanatory texts were needed for the new profession of systems analyst to be able to design the transaction orientated computer-based systems that were replacing manual accounting, payroll, inventory control and similar systems. On the other hand, scholars debated long term possibilities and their likely organizational effects (Whisler 1967).

Then, generation shifts in information technology produced new challenges for the practitioner and previously unimagined prospects for the theoretician. Concepts moved beyond transaction processing to information facilitating. Essentially transaction orientated systems supported the basic operations of an organization, recording changes in some resource, providing management information on position and performance. Information facilitating turned the search process around. Those wanting information no longer needed to be the passive recipients of reports with predetermined content: they could initiate their own searches of the data base.

Further technological developments in personal computers, global telecommunications, local area networks, decision-support systems (DSS), expert systems and other supporting software led to yet more proliferation of the serious literature and the search for meta-theories to codify, integrate and explain information systems phenomena.

The importance of information systems in some industries, (airlines, finance, distribution, for example) brought the recognition of their strategic significance and led to the discussion of whether IS was now a strategic advantage or a strategic necessity.

But in all this focussing and refocussing on the information systems field there was an underlying and unwritten assumption, namely that the prime mission was the application of information technology and the management of data for the benefit of the enterprise.

2.4 THE NEED FOR A NEW PARADIGM

But perhaps such assumptions have been a constraining element in thinking about the field. Could it be that the computer-centered and data-based concepts that are the information systems expert's stock in trade have led to a myopic failure to see a wider rationale?

What is at the core of an information system? Is it a computer (which would undoubtedly have been the answer in the early days), databases, a telecommunication network linking user nodes and data bases internationally, a decision support system with expert system capabilities, or all of these – or none of them?

What if the belief that the prime focus should be on the efficient use of information technology and effective management of data has been a siren song luring practitioners and scholars away from conceptual alternatives? What might a longer field of vision show?

2.5 INFORMATION AND ORGANIZATION

A close association between ideas of organization structure and systems concepts has been apparent throughout the history of MIS and information technology developments. Some have argued about the effect of information systems changes on organization structure and the locus of power (Mintzberg 1979), some have worked on organizational support systems for management decision making (Keen & Scott–Morton 1978), whilst others have suggested information processes as an insight into organization (Boisot 1987).

However, a thread that was apparent in the early information systems literature seems to have been truncated. This was the notion of the organization as an intelligent organism. Stemming from the general systems concepts of Boulding (1956) and others, rich analogies were drawn between systems.

In his work on cybernetics, Beer (1966) drew illuminating comparisons between an organization and the human body, drawing anatomical parallels between top management, board level decision taking and the brain, and identifying information systems with biological nervous systems. But whilst the analogy was illuminating, at that stage of technological development it had little operational significance.

Subsequent writers have used the notion of the 'brain of the firm'. Garratt (1987), in emphasizing the importance of what he calls learning organizations, able to adapt to changing circumstances, drew on the brain of the firm metaphor but principally in exhortatory recommendations to top management rather than in a discussion of information systems.

In a lesser known, but nonetheless seminal work, Wilensky (1967) wrote about organizational intelligence. In retrospect this might have been a somewhat confusing term, given a too ready association with work in human intelligence, intelligence testing and artificial intelligence. Wilensky had none of these concepts in mind; rather he was referring to intelligence in the military sense – the process of collecting information, much of it not readily available, to be aggregated into the intelligence necessary for the battle commander to plan and control his campaign.

Organizational knowledge might be a more appropriate term today. Could the notion of organizational knowledge and its management be useful as an alternative conceptual framework for information system developments?

2.6 THE IDEA OF ORGANIZATIONAL KNOWLEDGE

What might a framework for organizational knowledge contain?

Rather than being databased, emphasizing information for management decision and control, it would focus on what was known or knowable in the organization, and on making the process effective. Consequently it would embrace operational transaction-orientated systems, databased information systems, decision-support systems, indeed any of the existing processes for handling data and providing information. But these would be just part of the organizational knowledge system.

The prime focus would be on managing organizational knowledge. Such a system would facilitate an understanding of issues, threats and opportunities without being orientated towards specific decisions. A DSS is designed to provide support in the area of specific decisions that need to be made; an organizational knowledge system would encourage scanning and browsing outside the decision context.

As Mintzberg & Waters (1985) have suggested, strategies tend to emerge through time as a result of casual interaction and unpremeditated information, rather than as the result of a programmed planning process. Decisions to choose between alternative policies come subsequently. Simon (1960) made a similar distinction between programmed and non-programmed information; but again at the time of writing there was neither the technological power nor the theoretical expertise to do much about it. Now there is.

Managing organizational knowledge accepts the notion that organizations learn as they adapt to changing environments. That learning takes place as the result of acquiring knowledge. Moreover, the process has to be managed if it is to be effective in a complex organization.

In practice the system would presumably identify the stores of knowledge that exist in the organization, which could be in databases, files, records, reports, minutes, letters and, particularly, in peoples' memories. Such knowledge would be codified and stored, frequently updated and accessible to those who need to know.

2.7 THEORIES OF ORGANIZATIONAL KNOWLEDGE MANAGEMENT

Before proceeding to further discussion of the implications of managing organizational knowledge in practice, a tighter definition of the way we are using the concepts of knowledge, information and data is essential, particularly since these terms can be interchangeable in some circumstances.

Data, the plural of datum, is used to refer to things that are known – temperature readings, dates, names, car registration numbers, quantities, a map reference, for example – either as individual elements or as files of data. Data can be hard – that is precise, verifiable, often quantitative; or soft – that is involving judgemental, often qualitative assessments. Data is an entity. It can be captured, stored, retrieved and transmitted. Data has a cost and can be sold. It can also be lost or stolen.

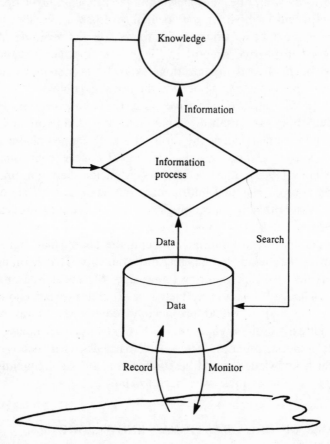

Fig. 2.2 The knowledge creation process.

Information, although often used as a surrogate term for data, is used in a different and specific way here. Information is not an entity. It is the outcome of a process. Information is the result of the action of informing or being informed. Information is a function of data available, the user of that data, and the specific situation in which it is used. The idea of information involves an activity. Information has a value – to the user in the specific context. As Koestler (1964) has shown, albeit in a different context, the unexpected can have a high information value; so can rarity and scarcity.

Knowledge is the sum of what is known, the state or condition of understanding (Shorter Oxford Dictionary). Knowledge is the aggregate of the data held with understanding.

The dynamics that unite data, information and knowledge are depicted in Fig. 2.2. It will be seen that, in effect, this is a model of the learning process.

2.8 THE PRACTICE OF ORGANIZATIONAL KNOWLEDGE MANAGEMENT

Of course, organizational knowledge exists wherever there is an organization. As Earl & Hopwood (1980) point out, managers acquire the information they need to function from a variety of sources. Far from being dependent on the formal data from official reports, they utilise a wide range of alternatives, as illustrated in Fig. 2.3.

Part of every organization's processes includes routine and *ad hoc* meetings, with agendas ranging from the highly formal to the casual. One of the vital, but usually unrecognized, aspects of all meetings is the need to exchange information and, through discussion, add to organizational knowledge.

Peters & Waterman (1982) describe one of the attributes of managers displaying 'excellence', as the ability to 'walk about'. This provides them with the opportunity to motivate, but also the chance to acquire information, insights and ideas.

Most organizations have a far richer store of such knowledge than is ever utilized for the benefit of the enterprize as a whole, because it is piecemeal, is dispersed throughout the organization and is held principally as unrecorded impressions and insights in the heads of individuals.

	Routine	Non-routine
Official	MIS Management accounting systems Production control systems	Access facilities Task forces Liaison roles
Unofficial	Black books Just in case files	The grapevine Lunch table chats

Fig. 2.3 Earl & Hopwood model.

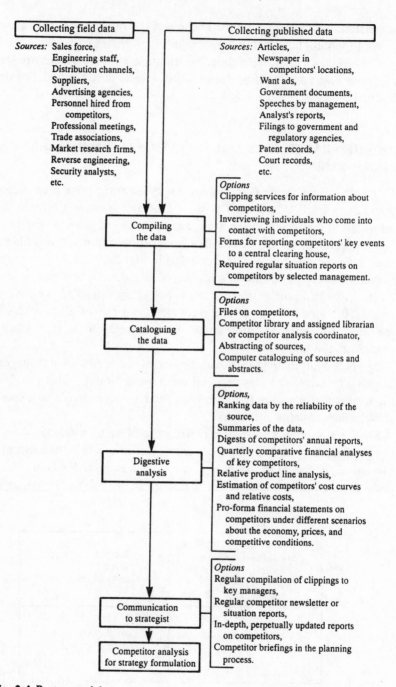

Collecting field data	Collecting published data
Sources: Sales force, Engineering staff, Distribution channels, Suppliers, Advertising agencies, Personnel hired from competitors, Professional meetings, Trade associations, Market research firms, Reverse engineering, Security analysts, etc.	*Sources:* Articles, Newspaper in competitors' locations, Want ads, Government documents, Speeches by management, Analyst's reports, Filings to government and regulatory agencies, Patent records, Court records, etc.

Compiling the data

Options
Clipping services for information about competitors,
Inverviewing individuals who come into contact with competitors,
Forms for reporting competitors' key events to a central clearing house,
Required regular situation reports on competitors by selected management.

Cataloguing the data

Options
Files on competitors,
Competitor library and assigned librarian or competitor analysis coordinator,
Abstracting of sources,
Computer cataloguing of sources and abstracts.

Digestive analysis

Options,
Ranking data by the reliability of the source,
Summaries of the data,
Digests of competitors' annual reports,
Quarterly comparative financial analyses of key competitors,
Relative product line analysis,
Estimation of competitors' cost curves and relative costs,
Pro-forma financial statements on competitors under different scenarios about the economy, prices, and competitive conditions.

Communication to strategist

Options
Regular compilation of clippings to key managers,
Regular competitor newsletter or situation reports,
In-depth, perpetually updated reports on competitors,
Competitor briefings in the planning process.

Competitor analysis for strategy formulation

Fig. 2.4 Porter model.

Porter (1980) confirmed this situation in his work on competitive strategy, emphasizing the importance of knowledge about competitors' positions and possible strategies. He advocated a competitor information system (Fig. 2.4) which would enable such diverse bits of information to be collected, consolidated and made available.

Indeed, this *is* the process of managing organizational knowledge, although Porter does not use that phrase and is more interested in the strategic advantages to be derived from the use of information than the process of managing the knowledge *per se*.

How might an organizational knowledge based system be created?

Perhaps the first step would be to recognize that every organization has one already – one that is part of the rationale for organizational structure and management style. So the question might be better stated as: how can the organizational knowledge base be made more effective?

What elements might such a system contain?

Certainly it will include the existing transaction-based information systems and standing files. Presumably it would also include those management reports, statistics and summaries that are considered worth keeping. It might also involve meetings, video conferences and electronic mail interactions to exchange experiences and collect new organizational knowledge, which could then be stored.

The traditional MIS tends to look inwards, recording states and changes inside the enterprise, whereas the organizational knowledge system would be additionally (and possibly mainly) externally orientated, recording what is known about the changing technological, economic, social and political worlds and about the markets, the customers and the competitors of the enterprise.

In practice such an organizational knowledge system would probably not be held as one concentrated, comprehensive information system. More probably it would have an organizational dimension (to identify knowledge wherever it existed and to create the knowledge base), plus an information dimension (to provide a cataloguing, indexing, and abstracting service to enable the members of the enterprise to pursue lines of inquiry relevant to their functional responsibilities and organizational position).

In the information systems model of Ives *et al.* (Fig. 2.1), the organ-

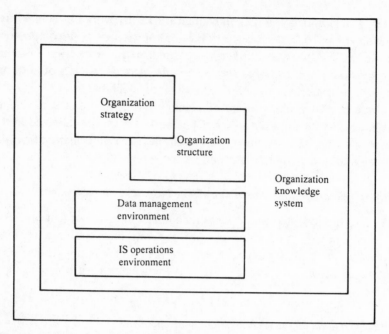

Fig. 2.5 Organizational knowledge model.

ization provides the external environment for the information system. By contrast, in the organizational knowledge model proposed here, the organization and the people in it are an integral part of the model (Fig. 2.5).

Close parallels to the organizational knowledge systems suggested here are strategic intelligence systems used by the military and criminal surveillance records built up by police forces. In both cases data from many sources are monitored, captured, cross referenced and stored for use in building up knowledge about a particular military strategic situation or about criminal activity.

2.9 SOME ISSUES IN ORGANIZATIONAL KNOWLEDGE MANAGEMENT

In police and military intelligence systems every scrap of information – observable fact, opinion and hearsay alike – is collected, compared and then evaluated. Judging the reliability and credibility of the information available is a component of the system. The organizational knowledge system must have similar attributes. Not all of the material available will be hard, measured data. Indeed, perhaps the most valuable sources of knowledge will be soft and qualitative.

Thus a crucial question in managing organizational knowledge is who is to have this responsibility? The answer must be consistent with the organization's strategies, structures and culture.

The importance of security and secrecy is apparent. Access to an organization's knowledge opens the door to knowledge of the entity's current situation and to its view of itself and its strategic situation. Another crucial question is who is to be keeper of the corporate knowledge? And another is who is to have access to the organizational knowledge? The need to know for each role and each level in the organization will have to be determined.

Then there is the other side of the coin – the need for regulation and accountability to protect the interests of society and the other stakeholder groups.

An illustration of the potential significance of such matters can be seen in banks that operate globally. They have rich intelligence on their customers' business affairs. If such information is made available around the organization, for example to foreign exchange traders or institutional investors, conflicts of interest and potential insider dealing situations could arise. Regulation of activities in the global context presents some major problems.

The firm which can effectively manage its organizational knowledge, however, will clearly have a competitive advantage over others.

2.10 CONCLUSIONS

In this chapter, it has been argued that thus far information systems studies have tended to confuse the means with the end. Concentration on the utilization of computers and the other aspects of information technology, and on managing data and supporting decisions with what has been called information, has focussed attention on the means. The end is not more data, held more accurately, made available more quickly and more widely; it is not even better informed decision makers. The end is a more knowledgeable organization, better able to fulfil its purposes efficiently and effectively. The concept of managing organizational knowledge may provide a means for harnessing information and organization in new and fruitful ways. It would certainly provide an agenda for further research.

Chapter 3

Information Systems Epistemology: An Historical Perspective

R.A. HIRSCHHEIM

London School of Economics
(currently University of Houston)

There are some important issues associated with knowledge and its acquisition which if realised could lead to quite a shift in our thinking about what constitutes valid research in information systems. They have a rich historical tradition and are fundamental to our understanding of nature and society. This chapter takes an historical perspective on information systems epistemology; in so doing, it hopes to expose some of the hidden assumptions which lie behind our conception of valid research and valid research methods.

3.1 INTRODUCTION

The information systems community is a loosely connected group of individuals trying to advance the state of information systems knowledge. Many of us are concerned that the state of information systems knowledge is not what it should or could be. Moreover, we feel a large part of the problem is directly related to what constitutes valid research. We need to explore the issue of whether there is a requirement for a shift in the information systems research paradigm, and at the very minimum to identify what alternatives to the current orthodoxy exist.

In this chapter, I should like to offer my thoughts on the salient concepts of information systems epistemology this book is trying to address. It is my contention that information systems epistemology draws heavily from the social sciences because information systems are, fundamentally, social rather than technical systems.

Thus, the scientific paradigm adopted by the natural sciences is appropriate to information systems only insofar as it is appropriate t the social sciences. If one contends that the social sciences embrace an epistemology which is different from their natural science counterparts, then so too is the case for information systems. I should like to argue in favour of such a contention. To do so requires a brief excursion into the history of social science epistemology.

3.2 FUNDAMENTAL ASPECTS OF EPISTEMOLOGY

Epistemology refers to our theory of knowledge, in particular how we acquire knowledge. There are two basic points which need to be looked at:

(1) what is knowledge;
(2) how do we obtain 'valid' knowledge.

Let me address each in turn.

Knowledge (which I consider to be roughly synonymous with understanding) has been an integral part of life and has been sought by humans since the dawn of mankind. The Greeks chose to classify knowledge into two types: 'doxa' (that which was believed to be true) and 'episteme' (that which was known to be true). Science, they believed, was the process of inquiry which transformed 'doxa' into 'episteme'. Of course, a major philosophical problem is how do (or could) we know something is true, i.e., how do we really know what we know? The Sophists were perhaps the first to raise this question, which has troubled philosophers for centuries.

The problem is a straightforward one: since man cannot transcend his language and cultural system, he cannot obtain any absolute viewpoint. The solution is to define knowledge in an alternative fashion, one where knowledge is only 'asserted'. It is supported by evidence (usually of an empirical variety), and knowledge claims are conceived of in a probabilistic sense. Knowledge is therefore not infallible but conditional; it is a societal convention and is relative to both time and place. Knowledge is a matter of societal (or group) acceptance.

The criteria for acceptance are an agreed set of conventions which must be followed if the knowledge is to be accepted by society. The set of conventions are not arbitrary; they are well thought out and have historically produced knowledge claims which have withstood the test of time. In any society there are a myriad of knowledge claims; those which are accepted are those which can be supported by the forces of the better argument. They are an agreed best understanding that has been produced at a particular point in time. Such knowledge claims may become unaccepted as further information is produced in the future.

The second point – how knowledge is acquired – is more polemical. This is the role of science. Because it is related to knowledge it too is based on societal (or communal) agreement. Science is a convention, related to societal norms, expectations, values, etc. In its most conceptual sense, it is nothing more than the search for understanding. It would use whatever tools, techniques and approaches are considered appropriate for the particular subject matter under study.

The consequence of this conception of science is that virtually any 'scholarly' attempt at acquiring knowledge could be construed to be 'science'. The distinction between science (normal science) and non-science or quasi-science (pseudo-science) is therefore blurred. In the West, however, this line of demarcation is relatively clear: for something to be considered scientific it must use the agreed set of conventions – the scientific method. It is the manifestation of the positivistic conception of science/inquiry or 'positive science' and has a long history of providing an accepted understanding of nature.

In other cultures, alternative forms of inquiry are considered appropriate, for example meditation or consulting an oracle. We might consider this form of knowledge acquisition 'unscientific' because it does not match our conception of science. But since science is simply the process by which an understanding is obtained, we cannot necessarily dismiss these attempts as unscientific because our culture is different from others. If a particular process is widely considered appropriate then that *is* science. According to Snyder (1978): 'Science is something that people do. It is not a particular set of assertions or theories, but a set of activities that may or may not produce organized theories'.

One might argue that science requires certain conventions which alternative forms of inquiry do not follow, such as replicability, that it is empirical in nature, and so on. Meditation, therefore, would likely be unacceptable to us as a scientific method irrespective of its acceptance elsewhere. These conventions are *our* conventions, based on our past experiences at acquiring knowledge. The conventions we agree to are those that have proved successful in the past. If, however, the conventions – and therefore our scientific process – cease to be successful then it would be time to reconsider.

This appears to be precisely what is happening in our attempt at obtaining an understanding of human and social behaviour. Chinks have begun to appear in the armour of the accepted scientific method, leading many to question its validity in various disciplines (even, for example, in physics). The very presence of Part 1 of this book is a good indication of exactly this point. Part 1 is included because we want – and need – to have a better understanding of how to advance the state of information systems knowledge. Many of us are concerned that the present accepted research methods are no longer appropriate for the subject – indeed, they may never have been. What is needed is a fresh look at the field; in particular what is the most appropriate epistemological stance.

3.3 SCIENCE AND METHOD

As was stated earlier, information systems – because they are largely human or social in nature – share all the difficulties associated with the social sciences. Our accepted process of inquiry, involving the use of the 'scientific method', has yielded many knowledge claims but most do not have widespread community acceptance.

This is hardly surprising given the often contradictory findings of our studies. Payne (1976) makes the insightful point that in all the years of organizational behaviour research, only four knowledge claims may have any 'real' validity or acceptance. In fact, many social scientists are convinced that the reason we have made so little progress is precisely because of our very conception of science. It is too limiting and not appropriate for their subject of study, i.e., human beings. The 'scientific method' may therefore be appropriate for the natural sciences but not necessarily for the social sciences.

A number of writers have proposed the need to change our conception of science. Some have suggested that science may be more appropriately described in terms of problem or puzzle solving (Kuhn 1970; Toulmin 1972; Laudan 1977). Science, in this conception, is simply a problem solving activity which uses certain conventions in the process. If this posture is adopted, many of the problems associated with research methodologies disappear, since the emphasis shifts away from aspects such as correlations, statistical significance and the like. One is simply looking for an appropriate way to solve a particular problem (Laudan 1977).

Popper (1972) has a similar conception. He states: 'The activity of understanding is, essentially, the same as that of problem solving'. If such a conception is embraced, then science has less to do with specific methods and more to do with practical solutions to problems. This relates to what was said earlier about the blurring of science and psuedo- or quasi-science.

Some chose to view the process of problem solving as a craft (Pettigrew 1985). Within this context the researcher should be viewed as a craftsman or a tool builder – one who builds tools, as separate from and in addition to, the researcher as tool user. Unfortunately, it is apparent that the common conception of researchers/scientists is different. They are people who use a particular tool (or a set of tools). This, to my mind, is undesirable because if scientists are viewed in terms of tool users rather than tool builders then we run the risk of distorted knowledge acquisition techniques. As an old proverb states: 'For he who has but one tool, the hammer, the whole world looks like a nail'. We certainly need to guard against such a view, yet the way we practice 'science' leads us directly to that view.

There are many alternative modes of inquiry but they are considered ascientific by the research community. Yet it is precisely these alternative methods which may allow us to acquire a better understanding of the human realm, and thus should be considered scientific. The difficulty in changing the community's conception of science, however, is legendry.

Popper (1963), for example, decries pseudo-science as valueless. For Popper, pseudo-science is one or more knowledge claims which he refuted. He gives three examples: Marx's historical analysis, Freud's psychoanalysis, and Adler's 'individual psychology'. Popper notes these theories cannot be considered science since any and all data can be fitted into the theories; they could never be refuted. Einstein's theory of relativity was a pseudo-science at one time, but it has now become accepted as 'proper' science.

It is interesting to note that the examples of what Popper calls pseudo-science are all in the human realm. For something to be considered science, it has to follow certain conventions. It makes no difference whether the subject of study is human or non-human. If the conventions cannot be met, then what is produced is at best pseudo-science. It is interesting to speculate whether the whole of social science itself might be considered pseudo-science under such a

As pointed out above, in the West there is a fairly strict conc of science. It is based on positivism: an epistemology which posits beliefs (emerging from the search for regularity and causal relationships) and scrutinizes them through empirical testing. Positivism has a long and rich historical tradition. It is so embedded in our society that knowledge claims not grounded in positivist thought are simply dismissed as ascientific and therefore invalid.

Because of the dominance of positivism, it is imperative that we understand what it is, why it is at the root of our knowledge acquisition attempts, and what are the alternatives.

3.4 POSITIVIST SCIENCE

Positivism has been defined by numerous individuals over the years. Kolakowski (1972), for example, states that positivism embraces a four point doctrine:

(1) the rule of phenomenalism, which asserts that there is only experience; all abstractions, be they 'matter' or 'spirit', have to be rejected;
(2) the rule of nominalism, which asserts that words, generalisations, abstractions, etc., are linguistic phenomena and do not give new insight into the world;
(3) the separation of facts from values;
(4) the unity of the scientific method.

Burrell and Morgan (1979) define it as an epistemology 'which seeks to explain and predict what happens in the social world by searching for regularities and causal relationships between its constituent elements'. For the purpose of this discussion, positivism is summarized as being based on five pillars:

(1) the unity of the scientific method;
(2) the search for human causal relationships;
(3) the belief in empiricism;
(4) the value-free nature of science (and its process);
(5) the logical and mathematical foundation of science.

Forces of the faithful		Forces of the doubtful	

17th Century

THE ARRIVAL OF POSITIVISM

Bacon	1620		
Galileo	1632		
Descartes	1639		
Hobbes	1651		
Spinoza	1663		
Newton	1687		
Locke	1690		

18th Century

Leìbnïz	1710		
		1725	Vico
Hume	1748	1781	Kant
		1798	Fichte

19th Century

		1807	Hegel
Mill	1843		
Comte	1853		
Spencer	1873		
Mach	1886		
Avenarius	1888		

ENTER ANTI-POSITIVISM

		1844	Marx
		1876	Dilthey
		1879	Wundt
		1880	Brentano
		1889	Rickert
Pareto	1890	1890	James
		1892	Simmel
		1894	Windelbrand
Weber	1896	1896	Weber
Durkheim	1898		

Fig. 3.1 A short history of IS epistemology.

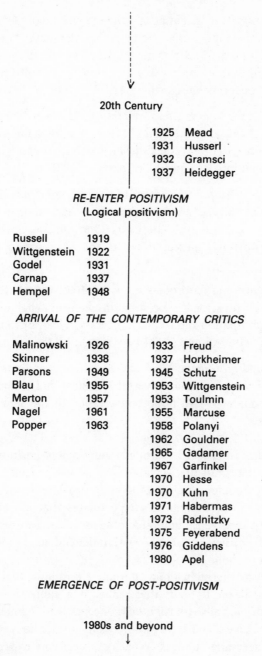

20th Century

1925	Mead
1931	Husserl
1932	Gramsci
1937	Heidegger

RE-ENTER POSITIVISM
(Logical positivism)

Russell	1919
Wittgenstein	1922
Godel	1931
Carnap	1937
Hempel	1948

ARRIVAL OF THE CONTEMPORARY CRITICS

Malinowski	1926	1933	Freud
Skinner	1938	1937	Horkheimer
Parsons	1949	1945	Schutz
Blau	1955	1953	Wittgenstein
Merton	1957	1953	Toulmin
Nagel	1961	1955	Marcuse
Popper	1963	1958	Polanyi
		1962	Gouldner
		1965	Gadamer
		1967	Garfinkel
		1970	Hesse
		1970	Kuhn
		1971	Habermas
		1973	Radnitzky
		1975	Feyerabend
		1976	Giddens
		1980	Apel

EMERGENCE OF POST-POSITIVISM

1980s and beyond

Fig. 3.1 *Continued*

(1) The unity of the scientific method means that the accepted approach for knowledge acquisition (the scientific method) is valid for all forms of inquiry. It does not matter whether the domain of study is animate or inanimate objects: human, animal or plant life, physical or non-physical phenomena, or whatever.

(2) The search for human causal relationships reflects the desire to find regularity and causal relationships among the elements of study. The process used is based on reductionism, where the whole is further and further reduced into its constituent parts.

(3) The belief in empiricism refers to the strongly-held conviction that the only valid data is that which is experienced from the senses. Extrasensory experience, conscious and unconscious organizing apparatus, subjective perception and the like, are not considered acceptable.

(4) That science and its process are value-free, reflects the belief that there is no intrinsic value position in science. The undertaking of science has no relationship to political, ideological, or moral beliefs. It transcends all cultural and social beliefs held by the scientist.

(5) Logic – and more generally, mathematics – provide the foundation of science. They provide a universal language and a formal basis for quantitative analysis – an important weapon in the search for causal relationships.

Positivism also embraces a particular ontological position. (Ontology refers to the nature of the world around us, in particular, that slice of reality which the scientist chooses to address.) The position adopted by the positivist is one of realism. It postulates that the universe comprises objectively given, immutable objects and structures. These exist as empirical entities, on their own, independent of the observer's appreciation of them.

This contrasts sharply with an alternative ontology, that of relativism or instrumentalism. It holds that reality is a subjective construction of the mind. Socially transmitted concepts and names direct how reality is perceived and structured; reality therefore varies with different languages and cultures. What is subjectively experienced as an objective reality exists only in the observer's mind. (The latter ontological stance is the one supported by anti-positivism which will be described in more detail later in this chapter.)

Through the centuries, positivism has enjoyed great success. It has had an especially happy relationship with the physical sciences where a tremendous growth in knowledge has been experienced. Its application in the social sciences has, however, been less than spectacular. Throughout history, individuals have sought to apply positivism to the human realm, bolstering or modifying its conception as necessary. Critics have surfaced to question its validity on numerous occasions.

An historical perspective provides an interesting view of the uneasy tension that has existed in the application of positivism in the social sciences. This perspective and tension I have tried to depict in Fig. 3.1. The rationale for such a view comes from Perrow (1973). His structuring of the important developments of organizational behaviour has provided the inspiration and model for my treatment of social science epistemology. Polkinghorne (1983), Burrell & Morgan (1979), Scruton (1984), Brown *et al.* (1981), Snyder (1978), and Clegg & Dunkerley (1980) have provided the details on the 'key historical players'.

In my attempt to structure the growth of epistemological thought I have had to grossly simplify and perhaps misrepresent various philosophers' contributions. This was unavoidable. It is not possible to do justice to this subject in a single chapter. The purpose of this treatment is to provide an overview of the key epistemological issues facing information systems researchers – something which I believe is long overdue. There has been little, if any, recognition of the importance of this subject. The only alternative epistemological treatment is found in Ivanov (1984). His historical perspective is summarized in Fig. 3.2.

3.5 THE SHORT AND GLORIOUS HISTORY OF INFORMATION SYSTEMS EPISTEMOLOGY

The historical perspective depicted in Fig. 3.1 divides the development of social science epistemology into four very loose stages, with a fifth just beginning to emerge. It should be noted that this perspective reflects Western epistemological development only. As Snyder (1978) quite rightly points out, there was a parallel growth in the East which could be considered to be every bit as rich as our own, particularly in the classic period 600BC–200AD.

I, on the other hand, have chosen to begin this historical review in the 17th century because it was from this period on that there has been the greatest influence on Western human science epistemology. This is

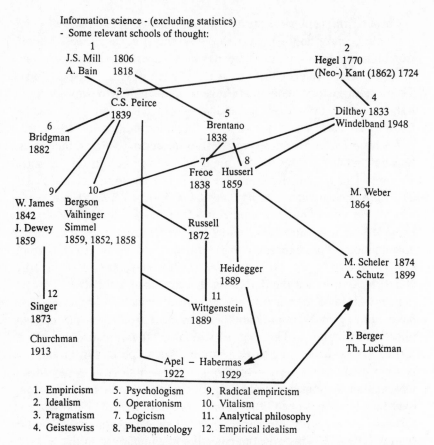

Information science - (excluding statistics)
- Some relevant schools of thought:

Fig. 3.2 Information science (excluding statistics) – some relevant schools of thought. (*Source*: K. Ivanov 1984)

1. Empiricism	5. Psychologism	9. Radical empiricism
2. Idealism	6. Operationism	10. Vitalism
3. Pragmatism	7. Logicism	11. Analytical philosophy
4. Geisteswiss	8. Phenomenology	12. Empirical idealism

not meant to understate the importance of the Greeks during the
formative stages of epistemological development. Their contributions
in the classic period, especially writers such as Pythagoras, Xeno-
phanes, Heraclitus, Socrates, Plato, Aristotle, Euclid, and Ptolemy,
are well known and appreciated. In fact, the writers appearing in the
left half of Fig. 3.1 – termed the 'forces of the faithful' – and largely
responsible for the development of positivist thought, can be traced
back to the writings of Plato and Aristotle. The right half – termed the
'forces of doubtful' – and largely responsible for the development of
alternatives to positivism, may be traced back to the Sophists (e.g.
Hippias, Protagoras and Proclicus).

The four stages of the historical perspective are referred to as:

(1) the arrival of positivism;
(2) the entering of anti-positivism;
(3) the re-entering of positivism (through logical positivism);
(4) the arrival of the contemporary critics.

A fifth stage just currently emerging is that of post-positivism.

3.5.1 The arrival of positivism

The period 200–1000AD is considered by most philosophers of science as the 'dark age' of Western scientific thought. The major area of intellectual activity during this period was theology. Questions about science were interpreted as questions about the nature of God. Scientific thought was greatly constrained by both political and religious forces, and although some of Plato's and Aristotle's writings had been translated into Latin, they were neither widely available nor known.

During the latter part of the 12th century, the Muslims allowed European scholars to have access to the entire body of Greek writings, which were then translated into Latin. Thomas Aquinas in the 13th century elaborated on Aristotle's work in physics and brought to the attention of the European scholars of the time the importance of Aristotle's writings. He was nevertheless constrained by the Church and needed to show how the Aristotlian notion of science was consistent with the Church's teachings and beliefs.

Nicholas Copernicus, in the early part of the 16th century, elaborated on the newly-translated Pythagorean works and postulated that the sun, rather than the earth, was at the centre of the planetary motion.

The 16th and early 17th centuries saw a great awakening in Europe on science. Critical debate about the Church and science burgeoned forward. Plato's work became influential. Copernicus challenged the Aristotelian world view supported by the Church and others of the so-called 'scholastic' period. Luther and Calvin broke away from the established Church. And Gailileo and Kepler attacked the accepted view about planetary motion. The Inquisition sought to re-affirm the Church's position, but by the 17th century it was clear that science would no longer be the sole province of the Church. Its intellectual authority had been irreparably damaged, and with it the door was opened for the development of positivist inquiry.

Foremost among the individuals to shape positivist thought was Rene Descartes (1596–1650) with his treatise *Discourse on Method* (1639). He felt that mathematics was the sole base on which a general theory of nature could be founded. All properties of material objects could be reduced to mathematical form. Descartes' most influential doctrine was the separation of mind (soul substance) and matter (physical substance). He felt one could be studied without reference to the other. The former would be left to theologians, the latter would consititute the subject of study for science. This distinction between mind and soul on the one hand, and the physical world on the other, laid the foundation of positivist thought for the next three centuries. Moreover, it was instrumental in the way human beings were to be studied. Out of Descartes' doctrine grew the mind-body division: the mind (the self) which was identified with conscious thought (awareness), and the body which was an essentially mechanistic object.

According to Koestler (1969) this caused the 'Cartesian catastrophe', the combination of the two doctrines that there is nothing in the mind which we are not aware of, and that the mind and body are two distinct entities. Nevertheless, Descartes' separation of mind and body has had an enormous effect on the development of positivist thought, and its application (and success) in the physical sciences. As Snyder (1978) notes:

'...the Cartesian framework carried natural science as far as it could in the attempt to understand nature as something wholly distinct from the human observer.'

The movement toward positivism and empiricism burst forth during the late Renaissance period. Francis Bacon's (1620) *Novum Organum* championed the inductive-experimental method as a replacement for Aristotle's methods. Galileo's (1632) *The Dialogue concerning Two Chief World Systems* noted that nature was consistent, not random. It could be seen in a systematic way and could be described using mathematics. Moreover, he suggested that teleological explanations should be abandoned; they were not needed to explain nature nor its 'purpose'. Isaac Newton's (1687) *Mathematical Principles of Natural Philosophy* stressed the need for experimental confirmation of theses. This was useful for a general understanding of the natural world.

The critical person of the age though, was probably Thomas Hobbes (1637) who was one of the first to state that humans could be studied using the same scientific methods as physical phenomena. Hobbes, in his *Leviathan* (1651), objected to Descartes' separation of mind and matter, stating that mind was simply part of nature and could be studied as such. He posited there was one universe made up of matter in regular motion which could be described by mathematical formulae. Studying human phenomena was no different from studying any other.

Two centuries later, positivism as an approach to human knowledge acquisition emerged as a more coherent theme. Prominent among individuals of this era was Auguste Comte (1798–1857). He posited that the study of human phenomena should reflect methods used in physical science. 'Positive' science was to be undertaken. The science of sociology – for discovering the laws of human behaviour – would be pre-eminent. It would be used to establish a perfect society based on these laws of behaviour.

Herbert Spencer (1820–1903), a 'positivist' in Comtean tradition, developed a biological analogy for sociology. Much of his work was based on the application of Darwin's theory of evolution to society. In *The Study of Sociology* (1873), he viewed society as a self-regulating system which could be studied and understood by the examination of its parts and how they interrelated. Evolution was the key to sociology for Spencer.

 John Stuart Mill's *System of Logic* (1843), provided a philosophical and logical foundation for empiricism as the ground of knowledge. For Mill, empiricism was as appropriate for the social sciences as the physical sciences. He wrote:

'The backward state of the moral sciences can only be remedied by applying to them the methods of physical science duly extended and generalized'.

Mill believed, however, that although the study of human nature should aspire to be like the exact (natural) sciences, they never would be.

'The science of human nature . . . falls far short of the standard of exactness now realized in Astronomy; but there is no reason that it should not be as much a science as Tidology is, or as Astronomy was when its calculations had only mastered the main phenomena, but not the perturbations' (Brown *et al.* 1981).

(Note the similarity of views on this point between Mill and Popper, as discussed earlier.)

Ernst Mach was largely responsible for the rapid growth of empiricism that took place in the 20th century. It was his advocation that knowledge should be limited to sensations, published in *The Analysis of Sensations* (1886), which gave empiricism its base. Mach contended that the only accurate description of the natural world is that which is experienced by one or more of the five senses. He noted that, while people may linguistically call the same object something different, their sense impressions of it are the same. For Mach, it is only man's sensations which are absolute and certain. Science, therefore, can only attain certainty if it is built on sensations.

Richard Avenarius, in his *Critique of Pure Experience* (1888), noted that pure experience was the sole admissible source of knowledge. Pure perception, 'the sensa', was necessary; metaphysical ingredients had to be eliminated.

Emile Durkheim (1858–1917), although often critical of Comte, was influenced by him greatly, particularly in his notion of the objective reality of 'social facts'. He also incorporated Spencer's organic analogy into his own analysis of society and its institutions. But Durkheim wanted to go beyond this: he stressed the need for causal analysis in addition to functional analysis. Like Comte and Spencer, he borrowed his methodology from the natural sciences, distinguishing between causes, functions and structures. In *The Rules of Sociological Method* (1930), Durkheim noted the importance of causation. He wrote:

'When the explanation of a social phenomenon is undertaken, we must seek separately the efficient cause which produces it and the function it fulfils'.

Vilfredo Pareto (1848–1923) was an economist who planned to apply scientific methods to the social sciences, 'to seek experimental reality . . . '. He used a social systems model based on the notion of equilibrium, thus basing his works on physical sciences instead of the biological analogy of Durkheim and Spencer.

During this period there was therefore a convergence of three philosophical traditions:

- naturalism (all phenomena can be explained in terms of natural causes and laws, without attributing moral, spiritual or supernatural significance to them);
- empiricism (that the experiences of the senses are the only source of knowledge);
- positivism.

3.5.2 Enter anti-positivism

In the latter part of the 19th century the anti-positivists entered the scene. They were particularly worried that the positivists' position failed to appreciate the fundamental experience of life in favour of physical and mental regularities. They neglected meaningful experience which was really the defining characteristic of human phenomena.

A number of individuals, such as Rickert and Windelbrand of the neo-Kantian Baden School, Johann Droysen and George Simmel, wrote of the need for something apart from positivism – hence the term anti-positivism. Perhaps the greatest exponent of this view was Wilhelm Dilthey. He suggested that individuals do not exist in isolation, but that they need to be understood in the context of their cultural and social life. This is the major theme that Dilthey and others developed.

Further, the notion of 'verstehen', which notes that humans recognize and understand meaning, became manifest in the writings of people like Wilhelm Wundt, Franz Brentano and, in particular, Edmund Husserl. William James in the early 20th century (with his notion of radical empiricism), and George Herbert Mead, in the 1930s (with his development of symbolic interaction), all played important roles in the development of anti-positivist thought.

Burrell & Morgan (1979) capture the spirit of the work of the anti-positivists. They write:

'In addition to focussing attention upon the essentially complex and problematic nature of human behaviour and experience, the work of this generation of theorists returned to the basic problems of epistemology identified by Kant, which confronted both the natural and social sciences. The positivist position came to be seen as increasingly unsatisfactory and problematic on at least two counts. First, within the natural sciences (Naturwissenschaften) it became clear that human values intruded upon the process of scientific inquiry. It was evident that scientific method could no longer be regarded as value-free; the frame of reference of the scientific observer was increasingly seen as an active force which determined the way in which scientific knowledge was obtained. Within the realm of the cultural sciences (Geisteswissenschaften) a second set of difficulties were also seen as arising, since their subject matter was distinguished by its essentially spiritual character. It was realized that man as an actor could not be studied through the methods of the natural sciences, with their concern for establishing general laws. In the cultural sphere, it was held, man was not subject to law in the physical sense, but was free . . . As a result of this disenchantment with sociological positivism, idealism assumed a new lease of life.'

Anti-positivist thought can be traced back to the following writers.

Giambattista Vico's *The New Science* (1725) offered an alternative to the empirical approach, stating that human phenomena knowledge can be gained through the study of our history. He believed the laws of historical development are laws of the structuring of meaning. He called for a study of the forms of social life developed by and created through human meaning.

Immanual Kant (1729–1804) has been called by Scruton (1984) 'the greatest phiiosopher since Aristotle'. In his classic work *Critique of Pure Reason* (1781), Kant outlined the problems associated with the empiricism of Locke and Hume, and the rationalism of Descartes, Spinoza and Leibniz. He believed the former placed primacy on experience to the detriment of understanding; the latter was the reverse. Neither could therefore provide a coherent theory of knowledge.

For Kant, knowledge is achieved through a synthesis of concept (understanding) and experience. He terms this synthesis 'transcendental', which gave rise to the philosophy of 'transcendental idealism'. In this philosophy, Kant noted a difference between theoretical and practical reason. The former dealt with the knowledge of appearances (realm of nature); the latter with oral reasoning (issues).

While Kant made no distinction between the physical and human science (he felt both were of the realm of nature) he left the door open for others to consider cultural phenomena within the realm of practical reason, since cultural phenomena were expressions of social meanings. Thus grew the Neo-Kantians who considered 'verstehen' a legitiate source of knowledge. The Baden School was the leading proponent of this contention.

Johann Fichte (1702–1814), a follower of Kant, proposed a version of subjective idealism hinged upon the notion that human consciousness is a never-ending stream of ideas, images and concepts which unite to form an external world. Fichte reasoned that, to understand this external world, one must understand the human stream of consciousness. His work has influenced much of contemporary social theory and philosophy.

Hegel (1771–1831), in his *The Phenomenology of Mind* (1807), postulated that knowledge was obtained through 'dialectics'. According to Scruton (1984), this is a term first used by Plato to describe the method of Socrates to obtain philosophical truth through disputation. Kant had also used the term, but in a somewhat obscure way, to describe the propensity to fall into contradictions. Hegel used it to refer to a method whereby truth is discovered by a progression from 'inadequate concepts' to more and more 'adequate' ones.

Scruton (1984) defines it thus:

'The dialectical process is . . . as follows: a concept is posited as a starting point. It is offered as a potential description of reality. It is found at once that, from the standpoint of logic, this concept must bring its own negation with it: to the concept, its negative is added automatically, and a 'struggle' ensues between the two. The struggle is resolved by an ascent to the higher plane from which it can be comprehended and reconciled: this ascent . . . generates a new concept out of the ruins of the last. This new concept generates its own negation, and so the process continues, until, by successive applications of the dialectic, the whole of reality has been laid bare.'

This attractive metaphor has had a great influence on the philosophical thought of the past two centuries. In terms of social science thought, Hegel (like Fichte) saw human consciousness as crucial to the understanding of the nature of society. Hegelian theory attempts to explain how human knowledge passes through several forms of consciousness, until finally a level of 'absolute knowledge' is attained. When this level is reached the individual is one with the 'absolute spirit' of the universe. For Hegel, human existence is a constant interaction between the individual's consciousness and its object form, the external world. These form a dialectical relationship – two sides of one reality. Hegel envisioned a perfect society, where all were subservient to the same 'absolute spirit' – the state.

CHESTER COLLEGE LIBRARY

Karl Marx (1818–1883) expanded on Hegelian theory and placed the individual rather than 'absolute spirit' at the centre of things. Marx argued that there existed no absolute above man. He and others of his day pointed out that the state, and even religion, were creations of man, not some 'absolute spirit'. Continuing this thesis, he explained how individuals could create and shape their own society through self-consciousness. This concept of the 'alienation of man' emphasized how societal constraints (man-made) were dominating the very being and nature of man. Later, Marx diverted his attention fron the idealist perspective to a much more realist-oriented view of nature and society.

Wilhelm Dilthey (1833–1911) was the principal architect of the anti-positivist movement. He believed in the need for empirical science to study human phenomena, but he disagreed with the positivists as to how humans should be studied. They need to be viewed within the context of a 'philosophy of life'. Life cannot be understood as a machine, as Hobbes suggested. Life is what we experience in our activities and reflections as we live out our personal histories. Life cannot be understood by using the explanatory model that classifies events according to laws of nature. He wrote: 'Because individuals do not exist in isolation, they cannot be studied as isolated units; they have to be understood in the context of their connections to cultural and social life' (quoted in Polkinghorne 1983).

Human scientists must seek to make explicit the principles of organization, the principles of 'categories of life'. They need to explicate the processes which make experience meaningful. Further, there is a need to explicate the processes, not seek causal connections. This differs from Mill's science which sought to trace causal genesis and to state the laws of explanation. Dilthey, then, sought to uncover the structures of meaning.

Dilthey also noted the need to extend the notion of 'empirical' as used by the positivists. Their position implied that what is perceived is the manifestation of physical objects, transmitted into consciousness by sensory apparatus. But there is another type of perception: that of recognizing meanings. When we read, we experience more than the visual sensation created by black marks on white paper. We perceive the meaning of the words and the message of the author. We see more than mere physical objects. We perceive the meaning in the world. This is the notion of 'verstehen'.

Johann Droysen (1858) noted a difference between physical and human science methods. The former used 'explanation' methods, the latter 'understanding' (verstehen) methods. These provide two different kinds of knowledge.

Wilhelm Windelband (1894) noted the existence of one realm, but it could be studied from two perspectives: 'nomothetic' (law) which addresses Droysen's notion of explanation (physical causation); and 'idiographic' (particular, distinct) – Droysen's 'verstehen' – which attempts to identify meanings and specific characteristics. The human sciences, thus, were not a different realm; they needed to be looked at through idiographic methods.

Heinrich Rickert (1809) saw the need to change from Dilthey's 'human science' to 'cultural science', since the former emphasized the study of individual experience to the detriment of the study of cultural aspects. He also noted that meaning cannot be understood except in terms of values. Values provide the meaning of individual events. He postulated that values are 'universal and ahistoric', something with which Dilthey disagreed.

Georg Simmel (1858–1918) introduced the notion of 'reciprocal effect'. He noted the existence of two forms of social life: 'content', relating to an individual's drives – love, hunger, etc., and 'actualizing forms', relating to reciprocal effects between individuals (e.g. cooperation, competition and solidarity). Experience is thus made up of these two forms of social life. To understand experience one must understand both forms.

He attempted an eclectic approach to sociological inquiry, a middle-ground between the theories of idealism and positivism. His middle-ground position strived for an analysis of human association and interaction. Simmel stressed the need for field study through interaction, examining and analysing the underlying reasons for societal behaviour. Epistemologically, Simmel leaned toward the positivist approach as his methodology was definitely nomothetic.

Wilhelm Wundt (1879) – often considered the father of psychology – noted a difference between physiological psychology and folk psychology. The former was clearly in the positivist's camp, the latter only partially. Wundt, although a believer in positivist methods, split with Mach's conception of science in that he did not believe science must be limited to 'sensa' data (i.e. pure perception). Subjective data were necessary particularly for folk psychology which dealt with feelings, affects and processes of volition (i.e. mental life). These were the higher operations of the mind.

Franz Brentano (1838–1917) believed the object of inquiry for psychology should be human experience in its fullness. He shared many of the ideals of the positivists, including the contention that psychology should be empirical. Brentano, however, wanted to recognize a special kind of experience that was not allowed in traditional empiricism. He noted two classes of phenomena: physical and mental. The former could be dealt with using traditional positivists' methods, since they were the objects of direct sense perception. The latter could not, as their primary characteristic was 'intentionality'.

Edmund Husserl (1859–1938) was the father of the phenomenological movement. He looked to the rationalist rather than empiricist tradition for help in understanding the organizing structures of consciousness. Husserl notes: 'What creates our lived experience are the essential structures or ideas that order and give form to experience'. His primary concern was with understanding the nature of these forms. To do this required an addition to empirical science, *viz* the establishment of a new rational science. The result was phenomenology, the science concerned with the essential structures of consciousness.

Phenomenology is based on the 'intuitive grasping of the esssences' of phenomena. An essence is defined as that which is necessary for something to be recognized as that thing. Husserl realised that sense data do not appear independent of meaning; they are the result of a constitutive process within consciousness. Thus, what is experienced is not essences but the result of the constitutive process. To uncover the essences, the phenomenologist must bracket away layer upon layer of the hidden structuring process which provide meaning to the experience. To express it differently, an essence 'is that which is constant as the "given" of consciousness in the constitutive process; furthermore, the essence is what remains "identical" in all possible variations of what is being investigated' (Polkinghorne 1983).

Essences are not physical entities, and cannot be studied as such. They are non-empirical and concerned more with 'how' and 'why' rather than 'which' and 'what'. For Husserl, the validity of phenomenological research comes from the self-validation of an insight into the phenomenon's essence that is communicated clearly and completely to the community. Knowledge is a sort of 'social intuition' rather than a set of hard facts. Its acquisition recognizes that:

(1) human experience is largely intersubjective in nature and these essences can be communicated to others;

(2) the process of understanding essences is historic: clarity is gained over time through successive studies.

Max Weber (1864–1920) believed that there existed a distinction between 'human action' and 'human behaviour'. Action embraces behaviour but is deeper in that the acting individual attaches a subjective meaning to his behaviour: behaviour guided by values and meanings. For Weber, meaning is not something which can be subjected to empirical observation. He thus distinguishes between two types of human understanding: 'direct observational' and 'explanatory'. The former reflects an understanding of human action where the purpose of the action is obvious to the observer; the latter, where it is not.

In explanatory understanding, the observer seeks an understanding of the action 'by placing the act in an intelligible and more inclusive context of meaning'. Weber argued that understanding and explanation were two sequential components of social science inquiry. Researchers first sought understanding, which became the basis of explanation. Weber believed the process of interpreting social action had to be undertaken with the same precision as that found in the natural sciences. This belief, however, led Weber towards a more empirical and positivist conception of human science which perhaps is exemplified in his discussions of an 'ideal type'. It is a construct which permits the irrational behavioural elements of human action to be recognised. One simply compares the actual observed action with the ideal action. The difference is attributed to 'irrational elements'.

William James (1842–1910), in *Principles of Psychology* (1890), developed and advocated the position of radical empiricism. An outgrowth of Mach's ideas, James contended that science should include all phenomena which are directly experienced. He felt that there were organizing patterns of the conscious which interpreted and ordered what was directly experienced from the senses. These organizing or structuring patterns that form part of the organized nature of experience needed to be seen as part of direct experience and thus appropriate for inclusion in science.

George Herbert Mead (1860–1949) was the father of symbolic interaction. Mead noted the need for a methodology of human science which would recognize the importance of symbols and their significance in understanding human behaviour. Symbolic interaction was his proposed approach to deal with these symbols.

According to Mead, individuals do not respond directly to stimuli.

Instead, they react to the meanings they assign (consciously or uncon-
sciously) to these stimuli. Meanings do not emerge in isolation but are
derived from social interaction. As such, they are shared amongst
members of the group and provide general guidelines which govern
social action. Mead noted that people modify their behaviour in line
with social influences. Their action is a result of an interplay between
the psychological forces 'I' and 'me'. To obtain an understanding of
the action, Mead felt the social actor's own view of his world and the
meaning his behaviour has for him, had to be included.

Antonio Gramsci (1891–1937) blended features of structure and
consciousness, philosophy with sciences, and subject with object.
Gramsci was critical of the Marxism of his day; he felt it had lost its
vital revolutionary quality due to the adoption of positivist notions and
other ideals. He wanted a theory which would transcend the classical
theories of philosophy (particularly the antinomies of voluntarism
versus determinism, idealism *versus* materialism and subjectivism
versus objectivism). His goal was a world view theory, a 'philosophy of
praxis' as he termed it. Gramsci saw this philosophy as complete and
all-encompassing; within it were all elements necessary for the sciences
as well as political concerns of life.

3.5.3 Re-enter positivism

In the 1920s, a movement to counteract the development of anti-
positivist thought emerged, known as the Vienna Circle. Positivism re-
entered (not that it ever really died). Its rejuvenation came primarily
from the work of Bertrand Russell. The Circle took Russell's new
logic, merged it with the positivism of Mach and the development was
called the 'received view'. It is now commonly referred to as 'logical
positivism'. Prominent members of the Circle were Carnap, Feigl and
Godel. Other people associated with this movement, although not
from the Vienna Circle itself, were Carl Hempel, Hans Reichenbach
and Alfred Ayer.

Wittgenstein's *Tractatus Logico-Philosophicus* was the inspiration of
the logical positivists. According to Giddens (1976):

'The Tractatus influenced the growth of logical positivism particularly with respect to the argument for the distinction between the
analytic and synthetic. There are no synthetic *a priori* judgments.

Systems of logic or mathematics, deductively derived from axioms, are essentially tautological; any other general claim to knowledge is synthetic, which means that it can be counterfactually shown to be false'.

The development of logical positivism (or neo-positivism as it is sometimes referred to) has had a great influence on today's notion of science. In fact, it is commonly considered to be the dominant epistemology of contemporary science. Although it has evolved over the past sixty years, it is still firmly rooted in the positivist camp.

Problems arising from its held beliefs have caused refinements to be developed and changes to be made. For example, there has been a move away from the classic positivist position of phenomenalism (where the only acceptable data come from experience), to physicalism (where data are seen to emanate from the world and not merely private experience; intersubjective agreement on objects is allowed). This movement also gave rise to a name change, from logical positivism to logical empiricism. (The two terms are, however, used interchangeably.) Concomitantly, the move to physicalism signalled the end of the classic claim that knowledge had to be indubitable. It was now acknowledged that intersubjective agreement provided sufficient justification for knowledge.

A second refinement to logical positivism shifted the goal of science away from individual explanation (or laws) to theoretical networks of knowledge statements linked together through deductive logic and grounded in direct observation. The accepted realm of inquiry included sense data and logical relationships. The purpose of scientific inquiry was to 'rationalize reality'. The fundamental model for scientific explanation was the deductive-nomological model of Hempel and Oppenheim. Its widespread adoption in the majority of research done today (i.e., using the hypothetico-deductive model) is visible proof of its impact.

There have been numerous individuals who played an important role in the adaptation and application of logical empiricism to the social sciences. Some of the more prominent are discussed below.

Bronislaw Malinowski (1926) was instrumental in establishing the usefulness of fieldwork in research. He proposed that the appropriate way of studying and understanding society was by analysing the various parts and their role within a culture. In order to comprehend a social system, one had to understand the functions which are performed. The term 'functionalism' was coined by him to describe this approach. It had a definite positivist orientation.

Skinner (1938) is most immediately associated with behaviourist theory, where he did extensive research into stimulus and response. Skinner viewed man much like a machine, simply responding in a deterministic way to external stimuli. Very much a proponent of experimental methods used in the natural sciences, he disregarded subjective states of mind. His research resulted in the formulation of many universal laws and patterns about human behaviour.

Another psychologist of the logical positivist genre was Clark Hull, who attempted to build a theory of psychological learning. In his book *Hypnosis and Suggestibility: an Experimental Approach* (1973), Hull argued for a strict adherence to the hypothetico-deductive method, utilising rigorous experimentally deductive reasoning. Postulates are formulated from which experimentally testable results are deduced and then subjected to rigorous experimental testing. Hull believed that psychology should be as objective a science as the physical sciences. The only way this could be achieved was through embracing and using the hypothetico-deductive method.

Radcliffe-Brown (1952) argued for the need to conceptualize society as a network of relations between its parts which he called 'social structures'. Using Durkheim's work as a starting point, he elaborated the analogy of biological organisms and society. He defined society in terms of the functions which are performed within its structure (i.e., recurring activities such as funerals, weddings, etc.) giving us the notion of 'structural functionalism'. In his examination of society he had a set of problems to solve, which led him to recognise the limitations of the organismic analogy. By noting these limits in the structural functionalist view he recognized the processual relationship of mutual influence between the structure and its functions, as well as the inherent danger in carrying the analogy of society and organisms to an extreme.

Talcott Parsons (1949) was a prominent social action theorist. He is credited with taking the so-called 'voluntaristic theory' of action and steadily making it more deterministic, eventually assimilating it into his theory of social systems: Social Action Theory, or Action Frame of Reference. Parsons' work is considered functionalist by Burrell & Morgan (1979) and Giddens (1976) who wrote: 'There is no action in Parsons' "action frame of reference", only behaviour propelled by need disposition or role expectation.'

Blau (1955), in examining the processes governing human association, attempted to link together the micro and macro levels of social analysis; that is, to bridge the gap between interactionism and social system theory. Blau subscribes to some of Simmel's 'interactionist' theories but resists his reductionist views of society in favour of a less segmented approach, where human action is viewed as an emerging social process. Fundamental to his work is the notion of social exchange which is analysed in terms of power differentiation and status.

Robert Merton (1957) is an integrative theorist who attempted to link conceptually different theories into a functionalist paradigm. Merton seeks a middle ground in order to link micro and macro levels of analysis as well as empiricism and grand theory. His research shows him to be a classic functionalist trying to strengthen some of the weak areas of functionalism.

David Easton, in his book *A Framework for Political Analysis* (1965), espouses the 'behaviourist' approach which holds a strong commitment to the assumptions and methods of empirical science. Easton hoped that a common unit of analysis could be found in social theory, which could be used in a similar way as molecules in the physical sciences. He states:

'The key idea behind this approach has been the conviction that there are certain fundamental units of analysis relating to human behaviour out of which generalizations can be formed and that these generalizations may provide a common base on which the specialized sciences of man in society could be built.'

The standard position of the logical empiricists is well summarised in the writings of Carl Hempel. In his book *Frontiers of Science and Philosophy* (1964), Hempel argues strongly for the unity of nomothetic explanation in scientific inquiry. Explanation, he posited, was the same in all scientific endeavours. He writes:

'... the nature of understanding, in the sense in which explanation is meant to give us an understanding of the empirical phenomena, is basically the same in all areas of scientific inquiry, and that the deductive and the probabilistic model of nomological explanations accommodate vastly more than just the explanatory arguments of, say, classical mechanics: in particular, they accord well also with the character of explanations that deal with the influence of rational deliberatism, of conscious and subconscious motives, and of ideas and ideals on the shaping of historical events. In so doing, our schemata exhibit one important aspect of the methodological unity of all empirical science.'

3.5.4 The arrival of the contemporary critics

Logical positivism, for all its attempts at providing a unifying basis for science, could not overcome a number of fundamental criticisms which were levelled against it by a variety of critics. These criticisms are fairly diverse and do not fit readily into any compartmentalized scheme. Perhaps the best source for an overview of the criticisms is in Suppe (1977), who listed nine specific points.

I should like to focus on just a few. First, logical positivism fails in its claims to provide observation reports which were theory-independent. That is, the veracity of observation reporting can be determined independently of the theoretical level. Both Quine and Achinstein have pointed out that the separation of observable from theoretical is extremely problematic. In fact, it is unlikely that observation can be theory-free. (See Hesse's (1980) insightful treatment of the theory-free argument.)

Second, logical positivism's attempt at grounding the scientific method on deductive reasoning to overcome the so-called 'problem of induction' has proved unsuccessful. The problem of induction, simply put, is that no matter how many sample instances are viewed, there is no way to infer that a given law is true. Laws, therefore, cannot be verified through the testing of deduced inferences.

The dismissal of inductive reasoning is a mistake, particularly considering that the practice of science since the 17th century has proceeded reasonably well using inductive reasoning. One of the major failings of logical positivism was its disregard for the history of science, in particular, the way scientists actually work. It was overly concerned with normative theory development and explanation and too little concerned with viewing science as a more pragmatic activity (*cf.* Toulmin 1953; Polanyi 1958). To have a better appreciation of a more pragmatic view of science, many philosophers turned to Peirce.

Charles Peirce (1839–1914), although a philosopher of the 19th century, had a considerable influence on many 20th century philosophers of science who were critical of logical positivism (*cf.* Habermas,

Apel & Radnitzky). For Peirce, science was not 'systematised knowledge' but rather the activities performed by individuals to acquire knowledge. Because of this, he felt it was important to understand the process of scientific activity, including the motives of the scientists themselves. Science needed to be conceived of as 'a living historic entity'. In contrast to the logical positivists, Peirce thought science should place as much emphasis on the processes of discovery as with how theories are justified. Science embraced a dialectical interaction between these two. Moreover, the method of science was considered by Peirce to be an historic attainment, a scientific achievement in itself. Peirce used Kant's notion of 'pragmatic' to reflect his conception of science.

Peirce's contention that science is a human activity which takes place in an historical context gave rise to what Suppe (1977) calls 'historical realism'. This is an epistemological development which attempts a reformation of the notion that knowledge is related to one's perspective or world view (Weltanschauung) and therefore inextricably bound up with one's historical and cultural situation. Science, in this context, produces the best alternative for bringing belief closer to reality – hence the notion of 'historical realism'. The philosophers most closely concerned with this point of view are Lakatos, Radnitzky, Toulmin and Laudan. Each looks at science from a slightly different perspective, but there is great similarity in how science is conceived, particularly in terms of how knowledge is incrementally advanced through history.

A third major problem with logical positivism is related to the basic issue of values. One of the fundamental pillars of positivist thought (including the latter refinements) is that the process of scientific inquiry is (or should be) value-free. The scientist must keep his values separate from his inquiry. The logical positivists felt there was a clear distinction between fact and value. Scientists must confine themselves to empirical-based studies of the facts; moral or political issues (values) are to be excluded.

Many contemporary critics strongly disagree. Gouldner (1962), for example, suggests that not only is it impossible to keep values out of social scientific inquiry, it ought not to be tried. Social scientists have a duty not to retreat from involvement in social issues and political practice. An apparent detachment by the researcher only seeks to further obscure underlying values. Under the guise of neutrality, the researcher is in fact tacitly supporting the *status quo*.

Fay (1975) argues vociferously: 'The conventional practice of viewing knowledge on the one hand, and the use of knowledge on the
other, as conceptually distinct is fundamentally misguided.' Fay be-
lieves this point is rather apparent yet is ignored by mainstream social
science, where the main concern is with methodological questions.
This naive view of science has caused the growth of Critical Theory –
found in the writings of the Frankfurt School – which has a rich history
(see, for example, the works of Gramsci, Lukacs, Marcuse, Hork-
heimer, Adorno, Fromm and Habermas).

Another writer who is critical of the value-free position is Hesse
(1978) who suggests values play an important part in developing
theories in social science. She contends that theories are not *fully*
determined solely by facts. Value judgements are needed for selecting
theories for attention. She writes: 'The proposal of a social theory is
more like the arguing of a political case than like a natural science
explanation.'

Some of the arguments of other prominent writers critical of the
logical positivists' position are summarised below.

Wittgenstein's well-known criticisms of logical positivism provided
the basis for further attacks on its fundamental beliefs by many commentators. In *Tractatus*, Wittgenstein postulated that there existed
some words in language that directly named parts of reality. Not long
after this work was published and became widely acclaimed, Wittgenstein began to doubt that such a relationship was possible. It occurred
to him that the meanings of words were determined by the contexts in
which they were used. The reason why certain words were understood
between individuals was because they shared a similar world view or
'language game'. Meanings were intersubjectively determined, not
given. They are inextricably bound up with social activity (*cf.* Whorf's
thesis).

Wittgenstein's dramatic change, discussed in *Philosophical Investigations* (1953), has been seen as the impetus behind the writings of many
contemporary critics such as Feyerabend, Kuhn and Lakatos. For
Wittgenstein, the meanings of words in language are obtained from the
language games in which they participate. Thus, all observation statements are theory-dependent, not statements of 'reality'. Moreover, the
truth of observation statements – or science in general – is related to
an individual's language game. And Wittgenstein would contend there
is a plurality of truths.

For the social scientist, then, the task is one of elucidating the values, propositions, beliefs, etc. which are felt to be true within a particular communication community or language game.

Winch challenges the belief in the unity of the scientific method in his *The Idea of a Social Science* (1958), in which he argues the need to consider the special differences which exist between the natural and the social sciences. He repudiates Mills' view that human behaviour could be predicted and generalized. For Winch, human action involves, inherently, social meaning. As such, the researcher can only truly understand this 'from the inside'. It is not simply a matter of observing such action 'from the outside', as is the case in the physical sciences.

Mills (1916–62) was critical of those social scientists who were trying to adapt methodologies of the natural sciences to the social sciences. He felt they let methodological concerns dominate their work and he coined the expression 'abstracted empiricism' to describe this phenomenon. Put concisely, abstracted empiricism is the use of nomothetic methodology (i.e. one that looks for general laws to cover whole classes of cases) to test a theory which embraces ontologically a subjectivist theory of human nature.

Alfred Schutz (1899–1959) was greatly influenced by Weber and Husserl. He tried to apply the concept of phenomenology to sociological problems. Schutz contended that Weber's concept that the main function of the social scientist was to interpret, did not go far enough. He believed the main characteristics of social science must be 'understanding', 'subjective' meaning and 'action'. Schutz looked for meaning in the 'stream of consciousness', a concept modelled after Bergson, which eventually developed into his concept of 'reflexivity'. Reflexivity, simply put, is the idea that only through retrospective examination can meaning be attached to an experience. Bergson applied this notion in his theory of typification, which enables one to understand the behaviour of others.

Gadamer (1981) reshaped the hermeneutic position by examining the circle of understanding (*cf.* Dilthey). He argued that it is not a 'methodological' circle, as was previously thought, but a description of an 'ontological structural element of understanding itself'. Gadamer sees language as the transmitter between actual experiences, traditions, etc. and the process of understanding. Language takes on an ontological role, shifting his view of hermeneutics nearer to the phenomenological realm. Language ceases to be a mere system of sounds and symbols – it becomes the expression of being.

Habermas (1971) is a prominent exponent of contemporary critical theory. Habermas was critical of interpretative soiology and socio-logical positivism, seeing them as self-serving and inadequate. His own notion of critical theory is adapted from Parsonian system theory and Gadamer's hermeneutics, with additional elements taken from psychoanalysis.

Habermas is deeply interested in language, its use and structure, and how these formulate and affect society. His theory of 'communicative competence' uses elements of hermeneutics to bridge the political micro-structure of speech, and speech within the context of symbolic interaction. In his analysis of communication he identifies the need for an 'ideal speech situation', which is free from 'communicative distortion'.

For Habermas, work is seen as a kind of 'communicative distortion' characterised by an asymmetric choice in the use of speech acts – a reflection of unequal power and relationships. The alternative is 'inter-action' which is based on communicative action between individuals where shared norms are developed and reflected in an intersubjectively shared language. For this to happen, social action must be 'eman-cipated' and free from domination. The ideal speech situation provides the context through which 'interaction' is made possible.

Lessnoff, like Winch, does not think the logical positivists' model is appropriate for the social sciences. This is because the subject matter of inquiry is social in nature and involves such mental phenomena as thinking, meaning, purposive action and categorisation. Because people have conscious minds and free will, the model of physics is inappropri-ate for providing an understanding of human behaviour.

Lessnoff, in his *The Structure of Social Science* (1974), argues that one *could* study human beings using the model of physics by disregard-ing the mental aspects of behaviour in favour of the physical, but this is not desirable. He writes: "Undoubtedly human beings could be scienti-fically studied on this basis – but not, I believe *as* human beings, and certainly not as social beings.' Social science needs then to be interpre-tive, understanding the mental aspects associated with social action.

Reason and Rowan, like Lessnoff and Winch, challenge the notion that the logical positivists' scientific method is appropriate for the social sciences. In their book *Human Inquiry* (1981), they argue that much of the current orthodoxy is open to severe criticism, particularly as it relates to the study of human beings. Their eighteen point critic-ism presents a practical view of the problems of social science.

For example, the orthodoxy's 'model of the person' is too simplistic.

They write: 'People are seen as isolatable from their normal social contexts, as units to be moved into research paradigms, manipulated, and moved out again. People are seen as alienated and self-contained, stripped of all that gives their action meaning, and in this way they are trivialized.' Moreover, they see problems with its epistemological stance: 'The whole language of "operational definitions", "dependent and independent variables", and so forth is highly suspect. It assumes that people can be reduced to a set of variables which are somehow equivalent across persons and across situations, which doesn't make any sense to us.'

Burrell and Morgan, in their book *Sociological Paradigms and Organizational Analysis* (1979), are of the same mind:

'Science is based on "taken for granted" assumptions, and thus, like any other social practice, must be understood within a specific context. Traced to their source, all activities which pose as science can be traced to fundamental assumptions relating to everyday life and can in no way be regarded as generating knowledge with an "objective", value-free status, as is sometimes claimed. What passes for scientific knowledge can be shown to be founded upon a set of unstated conventions, beliefs and assumptions, just as everyday, common-sense knowledge is. The difference between them lies largely in the nature of rules and the community which recognizes and subscribes to them. The knowledge in both cases is not so much objective as shared . . . Scientific knowledge here is in essence socially constructed and socially sustained; its significance and meaning can only be understood within its immediate social context.'

3.5.5 The emergence of post-positivism

During the past few years, a growing number of researchers have begun to argue the need for a change in direction. Most are engaged in social science research and believe orthodox science is not appropriate for their subject of study. Conferences have been held, books written, special issues of mainstream social science journals published, all on this subject.

This new breed of sceptics is coalescing and arguing for supplanting positivism in favour of a new conception of science. Some have referred to it as 'post-positivism' (Giddens 1978; Koch 1980; Polkinghorne 1983). This movement asserts the need to do away with the physical science model as the only acceptable vehicle for knowledge acquisition, particularly for the social sciences. It hopes to transcend the limitations of positivism. It challenges the tradition that knowledge is actually apodeictic, asserting instead that knowledge claims are simply those accepted by the community. They possess the power to convince the community that they do, in fact, represent an improvement on our previous understanding.

Post-positivism is more a belief about knowledge; it is not a particular school of thought with any agreed set of propositions or tenets, although perhaps that is something the information systems community might wish to pursue.

An interesting part of post-positivist thought is its belief in what might be termed 'methodological pluralism' – the assertion that there is no one correct method of science but many methods (Morgan 1980; Polkinghorne 1983). The 'correct' method is contingent on the problem being studied, the 'kind' of knowledge desired, and so on.

Kuhn (1970) argues this point strongly:

'The pull towards a single methodological perspective, with its clearly defined tools, needs to be resisted because this single perspective designed for research in "normal science", overlooks the anomalous quality of human experience. The difficulty for human science arises not from the need to change from one paradigm to another but the need to resist settling down to any single paradigm'.

Methodological pluralism is one theme we can and should support regardless of our epistemological biases. This chapter has sought to make the case for methodological pluralism irresistible, and the argument will be taken up and placed even more firmly in the context of information systems research in Chapter 8.

Chapter 4

Can the Field of MIS be Disciplined?

CLAUDE BANVILLE

Université du Québec en Abitibi-Témiscamingue

AND

MAURICE LANDRY

Université Laval, Québec

Preoccupations about the present and future evolution of management information systems (MIS) as a scientific field seem to be
gaining popularity among researchers. This chapter contends that
most models used by the investigators of the MIS field have been
based on an inappropriate monistic view of science.

4.1 INTRODUCTION

A number of active researchers of management information systems
(MIS) have recently expressed preoccupations with the actual state
and future evolution of MIS as a scientific field. Preoccupations of this
type have been around for quite a while, but they seem to have gained
in popularity and acuteness in the last few years as witnessed by the
frequency of exchanges related to this topic, whether it be through
papers, colloquia, or private and public conversations.

Some of those expressing concern assert that MIS researchers too
often work on non-pertinent (Bjorn-Andersen 1983; Huber 1983) or
unrelated topics ('gadget of the week'), while others (Klein 1984;
Weick 1984) question the research methods. Some will propose
frameworks (Ives *et al.* 1980; Mason & Mitroff 1973; Nolan & Wetherbe
1980) that should bring unity to a field they see as characterized by too
much dispersion. Others (Dickson *et al.* 1982) will react to an apparent
proliferation of frameworks and contend that 'we have enough conceptual frameworks'. It is time to test, enhance, and embellish these
frameworks with empirical research results'.

Keen (1980), the opening speaker at the First International Conference on Information Systems, asks for no less than a clarification of reference disciplines, a definition of the dependent variable, the building of a cumulative tradition and the solution to corollary problems such as the relationship of MIS to technology, the relationship between MIS research and practice and the establishment of publication outlets. Others, explicitly adopting Kuhn's model of the development of science (1970), announce the advent of (Farhoomand 1986, 1987) or ask for the establishment of (Weber 1985) or for efforts leading to a clear definition (Van Gigch & Pipino 1986) of a paradigm for MIS.

This list could be extended to contain concerns about the establishment of journals (Bullen 1986) or the organization of colloquia (McFarlan 1984; Mumford *et al.* 1985) or other such manifestations. It is probably sufficient, however, to show the pervasiveness among some of the most active members of the MIS field, of the interest for the actual state and future of MIS as a scientific field.

A major driving force underlying the concerns of these authors is a preoccupation with the idea of progress and maturation of the MIS field. Indeed, their comments are aimed at one or both of the two following goals: first, to point at what they perceive as obstacles to progress within the field and to propose means to eliminate them; second, to suggest actions deemed appropriate for accelerating the pace of progress in order for the field to mature more rapidly. In both cases this implies a legitimate need to understand and evaluate the present state and foresee the future of the MIS field. Indeed, members of any scientific field, and particularly those belonging to fields struggling for recognition such as MIS, have to worry about the social and scientific status of their discipline.

It must be realized that anyone attempting to assess the state of a particular scientific discipline must necessarily proceed with the implicit or explicit help of a model as to what a scientific discipline is and how it should develop. This model first leads one to focus on those factors in the situation under investigation that are deemed significant and, second, helps pass judgement, positive or negative, on these factors in order to suggest appropriate courses of action. So, the model one uses to assess the present state of a discipline and present possible solutions is of crucial importance and should therefore be carefully selected and explicitly stated.

Furthermore, if the investigator, as is usually the case, feels the necessity of comparisons with other disciplines, this model should be general enough and somehow be able to take into account and reflect intrinsic differences between the investigated disciplines, which can be as diverse as physics, computer science, management theory, MIS, sociology and others.

It is our contention that most models used until now by MIS investigators have been based on an inappropriate monistic view of science. This is a direct consequence of an explicit or implicit adoption of the Kuhnian model of scientific development based on the notion of paradigm and a narrow definition of the concepts of scientific progress and maturation which results in recommendations for the future development of MIS that are not, in our view, always appropriate.

Using Kuhn's well-known model as an illustration, this chapter shows how a monistic conception of the development of science is too restrictive to help understand the present state of MIS. Later, we will use a model adapted from Whitley's work on the sociology of knowledge (Whitley 1984a) as an example of a more general view of the development of scientific fields, and show how such a model can be used with great benefit to investigate our scientific field and to draw certain conclusions.

4.2 THE INADEQUACY OF A MONISTIC VIEW OF MIS: THE KUHNIAN MODEL

The concept of paradigm is the key to understanding the essence of Kuhn's model of scientific development. This model has been summarized by Chalmers (1982) as: pre-science – normal science – crisis-revolution – new normal science – new crisis. A paradigm is said to reign during periods of normal science and is brought under severe challenge during periods of crisis–revolution. The pre-science phase is characterized by the absence of a paradigm. The way Kuhn defines and delineates the term paradigm is thus central for a good understanding of his model of the transformation of a scientific discipline.

Unfortunately, the term paradigm has been used with many different significations throughout Kuhn's writings. Toulmin (1972) presents 'five distinguishable phases' in Kuhn's use of this term between 1957 and 1970. These phases are seen as being closely related to the changes in Kuhn's conception of *revolution* as it became more and more evident that he really meant *evolution*.

During this period, Kuhn went from seeing paradigms as dogmas and changes of paradigms as equivalent to religious conversion (re-volution), to paradigms as exemplars and changes of paradigms as logically construed endeavours (evolution). As to the numerous meanings of the term paradigm, Masterman (1970) produces a non-exhaustive list of citations from the first 1962 edition of *The Structure of Scientific Revolutions*, indicating twenty one connotations.

Kuhn's followers' interpretations have resulted in the diffusion of additional meanings. So much so, in fact, that De Mey (1982) classifies some of them in three groups labelled through 'their activity as paradigm-hunting, paradigm-detection and paradigm-dissection'.

The paradigm-hunters are those 'enthusiastic Kuhn followers who hope to remedy a deplorable state in their field by providing a paradigm or by promoting the search for it'. Paradigm-detectors track down groups of interacting scientists through bibliometric or sociometric methods. Paradigm-dissectors see this concept as central to the cognition process and analyse it for its contribution to the understanding of this process.

Sharing what can be seen as the most widespread definition (even though it is not found as such in Kuhn's writings), the MIS researchers referenced in the introduction seem to use the term paradigm as meaning that members of a scientific discipline endowed with a para-digm always know precisely the relevant research topics in their discipline, the appropriate research methods and the proper inter-pretation of results. Therefore, a paradigm should dually indicate problems and methods not belonging to a discipline. An example of such a definition is provided by Ritzer (1975) for whom:

'A paradigm ... serves to define what should be studied, what questions should be asked, and what rules should be followed in interpreting the answers obtained. The paradigm is the broadest unit of consensus within a science and serves to differentiate one scientific community (or *subcommunity*) from another.'

This restrictive view of science explains why philosophers of science generally agree that Kuhn's vision of science is monistic: it allows only one dominant view to reign during periods of 'normal science'. As stated by Kuhn (1970) himself: 'The new paradigm implies a new and more rigid definition of the field. Those unwilling or unable to accommodate their work to it must proceed in isolation or attach themselves to some other group'. But then, it is generally agreed that our discipline is made up of what has been called subfields. Culnan, using an analysis of cocitations of the most often referenced MIS authors, has identified nine of these subfields in one study (Culnan 1986) and five in a subsequent one (Culnan 1987).

This brings the first considerations on the dangers in the claim for a paradigm for MIS if this notion of paradigm is to be understood in the original Kuhnian perspective. These refer mainly to the identification of the community of owners of a paradigm, to the means of establishing a paradigm and to the scientific discipline used as an implicit standard of comparison in Kuhn's model.

If one is to build a paradigm, then the scientific community to which it will apply has to be identified. But then, who are the members of MIS? Traditionally, MIS has attracted scientists from *a priori* apparently weakly related disciplines such as computer science, decision theory, management theory, economics, psychology, and others. Each researcher would bring along concepts and methods from his background discipline and, often, would continue doing research which is closely related to it. This could explain why Culnan was able to identify so many subfields in one study (1986) and five in a subsequent one (1987).

It might be argued that this dispersion has been a major factor in the rapid growth (be it only for the number of MIS researchers) experienced by the discipline in the last two decades. If a paradigm is to specify, as expected, the way in which research is to be conducted as well as how results are to be interpreted, then it seems doubtful that we could end up with a paradigm that could include the different approaches currently found in the MIS field. A large number of MIS members would face the choice of either leaving or converting to (in its religious sense) the emergent paradigm. Nobody could say for sure, at the time of this split, which branch(es) will eventually be considered as MIS – the one created by the paradigm or the more or less formal groups created by those leaving.

Those claiming a paradigm for MIS seem to think that it could be created by a group of persons (which one would it be in MIS?) through simple force of will and adherence to a strict set of rules. Most scientists are concerned with contributing to their discipline, not with building paradigms. As stated by Chalmers (1982): 'Because of the way he is trained, and needs to be trained if he is to work efficiently, a typical normal scientist will be unaware of and 'unable to articulate the precise nature of the paradigm in which he works'. Stegmüller (1976), whose understanding of the term paradigm as exemplars was recognised as 'captur[ing] precisely my original intent' by Kuhn (1977), expresses similar ideas: 'Normal scientists never examine their paradigm critically, in particular the paradigmatic theory. They simply use the theory uncritically as an instrument for puzzle solving'.

A paradigm can only be observed *hic et nunc*; it is a result of the action of the forces at work in a scientific field. In the Kuhnian model, a paradigm appears after the pre-paradigm phase or after a crisis-revolution; a call to arms therefore seems absolutely useless as a paradigm will emerge only if certain conditions are met. Even when adhering to such a model, one should always remember that paradigms are largely a matter of implicit social consensus and that their emergence requires time and the combination of many favourable factors which can, at best, be facilitated.

The direct consequence is that one should not distract researchers from their daily activities and ask them to try to set up a set of rules to be called a paradigm; rather, one could observe how these researchers proceed, elaborate a model and propose it as a paradigm. We argue here that Kuhn's framework cannot, at the present time and in a foreseeable future, represent such a model for MIS.

In this regard we refer to a comparable debate that took place in the field of management theory at a symposium held more than two decades ago. Similarities between management theory and MIS are worth noting: the members of both fields have varying backgrounds, work on apparently unrelated topics with different research methods and their results are often interpreted in divergent ways. These similarities justify a comparison of the history of this recent yet older field of management theory.

At this symposium Harold Koontz (1964) proposed ways and means to get his discipline out of a: 'confused and destructive jungle warfare . . . It is important that steps be taken to disentangle the management theory jungle. In a field where the many blunders of an unscientifically based managerial art can be so costly to society, delays cannot be tolerated'. This sounds much like what one now hears in MIS.

Herbert Simon's answer was a call to patience and it stressed the fertility of the multitude of points of view for a young discipline. He first stated that 'confusion, by another name, is progress to which we have not yet become accustomed'; in other words, we should not be so sure that the relative calm of a paradigmatic period is a lot better than the turmoil of a crisis. Simon later added: 'Science, like all creative activity, is exploration, gambling, and adventure. It does not lend itself very well to neat blueprints, detailed road maps, and central planning. Perhaps that's why it's fun'. This conception is radically different from the rather monolithic view of normal science built into the Kuhnian model, and deserves consideration.

Equally interesting was Robert Dubin's statement at the same symposium: 'I happen to be an intellectual free enterpriser. I would like to put in a plea for free enterprise in perhaps one area where it still can exist, namely, in the affairs of the mind, in the affairs of the intellect'.

History seems to repeat itself. Once more we find ourselves confronted with the problem of the delicate balance between a high degree of organization in a field and consequent possible sclerosis on the one hand, and free enterprise will and consequent risk of futile dispersion on the other hand. It is a contention of this chapter that the imposition of a paradigm in MIS, if at all possible, would be a risky move towards the former.

We also argue that MIS researchers should not long for a paradigm, as it rests upon assumptions of the Kuhnian model of science which imparts value to knowledge on the basis of the conformity of its methods and results to an explicit standard: physics. Physics is but one science and its largely recognized value stems more from the fact that, at least in a popular view, it is applied to so-called *hard* objects with very adequate methods that have been perfected by sharp minds over a number of centuries. The large social consensus on the status of physics as the 'Queen of Sciences' brings scientists to compare the state of their field to that of 'The Model' and it is no wonder, the basis of comparison being biased, that they end up feeling very uncomfortable.

This should not be so. Chalmers (1982) clearly states the position held in this chapter on this matter:

'Philosophers do not have resources that enable them to legislate on the criteria that must be satisfied if an area of knowledge is to be deemed acceptable or scientific. Each area of knowledge can be analyzed for what it is. . . . Each area of knowledge is to be judged on its merits by investigating its aims and the extent to which it is able to fulfil them. Further, judgments concerning aims will themselves be relative to the social situation.'

In conclusion, the idea of establishing a paradigm for MIS along the lines of the popular conception of Kuhn's model, if at all practicable would not bring about the effects expected by the very proponents of this idea. On the contrary, the most probable result would be a break-up of the field into rather hermetic factions and the consequent loss of the creativity generated by exchanges about research topics and research methods.

Furthermore, one can doubt that MIS paradigm-hunters would themselves be ready to accept all the consequences of an implementation of the full Kuhnian model commensurate with their view of the paradigm. In fact, they seem to long for a period of perpetual *normal science*, thus forgetting the cyclical nature of a process of transformation that would take them regularly through the pains of crisis-revolution.

4.2.1 The Kuhnian model as revisited by Kuhn

Kuhn has reacted to his critics (Lakatos & Musgrave 1970) and his ideas on the concept of paradigm have evolved after the publication of *The Structure of Scientific Revolution* (1970). In *The Essential Tension* (1977) he writes about the problems caused by the confusion around the concept of paradigm and stresses the importance of the notion of scientific community:

'Whatever paradigms may be, they are possessed by any scientific community, including the schools of the so-called pre-paradigm period. My failure to see that point clearly has helped make a paradigm seem a quasi-mystical entity or property which, like charisma, transforms those infected by it. There is a transformation, but it is not induced by the acquisition of a paradigm.'

This allusion to some magical properties possessed by a paradigm and its refutation by Kuhn himself should seem a sufficient answer to those asking for a paradigm in MIS on the basis that it will necessarily transform our field for the better. In the same text, Kuhn even proposed to drop the concept of paradigm and replace it with a new notion, that of a 'disciplinary matrix' constituted by:

(1) symbolic generalizations;
(2) common beliefs and models;
(3) shared values;
(4) exemplars and other elements (said to exist but not presented in Kuhn 1970).

4.2.2 Ambiguity of Kuhn's conception of progress

The creation of a paradigm is often claimed for the sake of progress in a discipline. However, an attentive reading of Kuhn (1970) raises questions about his vision of progress. For him, and as stated by Stegmüller (1976), there are two 'forms of pursuing science . . . normal science and extraordinary or revolutionary science'. Even though the periods of normal science are presented by Kuhn (1970) as parts of a 'cumulative enterprise', they also have been clearly characterized as being made up of mopping-up operations and puzzle-solving that produce no major novelties.

A paradigm is thus not necessarily the moving force that will propel a scientific discipline on the way to the test of critical hypotheses or the construction of new theories that will incorporate anomalies in observed phenomena. On the contrary, Kuhn states clearly that, during a normal science era, the typical normal scientist observes only what his paradigm tells him to observe and most of the observations that do not fit this very tight schema either go on unnoticed or are put aside as irrelevant, or, better for the sake of 'progress', as something that cannot be explained yet. To use Karl Weick's expression (1984), 'believing is seeing' during those periods which are characterized, in retrospect, by no great leap in scientific progress.

Progress is at best relative during periods of normal science, but it is said to be a '. . . universal concomitant of scientific revolutions' (Kuhn 1970). The great moments of the history of science seem to be, both in the general public's mind and all along Kuhn's book, the great revolutions brought by Newton, Lavoisier, Einstein, Darwin and others. These great moments could easily be considered the only moments of real progress and the preceding periods of normal science could be called quiet science. The reign of a paradigm might mean progress, but it refers to a very restricted type of progress.

Thus, it is not clear at all whether progress occurs most during periods of normal science (paradigmatic periods) or during periods of crisis-revolution in the Kuhnian model. To make matters worse, Kuhn discusses the difficulty of establishing an operational definition of scientific progress and concedes an inevitable circularity between what he considers progress and what he sees as science. To use Stegmüller's (1976) expression, in any struggle over what science should be, 'the victors are by definition the progressives'.

In summary, asking for the establishment of a paradigm in the name of progress for a scientific discipline rests on shaky grounds. There could be as much progress in the non-paradigmatic periods. As stated by Simon, science may progress (whatever that word means) better without 'neat blueprints, detailed road maps and central planning'.

4.2.3 The importance of the concept of scientific community

Kuhn (1970) recognized the importance of the concept of scientific community when he wrote that: 'If this book were being rewritten, it would . . . open with a discussion of the community structure of science, a topic that has recently become a significant subject of sociological research and that historians of science are also beginning to take seriously.'

> To him (1977): 'A scientific community consists . . . of the practitioners of a scientific specialty' and is a factual observation, not an *a priori* determination. These scientific communities are good candidates as the basic units of analysis: '. . . there is excellent reason to suppose that the scientific enterprise is distributed among and carried forward by communities of this sort.'

Operationally, these communities are created along both a social and a cognitive dimension. They can be observed through group membership, membership in professional societies, journals read, attendance at summer institutes and special conferences, preprint distribution lists, 'and above all to formal and informal communications and networks, including the linkages among citations'.

To recapitulate what has been said so far about Kuhn's model and its application to the field of MIS, it has been argued that, first, it is too restrictive in its application to bring a valuable contribution to our field; second, the advent of a paradigm does not necessarily guarantee progress in a field; and third, this model nevertheless contains the seeds for the elaboration of a more appropriate model which can be extracted from recent contributions to the philosophy of science.

One of these contributors, Caldwell (1984), probably sums up best what has been said when he writes:

'Though Kuhn's influence has spread far beyond the confines of the philosophy of science, some non-philosophers who are acquainted with his work have not been aware of criticisms of his position. This has the paradoxical, though hardly unusual consequence, given the information lags that exist among disciplines, that at present Kuhn's prestige is greater outside the philosophy of science than within it.'

Saying that the application of Kuhn's model to MIS would not be beneficial to our discipline does not imply that the quest that has taken us this far is futile. On the contrary, epistemological reflection is an essential and integral part of any scientific enterprise, but it should be done with great care and with the best possible means. This rebuttal of the Kuhnian model should not be extended to the reflections and discussions carried out by certain MIS researchers. Their task is legitimate but must be supported by more adequate models of the development of science.

4.3 THE SCIENCES AS INTELLECTUAL FIELDS

It is now widely recognized that the production of scientific knowledge is an endeavour that is simultaneously cognitive and social. Although the cognitive dimension has been quite extensively studied since the first days of epistemology, the social dimension is a more recent preoccupation that has been picked up mainly by sociologists of knowledge. As sociologists are interested in societies, the question of specifying the basic unit of analysis of societies of knowledge producers cannot be avoided. The concepts of scientific discipline and community have been used by some, while others would rather use the concept of field to capture the social object constituted by groups of scientists at work.

Böhme (1975) concentrates on the informal organization of disciplines for which he uses the expression 'communities of research'; argumentation is then seen as the main ingredient of the basic relation within these communities. Mulkay (1979) uses the terms 'scientific community' and 'intellectual community' on the same page. These are to be seen as the places where the meanings commonly used by groups of scientists in their scientific activities are constructed. A detailed description of this process of construction would be difficult as 'these meanings . . . are inherently inconclusive, continually revised and partly dependent on the social context in which interpretation occurs'. To Knorr-Cetina (1981) fields are the:

'relevant contextual organisation[s] of laboratory production which in principle transcend the specialty networks . . . [and] may include the provost of the university, the research institute's administrative staff, functionaries of the National Science Foundation, government officials, members or representatives of industry, and the managing editor of a publishing house.'

These fields

'not only criss-cross the borders of a specialty group, but also shrink and expand in response to the issues at stake'; they 'appear to be the locus of a perceived struggle for the imposition, expansion and monopolisation of what are best called resource-relationships.'

The expression refers to allocation of jobs among scientists, distribution of research money, dissemination and use of research results. . . . For Whitley (1984a), intellectual fields are:

'. . . the social contexts in which scientists develop distinctive competences and research skills so that they make sense of their own actions in terms of these collective identities, goals and practices as mediated by leaders of employment organizations and other major social influences.'

Finally, the definition of Audet (1986), in our view captures and comprehensively links all the main ingredients incorporated in the preceding definitions. To him, a field is a common ground on which field members compete to gain control of the definition of conditions and rules of knowledge production and validation and, at the same time, the system of their relations and relative positions.

According to this last definition, one would probably vainly ask for the constitution of a field around his own personal view of the appropriate research topics and methods, as his recommendations would necessarily become an object of debate. To Audet, the research topics and methods are themselves the result of the collective action of a field's contributors. In other words, a field cannot be created and evolve according to precisely pre-defined plans. Actions can be taken that would influence its constitution and evolution, but the field itself can only be identified and characterized by observing its contributors at work.

This assertion is in line with Newell's view when he observes that: 'scientific fields emerge as the concerns of scientists congeal around various phenomena. Sciences are not defined, they are recognized De Mey (1982, p. 145)'. Of course, the difficulty of identifying what constitutes a field is not without similarities with the difficulty of specifying the owners of a paradigm (is there a paradigm for the whole of physics or should it be restricted to nuclear physics?). Indeed, there remains the necessity of a recursive use of the concept since subfields can also be seen as fields on their own when they become the units of analysis. Clearly, the term field does not refer only to the traditional scientific disciplines such as biology, economics, sociology and so on, but can also be applied to artificial intelligence or molecular biology.

4.3.1 Fields as reputational systems

According to Whitley, the quite explicit aim of the members of intellectual fields is the production of new knowledge. This implies standards of a particular kind for organizing and controlling research, standards which are created by the members of the field through a particular structure called the reputational system.

The evaluation of one's contributions by colleagues can be recognised as part of this reputational system. The importance of the reputational system is great as it controls the access to rewards, be it money for research projects, academic promotion, invitations as guest speaker at prestigious conferences and so on. The search for a positive reputation is achieved through the use of a formal public communication system which comprises colloquia, journals, seminars, etc. Scientific research is then seen as a form of work organization, a special craft system (Whitley 1984a): '. . . distinguished by its combination of continual novelty production . . . with strong collective co-ordination of task outcomes through access to rewards being controlled by reputations based on the utility of results for colleagues' research'. Whitley even uses the expression colleague-competitors to show how one must reach and maintain an equilibrium between innovation and conformity to the established knowledge and methods.

4.3.2 Presentation of Whitley's model

The concept of field is intuitively appealing and surely seems relevant to scientists who are sensitive to the social aspects of their scientific world. Yet it should be evident that an operational definition could never exhaust such a rich reality; a field is perpetually subject to change as a result of the actions of inventive and interested human beings. That is why any model that tries to explain the actual state and possible evolution of scientific fields will probably turn out to be inadequate with time or upon intensive usage.

In this domain, models, as dominant as they may be at any particular time, eventually become obsolete and we agree with Pondy & Mitroff (1979) that: 'If we have begun to confuse the map with the territory, then it is time to change maps'. It is within this map perspective that we present a classificatory model based on Whitley's work and it is also within this perspective that it should be received. But, even though it is based on a model that has been received as over-ambitious by Pinch (1984) and of problematic applicability by Yearley (1986), in our view and for the time being, it is a map that captures and expresses a lot of what we can observe within our field and across fields.

As already hinted, Whitley applies the methods of sociology, more specifically of the sociology of work organization, to the intellectual enterprise (the public sciences) carried on by scientists. He has proposed a classificatory scheme that, according to him, highlights important differences between the various intellectual fields. He also uses a set of contextual factors to explain how the evolution of these fields can be explained or influenced through certain actions of internal or external agents.

There is a certain analogy between Whitley's concept of intellectual field and Kuhn's scientific community. The different public sciences can be classified in both Kuhn's and Whitley's models. Whereas Kuhn emphasizes the necessary evolution towards normal science, we will see that for Whitley, and in accordance with Chalmers as quoted above, each field possesses its own characteristics and pattern of evolution and none of these fields is *a priori* more valuable than any other.

4.3.3 Classificatory scheme

In his earlier works (1974, 1975), Whitley introduced the notions of cognitive and social institutionalization of scientific fields. While these two dimensions have become quite classic, they are not independent. Whitley has thus provided a new model in his most recent publications (1982, 1984a). This model uses four variables that express the cognitive and social dependence of members of a field through the way they produce knowledge and interpret each other's research results.

The strong link between some aspects of the social and cognitive dimensions of intellectual fields (Yearley 1986) justifies a simplification of Whitley's model with minimal loss of interpretative power. This reduced version uses only three variables as classification criteria and should thus be easier to understand and use. These three variables are:

(1) functional dependence;
(2) strategic dependence;
(3) strategic task uncertainty.

These variables are used to produce a typology of intellectual fields, as shown in Fig. 4.1.

(1) Functional dependence

Functional dependence, as used here, refers to (Whitley 1984a): '... the extent to which researchers have to use the specific results, ideas, and procedures of fellow specialists in order to construct knowledge claims which are regarded as competent and useful contributions' and to 'the extent to which work techniques are well understood and produce reliable results ...'. As functional dependence increases, one can observe:

'... greater specialization of research topics and tasks, standardization of work procedures, competence standards and communication structure, and co-ordination of task outcomes from different research sites for dealing with particular problems. The scope of problems tackled by individuals and research groups tends to decline as functional dependence grows.'

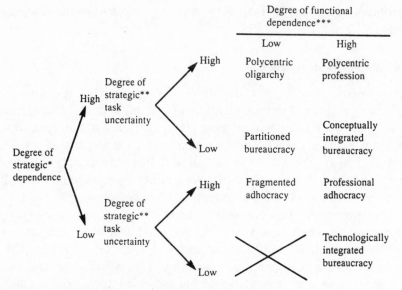

Fig. 4.1 A classification of intellectual fields.

* Strategic dependence is a measure of the political dependence of the members within a field. It is concerned with coordination, control and conflict.
** Strategic task uncertainty is a measure of the conceptual coherence within a field. It is concerned with relative importance of the different problems and the presence of schools of thought.
*** Functional dependence is a measure of the technical and procedural coherence within a field. It is concerned with the standardization of research tools, procedures and results interpretation. Adapted from (Whitley (1984a)).

The degree of functional dependence could be said to be a measure of the dependence on standard topics and methods of knowledge production.

(2) Strategic dependence

Strategic dependence refers to: '... the extent to which researchers have to persuade colleagues of the significance and importance of their problem and approach to obtain a high reputation from them'. Again,

'increases in strategic dependence are associated with greater concern over the relative importance of problems and approaches, and so intensify competition between groups for the domination of the field ... High strategic dependence implies a strong need to co-ordinate and interrelate research strategies and goals with those of specialist colleagues in order to gain important reputations from them.'

(3) Strategic task uncertainty

Strategic task uncertainty is defined in relation to the fact that: '. . . the stability of problem formulations, and of hierarchies of problems according to their importance and significance, varies across fields . . .'. Strategic task uncertainty is low when members of the field agree on a hierarchy of research problems, when there is a tight control over research goals and minimal local autonomy in the formulation of research problems and significance standards. Conversely, a high strategic task uncertainty is associated with the presence of loosely coupled schools of thought.

The different combinations of high-low values on the three variables produce eight possible configurations of intellectual fields. One of them is eliminated on the grounds that, according to Whitley (1984a), it is 'unstable and unlikely to become firmly established'. We are then left with seven valid entries. This classification is not necessarily exhaustive and unique but highlights some of the major differences between the scientific fields and helps explain such differences. Again it must be emphasized that these are unqualified differences: it is neither good nor bad for a discipline to qualify as high or low on any of the variables used for classification. A particular value on each criterion is to be seen only as a characteristic of the investigated field.

It is beyond the scope of this chapter to comment on each of these stable types and compare them. The names used by Whitley to designate them are, to a certain extent, self-explanatory and are further explained (1984a), where the interested reader may find a general description of each of these types. Some examples of scientific field classifications by Whitley may nevertheless be useful here.

A polycentric oligarchy in which contributors produce diffuse, locally coordinated knowledge, is exemplified by German psychology before 1933 with its many schools of thought. A polycentric profession appears with the emergence of a few dominant schools as functional dependence increases; experimental physiology is proposed as an example.

Seen as a partitioned bureaucracy, a rarely observed configuration, is the field of business finance. Low functional dependence is evidenced by the relative schism between field members over the all-important efficient market hypothesis and empirical research findings that continuously contradict its validity. Low strategic task uncertainty and high strategic dependence can be seen as a result of the growing influence of analytical economics whose 'intellectual goals and standards . . . have come to dominate the literature' (Whitley 1985).

Modern physics, on the other hand, is classified as a conceptually integrated bureaucracy, low on strategic task uncertainty and high on functional and strategic dependence; these are the characteristics of Kuhn's normal science. Management studies (or administrative sciences) is viewed by Whitley as constituting a fragmented adhocracy, high on strategic task uncertainty and low on functional and strategic dependence. This is a result of the relative failure of the attempt to apply the scientific methods to management problems. Administrative sciences are now (Whitley 1984b): 'to be seen as a largely academic enterprise with few connections to managerial actions and one which is highly internally differentiated . . . into separate ideas and approaches'.

Artificial intelligence is to be seen as a professional adhocracy, i.e., as producing highly specific and empirically focussed knowledge with (Whitley 1984a): 'a variety of problem formulations and conceptual approaches linked to particular skills'. Finally, modern chemistry, with its well-established industrial and academic research technology, very well illustrates a case of technologically integrated bureaucracy as its members concentrate on their particular problems, using quite standardized methods and tools and not showing a great concern about 'general contribution to the field as a whole'.

4.3.4 The contextual factors influencing the evolution of a field

It is interesting to know the means through which the characteristics of any field can be influenced. For example, according to Whitley, the centralization of funds or jobs increases strategic dependence, and decentralization does the reverse. Such a decrease in strategic dependence was the case in bio-medical research in the USA, especially for cancer and heart diseases, when governments started pouring more and more money into this research area, thus creating additional sources of research funds. Knowledge of the effect on our field's characteristics of external or internal decisions and of collective or individual actions should help us understand the implications of propositions such as the claim for the establishment of MIS journals or clarification of reference disciplines.

Whitley (1984a) has identified three sets of contextual factors affecting the structures of scientific fields that constitute the more dynamic part of Whitley's model. They are:

(1) degree of reputational autonomy from competing intellectual organizations and the wider social structure in setting standards: performance standards, significance standards and descriptive terms and concepts;

(2) degree of concentration of control over access to the means of knowledge production and validation: extent to which control over jobs, facilities, funds, and journal space, is dominated by a small number of employment units and research sites (horizontal concentration) and to which it is unequally shared between employees within those units (vertical concentration);

(3) structure of reputational audiences: variety of audiences available to get a reputation and extent to which such audiences are ranked in terms of prestige and importance.

A concrete illustration of the workings of these contextual factors is the use of mathematics or statistical methods which reduces task uncertainty, restricts audiences and gives access to prestigious audiences. In the same way, centralization of control over publication outlets can, at least until new outlets are created, increase the degree of functional and strategic dependence.

4.4 THE CASE OF MIS

We first have to ask if MIS qualifies as a scientific field. The following facts support a positive answer.

Many universities offer MIS programmes at both undergraduate and graduate levels. These programmes are managed by MIS departments that receive and use MIS research funds. Specific publication outlets have emerged such as *MIS Quarterly* and *Information & Management*, while papers published in other prestigious journals are identified as MIS papers. Prestigious conferences such as the International Conference on Information Systems are held on a regular basis and MIS sections are created in more general conferences such as the Administrative Sciences Association of Canada annual conferences.

The availability of a directory of MIS academics in North America (MISRC/McGraw-Hill, 1986) containing entries on 1696 members, 447 schools and 469 academic programmes stands as an additional indication that MIS qualifies as a field. Based on these characteristics, we feel justified in assuming that MIS is a field.

4.4.1 MIS as a fragmented adhocracy

We will now attempt to classify MIS within the model previously presentec. We will not try to prove that MIS is of type such and such; our intention is to bring forward indications as to the type that best fits our perception of our field. To us, knowing the exact situation of MIS within the model is not in itself as important as the results of the exercise of trying to figure out where our field stands on each of the pertinent variables and how this can be argued. The process of classification can thus be used as a basis for further discussion on the actual state of MIS.

It will be argued here that MIS is a fragmented adhocracy; it shows low degrees of strategic and functional dependences and a high degree of strategic task uncertainty. Whitley (1984b) has established the main characteristics of a fragmented adhocracy as the following:

- research is rather personal and weakly coordinated in the field as a whole;
- a researcher can gain a reputation by contributing in a way that is largely specific to a group of colleagues or a research site;
- the field is largely open to an educated public and amateurs can affect the field's standards;
- barriers to entry in the field are weak and going from one fragment to another is quite easy;
- reputations are fairly fluid, control of resources is unstable, coalitions are likely to be ephemeral and leadership is often of charismatic nature;
- common-sense languages dominate the communication system.

The classification of MIS can first be established on the basis of what its members say about the field, its research objects and its methods. As a matter of fact, these have been the themes of many papers,

colloquia or conferences and the resultant epistemological considerations of active contributors to the field constitute rich material for
this purpose.

Anyone could list quite a number of definitions of the central object
of our discipline – a management information system – by looking up
in textbooks or research papers, but no one seems to have taken the
trouble to examine extensively these often conflicting definitions and
their implications. On the other hand, complete definitions of the field
of MIS are scarce, if there are any. It is not easy to define a field
whose members '. . . still have not settled on what should be included
or excluded from [their] area' (Dickson *et al.* 1982).

On the same matter, Culnan & Swanson (1986) state that the field
of MIS is only emerging and have found 'no evidence . . . that a
consensus has emerged as to the body of MIS work held to be integral
to the field.' This is hardly a surprising situation for a discipline whose
members '. . . get diverted almost daily, by new research ideas, gee-
whiz applications, consulting, etc.' (Keen, 1980). In terms of the
model used here, this indicates a low degree of strategic dependence
and also hints at a low degree of functional dependence since researchers' contributions are driven more by the new technological
opportunities (the weekly technological events of Dickson *et al.* 1982
or research fads) than by concern over their colleagues' contributions,
evaluation and judgment.

Ein-Dor & Segev (1981) have proposed a paradigm for MIS (even
though the use of paradigm gives them trepidations caused by the
'recent disrepute into which this word has fallen'). Their book contains
93 propositions linking over 100 variables partitioned between success
of MIS, as dependent macro variable and many independent variables.
These propositions are extracted from an extensive review of the
literature related to MIS and are presented under seven loosely
coupled headings indicating a fragmentation of research topics.

The expression 'identity crisis' used in Dickson *et al.* (1982) to
characterize MIS, illustrates this situation in which a researcher can
build his contribution upon previous results of colleagues in one or
two of these domains, but most probably not in all of them. This
results in a low degree of functional dependence among members
of the field and stands as an indication of a high strategic task uncertainty, as it is difficult to build an overall consensus on an exhaustive hierarchy of all the topics included in this multiplicity of research
areas.

As to the research methodologies used in the field of MIS, one can refer to the proceedings of an International Federation for Information Processing (IFIP) colloquium (Mumford *et al.* 1985), at which methodologies ranging from surveys to phenomenology were discussed and in which 'a theme that emerged very strongly was that we should let many flowers bloom'. The conclusion drawn by Bjorn-Andersen in Mumford *et al.* (1985) is: '. . . the main conclusion has been that of methodological pluralism . . .'. This conclusion can be related to Keen's (1980) statement that in MIS 'there is no clear theoretical base and no match between theory and method'. These indicate a high level of strategic task uncertainty in the field as a whole.

Klein's (1984) opinion on information systems development methodologies refers to a topic that, although of relatively narrow scope, is of major importance as it is concerned with the central object of our discipline. Saying that 'disagreement about the right methods of IS development extends to the diagnosis of what causes the problems' directly expresses a high level of strategic task uncertainty in a fragment of MIS concerned with a rather concrete problem.

To document our case from another angle, let us go 'inside' the field of MIS and consider the 'cognitive styles' research theme which has been quite popular for nearly a decade. A number of research papers related to this theme have been published since the seminal contribution of Mason & Mitroff (1973). The popularity of this research area could have been easily interpreted as the signal of the emergence of a cumulation of research results. However, after an extensive review of this literature, Huber (1983) came to the conclusion that the results of these studies did not lead to 'operational design guidelines' and that future research on this theme could not result in a significant contribution to the establishment of these guidelines. To him, the bulk of these contributions amounted to much ado about nothing. Even though Robey (1983) did qualify Huber's conclusion, he nevertheless conceded the thrust of his argument. The fact that Huber had not been one of the main contributors in the cognitive styles 'fragment', but cared enough to undertake its evaluation, indicates the presence of a strategic dependence within the MIS field. Indeed, by so doing, he was in fact questioning the significance and importance of this problem for MIS as a whole.

This can be taken as an indication that strategic dependence is high enough within MIS to qualify it as a field, at least as far as this particular dimension is concerned. But then, the fact that this research theme was not fundamentally questioned for almost ten years by other members of MIS not directly involved in this area shows that strategic dependence could hardly be seen as very high. Moreover, as Huber indicates, these research results did not find their way into design methods. This is an indication of low functional dependence.

Fragmented adhocracies have been described as displaying weak barriers to entry. The fact that entry into the field of MIS is perceived as fairly easy by many, at least in the academic world, is exemplified by the content of a brochure presented by the American Assembly of Collegiate Schools of Business (1986) (Information Systems Faculty Development Institute). In the presentation by the 1987 Information Systems Faculty Development Institute that offers a highly intensive, four and a half weeks programme, it is stated that:

'The course is specially designed for terminally qualified business school faculty members whose specialization and training is not in MIS, but who wish to move in this area to teach and do research. Management scientists, accountants and organization behavioralists are examples of intended participants . . . [others] are faculty holding a doctorate from non-business fields such as mathematics, computer science, information science, the behavioral sciences and education who wish to shift to a business school position.'

Finally, some writings can be interpreted as a global opinion on the fragmented nature of MIS. For example, according to Culnan & Swanson (1986): 'Davis suggests . . . that MIS represents the intersection of six fields of knowledge: computer science, behavioral science, decision science, organization and management, organizational function and management accounting.' And the fragmentation has an impact on doctoral students who, according to Keen (1980): 'since there is no consensual core to MIS research . . . are often puzzled as to how to structure their preparation.'

In our view, all the considerations presented suggest a strong fragmentation of MIS in relation to the research themes and methods and support a classification of MIS as a fragmented adhocracy.

4.4.2 Contextual factors applied to MIS

The fact that MIS is not purely academic – that MIS departments are to a large extent vocational schools in that their graduates are eagerly recruited by a supportive business community – has a considerable impact on the actual and future states of our field. Whitley has documented the influence of practitioners in similar cases, namely that of management sciences (1987), of administrative sciences at large (1986), and of business finance (1985). One of the main consequences of this influence is that (1987): 'long term, theoretically oriented research programmes are not very likely . . . to be developed and followed in these sorts of fields'.

Maintaining links between academics and consultants or MIS employees within organizations (audiences with possibly divergent objectives and methods) will always result in the actual low functional dependence. This would then imply that those requesting a Kuhnian paradigm, thus a high degree of functional dependence, may implicitly be asking for a separation between academics and other members of MIS. This would result in the aforementioned possible break-up of our field, as it is currently constituted, with the academics forming a new field. The setup of a new information systems research journal by The Institute of Management Science (*MIS Interrupt*, August 1987) promotes such a separation. While this would probably result in higher functional and strategic dependences, chances are that this new field could rapidly resemble the actual operational research (OR) field (Whitley 1985, 1987).

On the other hand, maintaining links with practitioners does not necessarily imply that MIS will remain a perpetual fragmented adhocracy. A possible evolution is illustrated by the example of business finance. This field has maintained strong connections with the practitioners, whose problems have always been considered worthy research topics, and who, being educated by the academics, have always applied to their practical problems the sophisticated methods they had learned. These strong connections, also reinforced by the fact that academics have themselves often been very active as practitioners, account for a high degree of strategic dependence and reduced strategic task uncertainty.

This example suggests that MIS, even with its strong vocational character, might evolve towards something other than a fragmented adhocracy. According to Whitley (1985), the field of business finance has moved from fragmented adhocracy to partitioned bureaucracy but could return to a fragmented state if: 'scientific reputations in the field become less strongly determined by analytical standards, and/or valued resources can be obtained through other routes'.

Indeed, as stated earlier, analytical standards such as the use of mathematics or statistical methods, reduce task uncertainty, restrict audiences and give access to prestigious audiences. Thus, requesting the use of statistical treatment of empirical data as the only legitimate research strategy for MIS implicitly promotes a move toward the partitioned bureaucracy or the conceptually integrated bureaucracy types. This transformation would be facilitated by the induced reduction in the number of participants and by more precise and stable problem formulations as they would have to be amenable to empirical investigation and statistical treatment. The side-tracking of possibly valuable contributions by researchers not privileging statistical or empirical approaches, and the potential reduction in the issues addressed, have to be considered.

The creation of other prestigious MIS journals would have the effect of increasing the degree of functional and strategic dependences since MIS authors could refer more easily to other MIS publications and less to management theory for publication in *Administrative Science Quarterly*, less to computer science for publication in the Association for Computing Machinery journals, and so on.

In conclusion, the contextual factors constitute the more dynamic part of Whitley's model; any transformation in these may influence a field's status. But the mechanisms that produce these transformations are subtle. No individual member of our field can impose changes on these contextual factors and the resulting characteristics for MIS. A scientific field is perpetually created by the community of its owners and cannot be deliberately changed without the convergent actions of a large segment of its members. Given the fragmented nature of MIS and the relative strength of each of its many fragments, it seems unlikely that it will become a monistic scientific field in the near future. But the main lesson to be drawn from the application of Whitley's model is that a field should be accepted for what it is.

4.4.3 The value of MIS is independent of its classification

The classification scheme just presented is, from a strictly epistemological point of view, value-free. A conceptually integrated bureaucracy can never be said to be better than a professional adhocracy. Any change in the classification of a field brought about by a change in its characteristics should not be seen as either promotion or demotion; going from conceptually integrated bureaucracy to professional adhocracy is no worse or better than going from polycentric oligarchy to technologically integrated bureaucracy. On the other hand, saying that no one box of the Whitley model is better than the other does not mean that these boxes are equally comfortable for researchers. Fragmented adhocracy, as it is the most liable to identity crisis by its very nature, is understandably less comfortable to some of its members than others.

This leads us to Chalmers' opinion quoted earlier stating that any scientific field is to be judged relative to its aims, their social importance and their degree of fulfilment. The failure of management science (or operations research as it is also known) and its prestigious mathematical apparatus to solve the problems of the larger field of management theory should stand as a proof that success in a field can be as relative to the simplicity of its objects or aims as it is to the power of its tools.

As to the value of our field considered from the point of view of Chalmers' criteria, a few things may be said that could comfort those who feel uneasy about the importance of the contribution of MIS members to the accrual of knowledge. With an original perspective centred on either management, information, systems or a combination of these, MIS has made significant contributions in many domains of knowledge. There are ways in which such fields as psychology, computer science, decision science, organization theory, managerial practice and others have benefited from work done in MIS. Let us simply mention two examples.

In recent years, the field of decision science has probably been more inspired by the efforts in the development of decision support systems (DSSs) than by anything else. The actual works on end-user computing could very well result in concrete means for managers to (at last!) recapture the control over the very critical organizational resource that information is.

This list could be extended as every member of MIS can think of significant contributions, but it should be emphasized that, even though the length of the list is important, it is not the only, or even the main, criterion. It is paramount to realize that these contributions have been made by scholars, or practitioners, who were having the kind of good time Simon was referring to. Let us keep this kind of spirit alive.

4.5 CONCLUSION

A preoccupation with the actual state and possible future of any scientific field is a legitimate and necessary epistemological quest. However, it is not an easy task. Such a preoccupation should be received with great care as it can be loaded with questionable implicit assumptions about the very nature of science and scientific work. It can be supported by monistic models such as Kuhn's which may seem appropriate to the past and present state of certain scientific disciplines such as physics. But, as has been argued in this chapter, such a monistic model cannot be used to properly understand the actual state and possible future of the MIS field.

MIS is a fragmented field or, to put it in other words, an essentially pluralistic scientific field, especially in view of its vocational character. It can thus be understood and analysed only with the help of pluralistic models. Such models exist and Whitley's can be brought to contribute to MIS with great benefits. It has been used here in an attempt to analyse the characteristics of MIS and understand the ways and means of change in these characteristics.

Any scientific field is a perpetual and continuous social construction (Astley 1985) that can be influenced with the proper tools. MIS can be changed but it will never be by a simple decree aiming to reduce it to a portion of itself or to make it into something it is not. Changes will result from the action of colleagues-competitors working on both the foundations and the emergent parts of MIS. This field is attractive to many, including the authors, because of its great variety of approaches and their potential and actual cross-fertilisation.

For example, the practical implications of alternative perspectives on organizations (Astley & Van de Ven 1983; Burrell & Morgan 1979; Morgan 1986) or on IS development (Klein & Hirschheim 1987; Kling 1980) have not yet been fully drawn. Members of the MIS field should not refuse any help from other disciplines, given the richness and complexity of their main research object – management information systems – and their numerous facets. There is room in MIS, and so should it stay, for the indispensable free enterprise will.

The call for more unity in MIS has been made by some, on the grounds that MIS is presently degenerating in a so-called free-for-all situation. Those supporting that point of view are, in fact, predicting the death of MIS . . . unless something is done. For them MIS is presently too much of a free enterprise.

It is first interesting to note that some of those who make this plea implicitly assume that scientific knowledge has some intrinsic characteristics that distinguish it from other forms of knowledge. So the plea for more unity very often becomes an implicit plea to abide by the standards of good scientific practice and a call for less laxity in the field. Arguments tend to be rational and the assumption is made that colleagues are ready to accept changes if these arguments are correctly presented.

Unfortunately, such a set of intrinsic and permanent standards does not exist. The failure of all the attempts up to now to identify and formalize them since the 1930s by the Vienna Circle members and their followers (Audet *et al.* 1986; Caldwell 1984; Hirschheim 1985; Le Moigne 1985; Piaget 1967) is an eloquent testimony in this regard. Of course, scientific knowledge must abide by some standards, but these standards are socially defined and redefined with time. So that what was considered to be scientific knowledge 50 or 100 years ago may not be so today.

It is at this point that Whitley's model is interesting for MIS, since it points at factors that are likely to influence the position of actors in the debate for gaining control of the definition of conditions and rules of knowledge production and validation. By so positing the problem, Whitley's model is a good instrument for reflecting on the ways MIS may evolve.

As a last word, let us return to two of the central concerns of this chapter: maturation and progress. In our view, maturation is not a one-way street leading necessarily toward the conceptually integrated bureaucracy square of Fig. 4.1 that represents Kuhn's normal science. This is a too restrictive view for MIS. Progress, on the other hand, cannot be seen to occur only when there seems to be cumulation of research knowledge, as was the case during the early years of the cognitive styles research theme era. To see progress in this way would be, according to Popper (1972), assuming that '. . . our mind resembles a container – a kind of bucket – in which perceptions and knowledge accumulate'. Progress can also occur when cumulative research knowledge is challenged. On the matter of progress, we share the view of Hesse (1980) who observes that it is pragmatic success that cumulates in science, not necessarily the amount of knowledge.

Part 2

Researching Information Systems: Issues and Methods

Introduction

Having looked at the nature of information systems in Part 1, and having discussed some of the issues associated with what constitutes an appropriate research philosophy in our context, we now turn to the subject of the research which *has* been undertaken, and which various commentators believe *should* be undertaken, in the field. Part 2 considers not only the *object* of attention of our research (i.e. the 'what') but also the *approaches* being adopted (i.e. the 'hows'). It therefore builds on the subject matter of Part 1 and leads into that of Part 3 – which deals with some of the more practical issues associated with our research task.

Part 2 begins with a paper by Ali Farhoomand (Chapter 5). This explores the historical progress of information systems in the light of the accepted paradigms of the philosophy of science. As a result of this analysis, a classification of research strategies and themes for the period 1977–85 is produced. The trends in research methods adopted are identified for this period and a comparison is made regarding the information systems topics that were actually being researched during the period, as against the issues that were seen as being most important at that time.

The latter is the focus of the following chapter, Chapter 6, by Rick Watson and Jim Brancheau. In it, they bring us up-to-date with the findings of research into the beliefs of senior information systems executives as to the most significant issues they face as we move towards the year 2000. What is of particular interest here is the comparisons they make between beliefs in different parts of the world – something which we need to take into account when researching in the field of information systems in the context of multi-national corporations and the global economy. While there appear to be a number of similarities between the views of information systems executives in Australia, Europe and the United States of America, there are some quite different opinions given by their Singaporian counterparts. The whole issue of regional and cultural differences, as they apply to the subject of information systems, appears to be a rich vein waiting to be tapped from future research efforts in the field.

Chapters 7 and 8 refocus our attention on the question of research methods. Chapter 7, by Scott Hamilton and Blake Ives, reviews the approaches adopted by information systems researchers during the period 1970–79. While it may seem inappropriate for a chapter to be devoted to material that is now somewhat dated, it is nevertheless interesting to see the trends in approaches being used at that time. What is also important about this chapter is the fact that the authors provide a cogent argument in favour of the use of empirical approaches. Further, they argue that a need exists to establish a balance between alternative approaches. Given that they found that the case study approach was most common, they argue for the need to build on this, and on conceptual work, by testing the hypotheses that have emerged as a result by means of laboratory and field experimentation.

While Chapter 8, written by myself, argues for a broader range of approaches to be applied and questions the validity of the scientific paradigm in information systems research, it also picks up Hamilton and Ives' latter point by stressing the need to place one's research in the context of relevant research that has been undertaken previously and that which might be undertaken in the future in the light of one's own results. Both the design of the book cover and Fig. 8.1 (from which the cover design is taken) reinforce this point.

In addition, Chapter 8 attempts to bring the subject matter of Part 2 together by developing a taxonomy of information systems research approaches which are related to the research topics being studied. By this means, it provides some guidance as to the range of approaches which might most appropriately be adopted for a particular topic, bearing in mind the approaches that have been adopted previously, as well as the outcomes from previous research.

While Chapter 8 does not pretend to provide all the answers as regards how to choose appropriate research approaches for a particular context, it does attempt to pick up the theme of methodological pluralism introduced in Chapter 3 by Rudy Hirschheim, and to provide a framework which will help in making the choice of approach (or approaches) to be adopted.

Chapter 5

Scientific Progress of Management Information Systems

ALI F. FARHOOMAND
Concordia University

The objective of this chapter is to explore the historical progress of management information systems (MIS) from a philosophic scientific perspective. The study is based on the thematic analysis of research strategies of 536 articles published during the period 1977–85. The results of this survey indicate that MIS has been undergoing significant shifts in terms of the research strategies employed by researchers. More specifically, there has been a shift from non-empirical research to empirical studies over the past nine years. However, it seems that in spite of recent progress in the demarcation of its boundaries, MIS has not made very significant progress as a scientific discipline. The position is taken in this chapter that this state of the art will not change until MIS develops a body of substantive theories specific to its domain.

5.1 INTRODUCTION

The critical examination of the status of management information systems (MIS) began nearly two decades ago (Ackoff 1967). Since then we have been witnessing heated debates among MIS and non-MIS academics as to where MIS should be heading, what approaches it should take, and what fields of study should be used as its reference disciplines. Academics outside the field, in particular, have been vocal in their criticisms about the scientific *raison d'être* of MIS. Moreover, they have questioned the ability of MIS to improve decision making in the organization (e.g. Dearden 1970).

Some MIS scholars have also expressed concerns about the scientific status of the field. For example, a large portion of the articles appearing in the *Proceedings of the First International Conference on Information Systems* (1980) were dedicated to issues relating to the problems and challenges of MIS. More recently, the Harvard Business School's Research Colloquium on Information Systems (McFarlan 1984) was entirely devoted to highlighting the research needs of the field.

Although these ongoing debates have not produced a consensus, they have resulted in the development of several comprehensive research frameworks and considerable clarification of the boundaries of the field. More important, they have expedited the process by which MIS can further entrench its position as a scientific field of study in the halls of academia.

In the light of these developments, several recent studies have examined the scientific status of MIS. One group of studies has surveyed and analysed the literature in order to explore the intellectual development (Culnan 1986a), intellectual structure (Culnan 1986b), and research profile (Vogel & Wetherbe 1984) of the field. Another group of articles (e.g., Klein & Welke 1982; Weber 1985) has used the paradigmatic approach (Kuhn 1970) to evaluate the academic position of the discipline without providing any empirical evidence. No research study, however, has analysed the prevailing research practices in the field in order to determine the evolution of MIS from a philosophical scientific perspective.

This chapter contends that the nature of scientific progress of a discipline should be studied through the careful examination of its history of thought, and in the light of the accepted paradigms in the philosophy of science. The objective of this chapter, therefore, is to explore the historical progress of MIS. It does this by using the thematic analysis of research strategies of 536 articles published between 1977–85.

The paper begins with a short discussion of the nature of scientific discovery, then continues with a framework of study to investigate the status of MIS. In the context of this framework, MIS is defined, its scientific community is identified, and its disciplinary matrix is described. Next comes a comprehensive classification of research strategies and research themes of MIS-related studies, published in six academic journals over the past decade. Finally, using the results of the literature survey, in addition to the related concepts in philosophy of science, some insights are provided into the scientific programme of MIS.

5.2 THE NATURE OF SCIENTIFIC DISCOVERY

An examination of scientific discovery is particularly helpful in understanding the way interdisciplinary fields of study evolve. This investigation not only enhances our knowledge of the descriptive and normative models of scientific advancement, but also makes it possible to comprehend the nature of the problems faced by the scientific communities of newly emerging disciplines such as MIS.

In his well-known book, *The Logic of Scientific Discovery*, Popper (1959) presents a new set of doctrines pertaining to the nature of scientific discovery and growth. More specifically, he maintains that the problem of epistemology can be studied either as the problem of ordinary or commonsense knowledge, or as the problem of scientific knowledge.

Although Popper shares the viewpoints of some philosophers in that scientific knowledge is the extension of ordinary knowledge, he disagrees with them that ordinary knowledge is capable of analysing the most important problems of epistemology. In particular, Popper contends that the growth of science is not possible in the confines of commonsense knowledge and must be undertaken through scientific knowledge. His belief that theories can only be falsified and not confirmed leads to his conclusion that the growth of scientific knowledge is due to the proliferation of a variety of theories, which by definition are permanently tentative.

With regard to the evolution of science, Popper states that the advancement of science is usually in an inductive direction; that is, going from theories of a lower level of universality to theories of a higher level. However, he asserts that this inductive direction must not imply that there is a sequence of inductive inferences in the evolution process.

From a logical point of view, Popper contends, we cannot make universal inferences based on singular observations because it is unjustifiable to establish the truth of universal statements based on experience. So when we are making a declaration about the truth of a universal statement based on experience, we are reducing the truth of this universal statement to the truth of singular ones. Or to rephrase, discoveries are guided by theories rather than theories being discovered by observation. Therefore, the direction of scientific advancement, which Popper calls 'quasi-inductive', should be explained in terms of degree of testability and corroborability. In other words, a well-corroborated theory supersedes an old one only if it contains the old one (i.e. if it is of a higher level of universality).

Some philosophers contend that science should be regarded as an ongoing social enterprise with common bonds of language and methodology. Full epistemic understanding of scientific theories can only be achieved by observing the dynamics of theory development (to understand a theory is to understand its use and development). These philosophers of science indicate that there is a need for an analysis of theories which focus on epistemic factors controlling the discovery, development and testing of theories. In particular, such an analysis should be predicated on the premise that science is pursued from within a conceptual perspective that determines which questions are important and what types of answers are acceptable.

Stated differently, science is pursued from within a *Weltanschauung* (defined as a comprehensive conception of the universe and of man's relation to it); and in order to understand theories, one should first understand their *Weltanschauung*. In essence, this approach emphasizes the history of science and the sociological factors influencing the development, articulation, and *Weltanschauungen* in science.

Several philosophers of science subscribe to the *Weltanschauung* approach, and attempts will be made to highlight the major viewpoints of one of the prominent protagonists of this perspective. Kuhn (1970) asserts that the evolution of scientific *Weltanschauungen* is basically discontinuous. In situations where there is fundamental disenchantment with the existing theories, a new *Weltanschauung* replaces the old one. More specifically, Kuhn argues that scientific revolutions do not occur through accumulation; rather, they happen in a tradition-shattering manner when one well-accepted theory is rejected in favour of another. In the process, the concerned community in the field follows certain discernible steps:

- they recognize anomalies in the field and become increasingly dissatisfied with the existing framework;
- they search for a new set of alternatives which, after debates and discussion, are transformed to schools of thought;
- they accept one or some of the schools of thought as the dominating framework over the alternatives.

It should be noted that the genesis of Kuhn's doctrine is based on the concept of paradigm. In the postscript of the second edition of *The*

Structure of Scientific Revolution (1970), he revised his conception of paradigm by stating that the term should be used in two different but interrelated sociological and philosophical contexts. In a sociological context, a paradigm refers to the constellation of beliefs and values shared by a scientific community; and in this sense, it should be called a disciplinary matrix. In a philosophical context, on the other hand, the term paradigm: '. . . denotes one sort of element in that constellation, the concrete puzzle-solutions which, employed as models of examples, can replace explicit rules as a basis for the solution of the remaining puzzles of normal science'.

Later, Kuhn attempted to further disentangle the meaning of paradigm. He maintained that (Kuhn 1974): '. . . One sense of "paradigm" is global, embracing all the shared commitments of scientific group; the other isolates a particularly important sort of commitment and thus is a subset of the first one.' The concept of paradigm, he declared, should be closely linked to the scientific community, i.e. explication of a paradigm requires the understanding that scientific communities have an independent existence, and that a paradigm or a set of paradigms: '. . . account(s) for the relatively unproblematic character of professional communication and for the relative unanimity of professional judgment.'

More specifically, the first sense of paradigm in the above definition – disciplinary matrix – can be regarded as a kind of scientific *Weltanschauungen*. The second sense of paradigm is renamed exemplars and is referred to as (Kuhn 1970): '. . . achievements sufficiently unprecedented to attract an enduring group of adherents away from competing modes of scientific activity. Simultaneously, it was sufficiently open-ended to leave all sorts of problems for the redefined group of practitioners to resolve.'

It should be noted that disciplinary matrices (Suppe 1974) 'are acquired implicitly through the educational processes whereby one comes to be a licensed practitioner of the scientific discipline. This implicit acquisition comes from the study of one portion of the disciplinary matrix which can be explicitly formulated, the exemplars.'

Depending on the exemplars one holds, one sees the world differently and consequently one has different scientific values. During the initial establishment of a scientific discipline, because of the paucity of exemplars and the relatively limited scope and precision of the existing ones, a scientific community strives to enhance the exemplars so that they can be applied to a wider and more precise set of applications.

From an epistemological vantage point, the major commonalities in the viewpoint of several modern philosophers outweigh the ostensible differences in their ideological convictions. For example, if we compare Kuhn's theses with Popper's doctrines about the nature of scientific growth, we will notice that they basically share the same views, particularly in the revolutionary, rather than evolutionary, nature of scientific advancement where old theories are rejected and replaced by new ones.

5.3 A FRAMEWORK FOR STUDY OF SCIENTIFIC PROGRESS IN MIS

It is difficult, if not impossible, to examine the evolutionary process of any phenomenon in the light of definitional ambiguity. To this end, we shall define the term MIS before we establish a framework for study of its scientific progress.

The term MIS was originally introduced in 1968 to replace the term information technology. Since then, the concerned bodies in the areas have tried to provide precise definitions for MIS in order to differentiate it from other disciplines. For the purpose of this chapter we will employ the following definition (Davis & Olson 1985):

> 'MIS is an integrated, user-machine system for providing information to support operations, management, analysis and decision making functions in an organization.'

It is important to notice that both the label and the definition of a concept are instrumental in identifing a field's identity. The periodical challenge from proponents of title change (e.g. DSS) or definitional change is consequently helpful in better understanding the domain of the discipline, which may well expand beyond its original boundary.

Having defined the term MIS, we can now present our framework, which is predicated on a Kuhnian perspective (Kuhn, 1970). According to this doctrine, the examination of scientific progress of a discipline should follow these steps:

- identifying the scientific community of the discipline;
- delineating its disciplinary matrix;
- identifying the dominating schools of thought in the area.

In the following paragraphs we shall attempt to describe the specificities of these steps.

5.3.1 The scientific community of MIS

In order to regard a discipline as a unique field of study, we should be able to highlight the specifics of that discipline, including the commonalities of its members and the communication outlets which they use to exchange information. This position is congruent with Kuhn's doctrine, which regards the identification of the scientific community of a field as the first prerequisite for the study of evolution of that discipline. In this context, Kuhn (1970) states that a scientific community consists 'of the practitioners of a scientific specialty... [who] have undergone similar education and professional initiations, [and] in the process they have absorbed the same technical literature'.

The formation of the scientific community of MIS seems to be in its maturing stages, as we have recently witnessed new developments in this area. For example, there has been growing concern, both among academics and among practitioners, about a common curriculum of MIS education; and we have seen a convergence of opinions about the boundaries as well as the 'goals' of MIS in the specialised communications outlets.

Three major reasons can be cited as to why MIS does not possess a more entrenched scientific community. First, the pioneers in MIS education, who through their contributions have built MIS into an independent academic discipline, have themselves come from diverse backgrounds, i.e. they have not gone through similar education. Second, some of these members have invariably held their primary academic affiliations with the scientific community of their original field of study. Finally, the MIS practitioners, by and large, have historically concentrated on only one aspect of the discipline, i.e. design and development of information systems.

5.3.2 The disciplinary matrix of MIS

Kuhn identifies four major components of a disciplinary matrix as symbolic generalizations, shared commitments, values and exemplars. It is worth noting that the disciplinary matrix, in essence, is the base grounding of any field. Once one learns about various elements of the matrix, one can communicate in the same language with other members of this group about all problem situations. In what follows, the four major components of an MIS disciplinary matrix are summarized briefly. Detailed discussions of these components can be found in Klein & Welke (1982).

(1) Symbolic generalizations

Symbolic generalizations include the readily understood, formalizable components of the matrix. In MIS, they comprise programming languages, program and system flowchart symbols, and acronyms used to describe operational as well as procedural components of an information system.

(2) Shared commitments

Shared commitments are beliefs in particular models, along a spectrum from heuristic to ontological models. They help determine what will be accepted as explanations of solutions; conversely, they help in identification of unsolved problems. Although it is difficult to point to global shared commitments in MIS, we can cite examples of shared commitments in the specific sub-areas of MIS. For instance, a top-down approach or bottom-up approach to system analysis and system design, and the taxonomy of DSS can be viewed as examples of shared commitment in MIS.

(3) Values

Values refer to the standards which govern the quality of the work of the members of the community. The importance of values is manifested when there is a crisis and the members of the community have to choose between incompatible ways of practising their discipline. According to Kuhn, the identification of a scientific community is a *sine qua non* of every disciplinary matrix. Therefore the value system of a scientific discipline, which is a component of the disciplinary matrix, is determined and assessed by the opinions of its influential members such as the reviewers and editors of academic journals.

Owing to the infancy of MIS, however, its influential members come from diverse, non-MIS backgrounds. As a result, the value system governing MIS is, to a certain degree, a *pot-pourri* of the values of other disciplines. It follows then that MIS will not possess its own values until there is a consensus of opinion among the concerned bodies about the composition of its scientific community.

(4) Exemplars

Exemplars are problem solutions that a student of a discipline en-
counters during his/her training, including textbooks and the result of
research activities in the field. Kuhn maintains that 'more than other
sorts of components of the disciplinary matrix, differences between
sets of exemplars provide the community fine-structure of science'
(Kuhn 1970). He further states that via the study of exemplars the
student develops a similarity relation, which is used to model symbolic
generalizations to empirical situations. Although there are indications
that the number of MIS textbooks and of MIS-related articles published
in various journals has been growing in recent years, it is difficult to
point to many exemplars which are shared by the IS community.

5.3.3 Research practices

We examined 536 articles published over the nine-year period from
1977 through 1985, in order to get a better understanding of the
prevailing research practices in the area. Six journals were selected.
The entire collection of three journals (*MIS Quarterly, Information &
Management*, and *Systems, Objectives and Solutions*) were included.
For the other three journals (*Management Science, Communications of
the ACM*, and *Harvard Business Review*), a computer-based search
was performed.

The selection criterion was the observation of data processing,
management information systems, information systems, and decision
support systems or their corresponding acronyms in the title or in the
abstract of the articles. Eight articles from the *HBR* list and one article
from *Management Science* were deleted because, although they contained one of the search keys in their title or abstract, their primary
focus was on some non-MIS issues. We referred to the research
methodology section of an article whenever we had a problem classifying the research strategy of the article based on the content of
its abstract. Table 5.1 shows the characteristics of the six journals
examined.

The above research methodology is similar to content analysis used
by the Naisbitt Group (1982) in *Megatrends*. The roots of this method
can be traced to World War II when intelligence specialists tried to
gather information on enemy nations through use of public opinion
polls. In other words, monitoring public behaviour based on the

Table 5.1 Characteristics of journals examined.

Journal	Time period	Number of articles	% in total
MIS Quarterly	1977–85*	178	33.6
Information & Management	1977–84	171	32.3
Systems, Objectives and Solutions	1981–4	59	11.1
Communications of the ACM	1977–85	53	10.0
Management Science	1977–85	38	7.2
Harvard Business Review	1977–85	31	5.8
Total		530	100.0

*Does not include the last issue of 1985 (Vol. 9, No. 4).

analysis of the content of a society's newspapers is predicated upon the premise that the amount of space devoted to news in a newspaper remains fixed over time. When something new occurs, something else has to be omitted, i.e. a society can be preoccupied with certain problems and issues at any given time, and the collective news hole is the mechanism which it uses to reflect its priorities.

The Naisbitt Group made this observation based on a comprehensive analysis of a great number of local papers in different states. They argued that in addition to the above phenomenon, most of the social inventions occur in certain 'bellwether' communities, and the others are simply followers. Our rationale for using the above methodology was simple: the amount of space in academic journals devoted to MIS-related issues has not changed significantly over time. Few new academic journals had emerged during the period studied, and the MIS section of non-MIS journals seemed to have remained fixed in size. Although a few new academic MIS journals have emerged in recent years, some others have been discontinued after some time (e.g. *System*, *Objectives*, *Solutions* and *Technology and Human Affairs*). The number of MIS articles in *Management Science* has varied from 3 to 7 per year in the nine year period prior to the original publication of this article, in 1987).

Furthermore, there are indications that some publications are the 'bellwether' journals of MIS, as evidenced by the survey of Hamilton & Ives (1983) pertaining to journal preference among academics as well as practitioners.

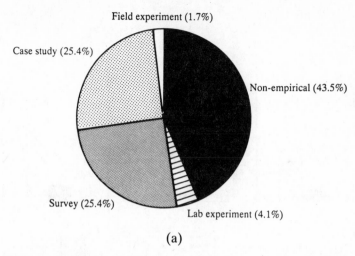

(a)

Fig. 5.1a Research strategy 1977–85.

Analysis of IS research strategies

The first purpose of our survey was to investigate the existing trend in MIS-related research strategies. We employed the research taxonomy utilized by Hamilton & Ives (1982) – and included in this volume as Chapter 7 – and classified the articles into five categories: case study, survey, field test, experiment and non-empirical. Because we were also interested in the trend of research strategies, we divided our timeframe into three 3-year periods (1977–79, 1980–82, 1983–5). We ensured the reliability of our procedure by having a random sample of the articles reassessed by a colleague who was given instructions about the classification procedure. We found the result of the sample classification generally in agreement with the original classification.

Figure 5.1a exhibits the MIS research summary by taxonomy category for all the articles in the nine-year period. Over 43% of the published research belongs to the non-empirical class, which is much smaller than the 70% reported by Hamilton & Ives. Two factors could have caused this change:

(1) different journal samples (we used only a subset of the sample of 15 journals used by Hamilton & Ives);
(2) true change in preference for other research strategies (our survey deals with 1977–85, Hamilton and Ives' survey focussed on 1970–79).

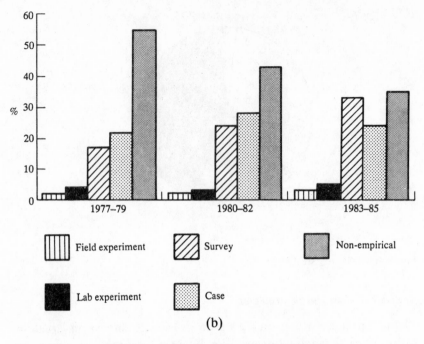

Fig. 5.1b Research strategy 1977–79, 1980–82 and 1983–85.

The majority of empirical studies are either case study or survey (approximately 25% each) and the remainder are divided between experiment and field test (4.1% and 1.7% respectively). Figure 5.1b shows the MIS research summary for the three periods. As was mentioned before, the non-empirical studies have continually decreased over time (from 55% to 43% to 35%); survey has increased consistently (from 17% to 24% to 33%); and case study has moved up in the second period but has decreased in the third (from 22% to 28%, then to 24%). Experiment and field test comprise a small portion of all the studies and have shown insignificant movement over the years.

Analysis of IS research themes

The second purpose of our study was to identify the dominating themes of research in MIS. We used the result of a thematic analysis of the strategy statements provided by twelve leading schools to the *Harvard Research Colloquium on the Information Systems Research Challenge* (McFarlan 1984). Table 5.2 indicates the important research

Table 5.2 Information systems research themes.

(1) Cost benefit analysis.
(2) Databases, systems, software design.
(3) Data management, information resource management (IRM).
(4) Decision support systems (DSS), decision theory.
(5) End-user computing (EUC).
(6) Expert systems, artificial intelligence.
(7) Human-computer interface.
(8) Impact.
(9) Implementation.
(10) Information requirements analysis (IRA).
(11) Interorganizational systems.
(12) Management of and planning for IS.
(13) Organizational design.
(14) Strategic use of IS.
(15) Technology transfer.
(16) Other.

themes. Because some research studies examined did not fall into any of these 15 themes, we added an 'other' class to the list.

We performed our thematic analysis by classifying articles according to the keywords provided for the articles. Since an article is usually accompanied by several keywords, we included all the associated keywords in the analysis without including a weight for the extent of contribution of a particular theme.

We counted the number of times a keyword was observed in articles and then calculated the percentage of articles related to a particular theme by dividing that number by the total number of articles. Of 46 articles (9%) which we could not classify into one of the fifteen categories, more than half appeared in *Information & Management*.

In order to facilitate presentation of the results, the top five (Fig. 5.2a) as well as the second five (Fig. 5.2b) dominating themes are grouped together. As can be seen in Fig. 5.2a, although data bases, systems, software design, and management of and planning for IS, lead the list as the two dominating themes, there has not been a consistent increase or decrease in their popularity over the years. On the other hand, the third top theme (human-computer interface) as well as the fifth top (DSS) have shown steady, increasing acceptance among researchers in the last nine years.

It is also interesting to note that the top three themes (design,

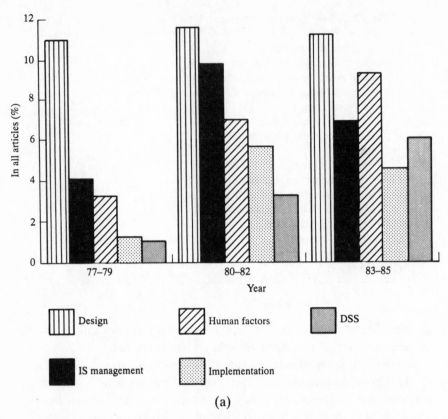

Fig. 5.2a Top five popular research themes.

management of IS and human-computer interface) each belong to one of the major MIS influences (technical, organizational and behavioural respectively), while the next two themes (implementation and DSS) could fit into all three categories. Six areas were found to have received little attention over the years: expert systems, artificial intelligence, interorganization systems, strategic use of IS, impact, cost-benefit analysis, and end-user computing.

It is worth noting that there is a large difference between the existing research practices and what practitioners deem important. Table 5.3 contrasts the ranking of ten top research themes with the ranking of ten key IS management issues, as identified by IS professionals and reported by Dickson *et al.* (1984).

We performed a Kendall rank correlation to see whether there is a correlation between these two rankings. This coefficient is used as a

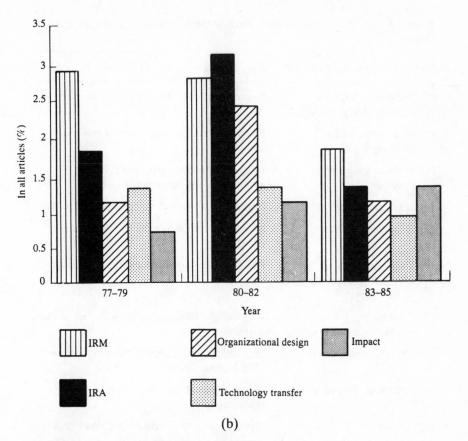

Fig. 5.2b Second five popular research themes.

measure of the agreement between the ranks assigned to the topics (Siegel 1956). In order to calculate the correlation coefficient, we had to drop information requirements analysis from the research theme list and end user computing from the key issues so that we could have nine topics common to both lists. We paired up the topics in the two lists as follows (research list numbers first): 1–4, 2–1, 3–6, 4–8, 5–10, 6–9, 8–7, 9–3, 10–5.

The rank correlation coefficient was found to be −0.11, indicating a very weak association between the two rankings. Although the key issues did not exactly match their counterparts in the research theme list, the weak correlation manifests the divergence of research practices over the previous nine years and what IS professionals regarded as important for the 1980s.

Table 5.3 Ranking of top research themes contrasted with ranking of top key IS issues.

Ranking of IS research theme	Key IS issue
(1) Databases, systems, software design	Improved IS planning
(2) Management of and planning for IS	Facilitation and management of end-user computing
(3) Human-computer interface	Integration of data processing, office automation and telecommunications
(4) Implementation	Improved software development and quality
(5) DSS, decision theory	Measuring and improving IS effectiveness/ productivity
(6) Data management, information resource management	Facilitation of organizational learning and usage of IT
(7) Information requirements analysis	Aligning the IS organization with that of the enterprise
(8) Organizational design	Specification, recruitment and development of IS human resources
(9) Technology transfer	Effective use of the organization's data resources
(10) Impact	Development and implementation of DSS

Several difficulties were confronted in the survey phase of this study. These limitations are classified into five broad categories, of which the first four are related to the methodological issues and the last one is associated with the predictive power of the results in terms of forecasting the status of MIS in the future.

(1) *Sample bias* As previously noted, we employed a sample of six journals out of IS journals identified as being important to the communication of MIS research. Although the sample includes the bellwether journals, it lacks completeness and consequently does not entice total credence with respect to generalizability. Moreover, the change in editorial policy of the journals over time could have affected the results.

(2) *Strategy classification* A large portion of case study articles in the sample introduce a model or present an argumentative/subjective discussion (Vogel & Wetherbe 1984) before conducting the empirical part. Since the taxonomy of the research strategies was treated as containing mutually exclusive categories, we classified this type of deductive study in the case study category. Therefore, the figure reported for this classification (25.4%) appears to be inflated.

(3) *Keyword classification* Because of the multidisciplinary, multi-dimensional nature of the majority of MIS studies, we had to classify them into several different research themes. The lack of a measure of the extent of contribution of a particular theme could have had some bearing on the results of the thematic analysis.

(4) *Key issues correlation* The lack of a strong correlation between the key IS issues and the prevailing research practices could be attributed to the time lag that exists between the conception of a research idea and the actual publication of the corresponding research study. It would be fruitful to conduct a similar study within three to five years to investigate any potential shifts which might have been created by the demand pull (i.e. the key issue) for certain types of research.

(5) *Predictive power* King & Kraemer (1984), in the context of theories of the social sciences, distinguish between evolutionist and evolutionary models of change. The former perspective 'assesses history as a developmental, progressive, and directional set of changes that increase in their complexity or perfection with the passage of time'. The latter perspective, by contrast, is concerned with mechanisms by which changes occur.

Because the framework presented in this paper is essentially based on an evolutionist view, it exhibits the strengths and weaknesses inherent in these types of models. In particular, one of the primary weaknesses of our findings appears to be the inability to explain why changes in research activities occur the way they do. This limitation, in turn, makes it difficult to extrapolate the results and predict the exact nature of changes in the future.

5.4 CONCLUSIONS

The results of our study point to certain discernible developments in MIS. More specifically, our findings suggest that there has been a steady movement away from non-empirical work to empirical studies. Furthermore, our thematic analysis of articles suggests that while design and management of IS have proved to be the most popular research themes, they have not consistently held that position over the nine years of the study. On the other hand, human-computer interface and DSS have gained increasing popularity during the same period. Finally, none of the three major MIS influences (technical, organizational and behavioural) seem to be dominating research activities, as evidenced by the equal distribution of the popular research themes among these major influences.

As previously remarked, in order to examine the scientific progress of a field we need to get an intimate insight into the domain of that field. In other words, understanding the dynamic interplay between theories and domains is essential, not only for explaining the theoretical structure of the discipline but also for understanding the boundaries within which the field is evolving. It is important to note that even though the domain of MIS is more or less distinguishable, its theoretical structure has not received a great deal of attention because of a severe lack of substantive theories in the area. The inter-logic of any scientific discipline is its theoretical underpinnings and, as Popper (1959) notes, scientific growth is possible only through proliferation of theories.

Not surprisingly, the rather insignificant scientific progress of MIS can be attributed, to a large degree, to the fact that MIS lacks articulated theories of its own. What is suggested here is in congruence with Keen's call for a cumulative tradition (1980) and Weber's call for paradigms in MIS (1985). That is, MIS will not make significant progress as a scientific field of study until it can both explicate its disciplinary matrix through development of its own theories, and enhance its exemplars so that they can be applied to a wider and more precise set of applications. It is only through well-grounded theories that the discipline will be able to shape the goals and boundaries of its domain structurally, not cosmetically.

As a corollary to this argument, it is asserted that the reason Nolan's Stage Growth Model has become so popular and at the same time so controversial (Benbasat *et al.* 1984; King & Kraemer 1984) is that this model is one of the few articulated theories in MIS. And irrespective of its ability to withstand scientific scrutiny, the Nolan model will be remembered as a major contribution to the field of MIS because it is the first theory that:

(1) has introduced a specific concept to MIS which is widely accepted and used by practitioners;
(2) has stimulated a great deal of fruitful debate in the academic circles about its validity.

In spite of the field's dire need for theories, the results of this study indicate that MIS researchers have concentrated mainly on either design-related studies or on purely inductive methods of research. As a result, the deductive methods of knowledge generation, as well as the essential interplay between these methods and the inductive methods, have received little attention in the area, thus leaving out an important component of any scientific discovery. Moreover, there are strong indications that a large portion of research in the field is still not well-grounded in the fundamentals of organizational behaviour and organizational theory (Culnan 1986). This has consequently prevented MIS from building a cumulative research tradition which would have, in turn, helped the field fulfil its basic mandate – effective support of decision making in the organization.

In short, the boundaries of the domain of MIS – i.e. its scientific community, its reference disciplines and its definition – seem to have gained general acceptance. However, what has hampered scientific progress in the field to a large extent is the lack of a substantive ideology.

If we apply Kuhn's notion of revolution to MIS, it appears that MIS is emerging from the period of professional insecurity, wherein the rules are increasingly scrutinized and the disciplinary matrix is questioned but not abandoned. The embarkation on the next stage of the evolution – i.e. proposals of alternative sets of ideas which will ultimately turn into schools of thought – will not be possible until MIS develops its own theories. Unfortunately, purely empirical research which is not based on solid theoretical foundations, or studies which are primarily preoccupied with technology, will not facilitate reaching this objective.

Chapter 6

Key Issues in Information Systems Management: An International Perspective

R.T. WATSON
University of Georgia
AND
J.C. BRANCHEAU
University of Colorado

The study discussed here compares and contrasts the findings of recent IS management studies in Australia, Europe, Singapore and the United States. It examines the key concerns of IS executives in these areas, focussing on identifying and explaining regional similarities and differences. IS executives in Australia, Europe and the USA show a reasonable level of agreement on the most critical issues they face. They take a mid- to long-range perspective on their function and are very concerned with planning and managing external relationships. Singaporean managers perceive that their problems are different and several explanations are put forward for understanding this difference. IS executives in multinational firms who are aware of regional differences should be able to manage the IS function more effectively. At a minimum, IS executives must be cognisant of the varying perspectives inherent in a global economy.

6.1 INTRODUCTION

The recent shift of economic power towards the Pacific rim, the approaching economic unification of Europe, and the eroding economic dominance of the USA are clear signs of the globalization of the world's economy. Executives of multinational organizations can no longer afford to view their information systems function within the context of national and regional boundaries. Managing information systems is no longer a domestic issue. IS executives must plan and coordinate their function's activities on a worldwide basis. To be effective in this broader role, they must be sensitive to national and regional differences in the social, cultural and economic climate. Such differences are often reflected in the key concerns of executives operating within national and regional bounds.

Studies of the key concerns of IS executives have been conducted in the USA (Ball & Harris 1982; Brancheau & Wetherbe 1987; Callan 1989; Dickson *et al.* 1984; Hartog & Herbert 1986); in Singapore (Rao *et al.* 1987); in Europe (Davenport & Boday 1988; Hirschheim *et al.* 1988); and Australia (Watson 1988). Many of these studies have restricted their scope to a national sample and most of the others have compared the results from a single region with results from the USA.

This study compares and contrasts the findings of recent studies in Australia, Europe, Singapore and the USA. The intent is to take a broader look at the key concerns of IS executives worldwide, to determine which concerns are global and which are regional in nature. Knowledge of regional similarities and differences can assist IS executives in effectively managing their increasingly global function. IS executives with purely regional or national responsibilities can gain some insights into why issues are important in their arena and not elsewhere.

6.2 THE REGIONAL VIEWS

The four studies selected for analysis represent the most current and consistent data available in each of the four regions. In the case of the USA, where several studies are available for analysis, the most recent Delphi study is chosen because of the strength of its approach, because of the authors' detailed knowledge of its results, and because it was used as a basis for at least two of the other studies reported here.

6.2.1 USA

The most recent Delphi study of key issues in the USA was conducted in 1986 by the MIS Research Center (MISRC) at the University of Minnesota (Brancheau & Wetherbe 1987). Closely following an established model (Dickson *et al.* 1984), the study involved a three round Delphi survey of IS executives from the Society for Information Management (SIM). For its starting point, it relied on a list of key issues generated and reported in Dickson's study. The final round of the study involved 68 IS executives from all regions of the USA (a 38% response rate).

The study reports that the major concerns of USA-based IS executives are:

(1) improving strategic planning;
(2) using information systems for competitive advantage;
(3) facilitating organizational learning;
(4) increasing understanding of the role and contribution of IS;
(5) aligning IS with the organization.

Historical trend data are presented to show that managerial/enterprise issues have begun to dominate technical/application issues in importance. The study concludes that USA-based IS executives are making the transition from managing their function to managing the relationship between IS and the enterprise.

6.2.2 Australia

Using the issues identified in the USA study as his starting point, Watson (1988) conducted a three-round Delphi survey of the chief concerns of IS executives in Australia's 200 largest organizations. Two modifications were made to the method used in the USA study. Respondents were asked to rate, rather than rank, each issue. In addition, the results of each Delphi round were fed back to non-respondents in an effort to improve the response rate. The final round of the 1988 study involved 48 IS executives (a 24% response rate).

The study reports that the major concerns of Australian IS executives are:

(1) improving IS strategic planning;
(2) specifying recruiting and developing human resources;
(3) developing an information architecture;
(4) improving the effectiveness of software development;
(5) aligning the IS organization with that of the enterprise.

The investigation suggests that these issues reflect strong awareness of managerial problems, with an emphasis on issues relating to the interface between IS and the rest of the organization. The study concludes that Australian IS executives need to view IS as an integral part of the business and that IS managers should concentrate on managing the relationship between IS and the organization.

6.2.3 Europe

Using issues similar to those of the SIM studies as their starting point, the USA-based Index Group conducted a single round survey of key issues of European IS executives in 1988 (Davenport & Boday 1988). It is possible that this study is indicative of UK views rather than those of Europe in general because native English speakers are more likely to respond to an English language questionnaire. The survey involved 75 high-ranking IS executives from among the 2000 European readers of the *Indications* newsletter (a 4% response rate). Despite the low response rate, the study's findings (in terms of issue rankings) closely parallel an in-depth study of 10 leading IS executives in the United Kingdom (Hirschheim *et al.* 1988). The parallel nature of the findings lends support for the validity of both studies.

The Index study reports that major concerns of European IS executives are:

(1) improving IS strategic planning;
(2) aligning the IS organization with that of the enterprise;
(3) increasing understanding of the role and contribution of IS;
(4) using information systems for competitive advantage;
(5) developing an information architecture.

Similar to the USA and Australian studies, it concludes that strategic issues dominate tactical issues and that managerial issues dominate technical issues.

6.2.4 Singapore

Rao *et al.* (1987) conducted a single-round survey of IS executives of the Singapore Data Processing Management Association in 1987. While the study involved only 19 executives (an 18% response rate), this number is reasonably high relative to Singapore's base population, which is two orders of magnitude less than that of the USA or Europe.

The study reports that the major concerns of Singapore's IS executives are:

Table 6.1 Mapping from the European study to international issues.

National issue	International issue
Strategic planning	Strategic planning
Aligning IS and corporate goals	Organizational alignment
Educating senior management of IS potential and role	IS's role and contribution
Using IS for competitive advantages	Competitive advantage
Developing an information architecture	Information architecture
Determining appropriate IS funding level	IS's funding level
IS human resources	Human resources
Managing organization changes caused by IS	Organizational learning
Telecommunications	Telecommunications
Integrating systems	Integrating systems
Measuring and increasing IS productivity	Measuring effectiveness
Data utilization	Data as a resource
End-user computing	End-user computing
Improving software development	Software development
Information security and control	Security and control

National issues (Davenport & Boday 1988) are listed only if they appear among the top ten issues in at least one of the studies reviewed.

(1) measuring and improving IS effectiveness;
(2) facilitating and managing end-user computing;
(3) keeping current with new technology and systems;
(4) integrating office automation, data processing and telecommunications;
(5) training and educating DP personnel.

The study suggests that substantial changes in the role of IS are in progress and concludes that Singaporean IS executives need a solid business orientation and strong organizational skills to manage the expanding role of their function successfully.

6.3 THE GLOBAL VIEW

To facilitate analysis across regions, the SIM-based issues are used as the basis for a standardized (international) set of issues. Selecting these issues permits use of the USA and Australian results without reinter-

Table 6.2 Mapping from the Singapore study to international issues.

National issue	International issue
Measuring/improving MIS/DP effectiveness	Measuring effectiveness
Facilitating/managing end user computing	End-user computing
Keeping current with technology/systems	Organizational learning
Integrating OA, DP and communications	Integrating technologies
Training and education of DP personnel	Human resource
Data security and control	Security and control
Disaster recovery planning	Security and control
Translating information technology into competitive advantage	Competitive advantage
Having top management understand the needs and perspectives of the MIS/DP department	IS role and contribution
Impact of new technology on people and their role in company	Organizational learning
Developing a three to five year IS Plan	Strategic planning
Use of productivity tools in systems development	Software development
Centralization v. decentralization	Organizational alignment

National issues (Rao *et al.* 1987) are listed only if they appear among the top ten issues in at least one of the studies reviewed.

pretation. Due to their probable bias in the SIM studies, the European results also easily map into the international issues (for details see Table 6.1). Mapping the Singaporean results into international issues is more difficult due to differences in the wording used to describe the issues. Nevertheless, careful review of the Singapore study enables a reasonably accurate mapping of the issues (for details see Table 6.2).

Table 6.3 presents the results of the four studies in terms of international issues. They are listed in ascending order based on average rank. Because the Singapore sample was so small and because values for some key issues were missing, the Singapore data were not used to compute the average rankings. The table includes all issues which rank among the top ten in at least one of the studies. The overall rankings suggest a surprising level of agreement on the top five international issues in Australia, Europe and the USA. It is immediately apparent that IS managers in Singapore have a quite different set of top issues.

To assist interpretation of the results, issues are classified along dimensions of management/technology, planning/control and internal/external. Where possible, issue classification follows the work reported

Table 6.3 International issues in IS management regional rankings.

Overall ranking	International issue	Australia 1988	Europe 1988	Singapore 1987	USA 1986	Average ranking	Standard deviation	Spread
1	Strategic planning	1	1	11	1	1.00	0.00	0.00
2	Organizational alignment	5	2	15	5	4.00	1.73	3.00
3	Competitive advantage	7	4	8	2	4.33	2.52	5.00
3	IS's role and contribution	6	3	9	4	4.33	1.53	3.00
5	Information architecture	3	5	—	8	5.33	2.52	5.00
6	Organizational learning	10	8	3	3	7.00	3.61	7.00
6	Human resources	2	7	5	12	7.00	5.00	10.00
8	End-user computing	8	14	2	6	9.33	4.16	8.00
8	Data as a resource	9	12	—	7	9.33	2.52	5.00
10	Software development	4	14	12	13	10.33	5.51	10.00
11	Telecommunications	13	9	—	11	11.00	2.00	4.00
12	Integrating technology	18	10	4	10	12.67	4.62	8.00
13	Measuring effectiveness	19	11	1	9	13.00	5.29	10.00
14	Security and control	17	18	6	18	17.67	0.58	1.00
15	IS funding level	27	6	—	20	17.67	10.69	21.00

Includes all issues ranking among the top ten in at least one of the national studies reviewed.

Table 6.4 International issues in IS management classification of issues.

Ranking	International issue	M/T	P/C	I/E
1	Strategic planning	M	P	E
2	Organizational alignment	M	C	E
3	Competitive advantage	M	P	E
3	IS's role and contribution	M	P	E
5	Information architecture	M	P	I
6	Organizational learning	M	C	E
6	Human resources	M	C	I
8	End-user computing	M	C	E
8	Data as a resource	M	C	E
10	Software development	T	C	I
11	Telecommunications	T	C	E
12	Integrating technology	T	C	E
13	Measuring effectiveness	M	C	I
14	Security and control	T	C	I
15	IS funding level	M	P	E

M/T indicates management (M) or technology (T) issue; P/C indicates planning (P) or control (C) issue; I/E indicates internal (I) or external (E) issue.

in the regional studies. For example, the management/technology dichotomy is based on Brancheau & Wetherbe's (1987) classification and the external/internal split is based on Hirschheim *et al.* (1988). Despite attempts to follow earlier studies, subjective judgement is involved, since some issues overlap categories. Table 6.4 illustrates the classification for each issue.

Among the top ten issues, all are predominantly management-related concerns; none reflect strong technological concerns. The top five issues indicate a very strong concern for long-range strategy and planning, while the second five issues suggest concern for mid-range tactical and control issues.

The majority of the top ten issues also reflect a strong external orientation. IS executives appear to be heavily concerned with managing external relations, i.e. managing the relationship between IS and the enterprise. In recent years, the external orientation has emerged as a dominant theme in the IS management literature (Benjamin *et al.* 1985; Hartog & Rouse 1987; Rockart *et al.* 1982). These results provide additional evidence of this trend.

Using the standard deviation as a means of quantifying the level of agreement, there appears to be broad agreement (standard deviation <3.0) on the relative importance of the top five issues in Australia, Europe and the USA. In contrast there appears to be low agreement (standard deviation > 5.0) on the importance of software development (=10), measuring effectiveness (=13), and IS funding level (=15). These issues tend towards the bottom of the overall ranking. Thus, while it appears that there is some consensus on the leading issues, agreement declines with issue ranking.

6.3.1 Key difference in national rankings

Variations in timing and methods across the four regional studies make it difficult to identify subtle difference. Several regional rankings, however, appear as 'outliers' in the data. For the purposes of this study, a regional issue is considered an outlier if it is ranked at least five ranks higher or lower than the next closest regional rank. Differences of this magnitude appear to reflect substantive differences of which IS executives, particularly those with multinational responsibilities, should be aware.

One factor that may influence the overall ranking of key issues in each region is the local culture. Some insight as to the possible impact of culture is provided by Hofstede's (1980) study of employees' attitudes in a large multinational US corporation and its overseas subsidiaries. Hofstede isolates four dimensions of national culture: power distance, uncertainty avoidance, individualism and masculinity. The values for these variables for Australia, Singapore and the USA are shown in Table 6.5. Because of the wide diversity of scores for these four variables in the countries of Europe, it is inappropriate to treat Europe as a single culture, and thus, it is not shown in Table 6.5.

Based on Hofstede's four dimensions, Australia and the USA have very similar cultures. Hence, we would not expect differences in their key issue rankings to be due to cultural factors. Singapore varies considerably from the other two regions in that it has higher power distance, lower uncertainty avoidance, and lower individualism. While the masculinity score is lower, it is not significantly different.

High power distance tends to result in organizations that are more centralized, taller, and have a directive style of management. Organizations in cultures with low uncertainty avoidance tend to be less structured, have fewer rules, employ more generalists, and be multi-

Table 6.5 Measures of culture.

Country	Power	Uncertainty	Individualism	Masculinity
Australia	36	51	90	61
Singapore	74	8	20	48
USA	40	46	91	62
All nations mean	52	64	50	50
Standard deviation	20	24	25	20

Source: Hofstede (1980)

form. Managers in these cultures are more involved in strategy, more person oriented, flexible in their style, and more willing to take risks. Employees in low individualism cultures expect organizations to look after them like a family member, and organizational procedures are based on loyalty and a sense of duty. Therefore, when analysing the differences in the ranking of key issues between Singapore and the USA or Australia, cultural factors must be considered.

6.3.2 Australia

Software development is a greater problem in Australia than in any other region (4 compared with 14-12-13 in other regions). Previous reports suggest that the root cause of the concern for software development is the continuing shortage of skilled IS personnel in Australia, which Watson attributes to the rigidities of the Federally funded Australian education system. Australian universities, short of qualified staff to teach IS programmes, are constrained by a centralized, regulated, wage-fixing system that makes it difficult for them to attract suitable staff, and they cannot meet the demands of industry and government (Macrae 1988; The Western Australian 1989).

As illustrated in Table 6.3, lack of human resources is the second most important concern in Australia. Because of personnel shortage, many Australian IS executives are forced to promote staff into positions for which they may lack the appropriate technical, managerial and political skills. The recent emergence of privately funded universities in Australia may provide the mechanism for responding to market needs.

Measuring IS effectiveness (19 compared with 11-1-9 in other regions) and integrating technology (18 compared with 10-4-10) are ranked markedly lower in Australia. From the data available we are unable to find a satisfactory explanation for these differences.

6.3.3 Europe

End-user computing ranks markedly lower (14 compared with 8-2-6 in the other regions). This low ranking is also reported by Hirschheim *et al.* (1988). It is possible that the relatively low ranking of end-user computing is due to lower levels of penetration by personal computers (their cost is generally higher in Europe than other regions). It might also reflect a substantive decline in the importance of end-user computing in recent years.

The European results are more recent than those of the USA (1986) and Singapore (1987). A recent single-round survey from the USA (Callan 1979) found that end-user computing has declined in importance in the USA to about the same level reported for Europe. IS funding level is of much greater concern in Europe than Australia or the USA (6 compared with 27-20). Again, given the data available, we are unable to explain this difference.

6.3.4 Singapore

The key issues of Singapore's IS executives are substantially different from those of the other regions. For example, strategic planning (11 compared with 1-1-1) and organizational alignment (15 compared with 5-2-5) are ranked much lower than in other regions. Furthermore, measuring IS effectiveness (1 compared with 19-11-9), integrating technology (4 compared with 18-10-10) and security and control (6 compared with 17-18-18) are ranked much higher.

Some of these differences may be explained by the relative newness of information systems in Singaporean organizations. Singapore boasts a recently industrialized and rapidly growing economy. Many of its organizations may be in the early stages of IS development. In terms of Nolan's (1979) stage model, Singaporean IS organizations could collectively be viewed as moving from a growth phase into a control phase. This would explain the heavy emphasis on measurement, control and technology as well as the low emphasis on planning and alignment.

In terms of the framework developed by Hirschheim *et al.*,

Singaporean IS organizations would appear to be in a 'pre-strategic' phase of their development. In this light, it is noteworthy that Singapore ranked 'competitive advantage' lower than any other region. This high ranking in Singapore of measuring effectiveness, end-user computing, security and control, and integrating technology is similar to the high ranking these issues received in Dickson's 1983 USA study, and this lagged temporal correspondence lends support to the premise that IS in many Singaporean organizations is moving from a growth to control phase.

Singapore is based on a centrally planned economy. Within IS, planning occurs from the top down. In 1986, for example, Singapore completed development of its integrated national information technology (IT) strategy. The existence of a national IT plan, backed by a strong central government, could create an environment in which strategic planning and organizational alignment are seen as less of a problem.

Another explanation for the Singaporean results may be the size of local organizations. Most Singaporean enterprises are relatively small when compared to those of the USA and Europe. Also, many Singaporean firms operate within a very small geographic area and may rarely confront the large-scale problems faced by the multinational organizations in the European and USA studies. While many Australian firms may confine their activities to the domestic market, they function in a geographically large area. As a result, Singaporean IS executives probably manage simpler organizations than their counterparts and issues such as strategic planning and organizational alignment may appear relatively simple to solve or not even apparent as key issues.

As we have already seen, the Singaporean business culture is different from that of the USA and Australia. The low concern for planning in Singapore can be explained by its lower uncertainty avoidance index. As planning is a means of coping with uncertainty (Cyert & March 1963), it is quite in order for members of a culture with a high tolerance for uncertainty to be less concerned with planning. It may also be that the high power distance of the culture means that IS managers accept the directive style of their superiors and, as a result, strategic planning and organizational alignment are not considered to be important issues because IS managers are conditioned by the culture to unquestioningly accept the decisions of more senior managers.

Table 6.6 Correlation of ranking of key issues Kendall's tau (probability).

	Australia	Europe	Singapore	USA
Australia	1.00	0.33(0.09*)	−0.53(0.012**)	0.30(0.13)
Europe		1.00	−0.44(1.06*)	0.36(0.06*)
Singapore			1.00	−0.05(0.82)
USA				1.00

* Significant at 10% level.
** Significant at 5% level.

6.3.5 Correlating the regional views

In addition to focussing on issue-specific differences, we can use correlation and correspondence analysis to examine overall regional similarities and differences. Kendalls' tau (Siegel 1956) can be used to compare issue rankings across all four regions. As presented in Table 6.6, this correlation analysis highlights a number of significant relationships ($p < 0.10$). Significant positive correlations in the importance of issues occur between the USA and Europe, and between Europe and Australia, while significant negative correlations occur between Singapore and both Australia and Europe. These data suggest a reasonable level of agreement by Australian, European and USA executives on key IS issues.

Interestingly, the data also indicate that Singaporean IS executives' concerns are nearly the opposite of their Australian and European counterparts.

Correspondence analysis is an exploratory technique for displaying the rows and columns of a data matrix as points in a one- or two-dimensional space (Greenacre 1984). The input data matrix to correspondence analysis normally contains frequencies, rather than rankings. The only strict requirement for correspondence analysis is a rectangular matrix with non-negative entries. Because greater emphasis is placed on cells with relatively higher frequencies, it is necessary to first reverse the rankings in Table 6.3.

As reported in Table 6.3, there are no rankings for Singapore for four issues. As the highest rank (least important issue) in Table 6.3 is 27, missing ranks are given an arbitrary value of 30, and Table 6.3 is then transformed by subtracting each rank from 31. The results of

Table 6.7 Correspondence analysis results.

	Eigenvalue	Percentage	Cumulative Percentage
	0.0784	75.19	75.19
	0.0210	20.23	95.42
	0.0047	4.58	100.00

	Mass	Inertia	Horizontal axis			Vertical axis		
			Coord.	Contrib.	Corr.	Coord.	Contrib.	Corr.
Region								
Australia	0.250	0.017	0.124	4.9	0.231	0.220	57.7	0.734
Europe	0.270	0.022	0.211	15.3	0.559	−0.180	41.5	0.405
Singapore	0.213	−0.060	−0.531	76.7	0.996	−0.030	0.9	0.003
USA	0.266	0.006	0.095	3.1	0.417	−0.001	0.0	0.000
Variable								
1 Strategic planning	0.087	0.001	0.073	0.6	0.795	0.037	0.6	0.205
2 Organizational alignment	0.077	0.001	0.122	1.4	0.970	0.001	0.0	0.000
3 Competitive advantage	0.082	0.000	−0.028	0.1	0.275	−0.019	0.1	0.123
5 IS's role and contribution	0.081	0.000	−0.004	0.0	0.089	−0.014	0.1	0.878
5 Information architecture	0.062	0.016	0.485	18.6	0.930	0.128	4.8	0.065
6 Organizational learning	0.079	0.003	−0.170	2.9	0.848	−0.026	0.2	0.019
6 Human resources	0.078	0.003	−0.122	1.5	0.348	0.090	3.0	0.188
8 End-user computing	0.074	0.005	−0.251	6.0	0.870	0.082	2.4	0.093
9 Data as a resource	0.052	0.013	0.459	14.0	0.847	0.145	5.2	0.085
10 Software development	0.064	0.003	−0.064	0.3	0.082	0.196	11.7	0.765
11 Telecommunications	0.048	0.011	0.482	14.3	0.992	−0.003	0.0	0.000
12 Integrating technology	0.065	0.006	−0.275	6.3	0.771	−0.146	6.6	0.218
13 Measuring effectiveness	0.067	0.000	−0.246	10.2	0.814	−0.154	7.4	0.160
14 Security and control	0.052	0.009	−0.416	11.4	0.975	−0.002	0.0	0.000
15 IS funding level	0.032	0.022	0.547	12.4	0.436	−0.613	57.8	0.546

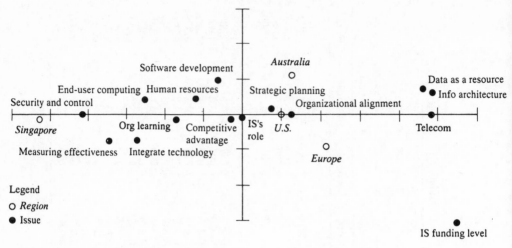

Fig. 6.1 Perceptual map of regions and key issues (all regions).

a correspondence analysis on the transformation of Table 6.3 are shown in Table 6.7 and the perceptual map is shown in Fig. 6.1. As procedures for correspondence analysis have only recently become available in common statistical packages such as SAS and BMDP, a reasonably detailed explanation of the results is provided.

The first two eigenvalues account for 95% of the total inertia (a measure of the overall spatial variation in the data) so that almost all the information in Table 6.5 is represented in a two-dimensional perceptual map (see Fig. 6.1). The horizontal axis explains 75% of the total inertia and the vertical axis some 20%. The perceptual map shows similarities and differences within each set of data (i.e. regions and issues) and the correspondence between sets. The perceptual map is based on the coordinates for each point (the coord columns in Table 6.7).

Readers should be aware that distances between points in the same set are chi-squared distances and when judging closeness one should look at vertical or horizontal distances between points and not at diagonal distances. Distances between points in different sets cannot be interpreted. The main purpose of the perceptual map is to graphically display those issues that are ranked similarly and those regions in which overall rankings are similar. No relevance can be attached to the particular quadrant in which an issue or region appears.

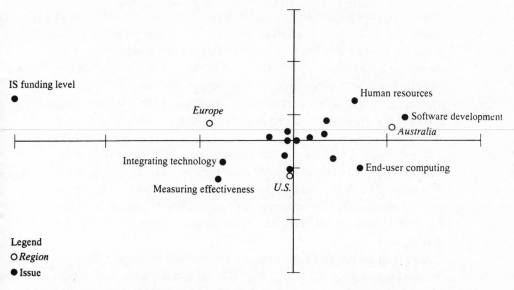

Fig. 6.2 Perceptual map of regions and key issues (excluding Singapore).

It is the relative vertical or horizontal distance between points that is significant.

Inspection of Fig. 6.1 shows that Australia, Europe and the USA are quite close together and Singapore is some distance apart. Key issues appear clustered in two groups. On the right side of the map are four issues (information architecture, data as a resource, telecommunications and IS funding level) which are quite close together when projected on to the horizontal axis. The other issues form an elongated cluster around the horizontal axis.

When we compare the two sets of data, we observe that regions tend to be close to their highly ranked issues. For example, measuring effectiveness and security and control, which rank quite high in Singapore (1 and 6 respectively), and low elsewhere, are very close to the point representing Singapore. Conversely, the unranked issues in the Singapore study, the four issues in a separate cluster on the right, are on the opposite side of the vertical axis to Singapore. Issues ranked low in Singapore and highly ranked in Australia, Europe and the USA (strategic planning and organizational alignment) are clustered around the points representing these regions.

It can be seen that the horizontal axis shows mainly how Singapore differs from the other regions. Examination of Table 6.7 indicates why this is the case. The absolute contribution of each point to an axis is shown in Table 6.7 under the heading Contrib, and we see that Singapore contributes 76.7% to the direction of the horizontal axis. In addition, the relative contribution, shown in Table 6.7 under the heading Corr, gives that part of the variance of a point explained by an axis and we observe that the horizontal axis explains 99.6% of the inertia of Singapore.

If we focus attention on the vertical axis, we see that it mainly discriminates between Australia and Europe, as the absolute contribution of each of these regions to the vertical axis is 57.7% and 41.4% respectively. For example, IS funding level – the issue of most disparity in ranking between the two regions – is closer to Europe than Australia.

A second correspondence analysis without the Singapore data gives the perceptual map shown in Fig. 6.2. The horizontal axis explains 77% of the total inertia and mainly discriminates between Australia and Europe as they contribute 55% and 45% respectively to the horizontal axis. This is to be expected as the vertical axis of the perceptual map with the Singapore data differentiates between Australia and Europe.

Australian and European IS managers differ in respect of two groups of issues. IS funding level, integrating technology, and measuring effectiveness are ranked higher in Europe than Australia. Human resources, end-user computing and software development are ranked higher in Australia than Europe. The remaining issues are quite close together and are not individually identified in the perceptual map. The USA appears to occupy the middle ground between Australia and Europe.

In summary, correspondence analysis of the rankings of the international issues provides an image of similarities and dissimilarities between the regions. The perceptual map in Fig. 6.1 highlights primarily that Singapore differs and shows how. When the Singapore data is removed, the differences between Australia and Europe emerge.

6.4 SUMMARY AND CONCLUSIONS

Overall, IS executives in Australia, Europe and the USA show a reasonable level of agreement on the most critical issues they face over the next 3 to 5 years. These executives are principally concerned with long-range issues such as IS strategic planning and aligning IS with the organization. Beyond the top five issues, medium-range issues, such as human resources and organization learning, emerge.

In general, IS executives in Australia, Europe and the USA are concerned primarily with the planning and management of the IS department's relationship with the organization. There is a striking difference in the problems that Singaporean IS executives perceive they face. We suggest that this disparate perspective may be due to the stage of development of IS in Singaporean organizations combined with the influence of the local business culture and the relatively smaller size of Singaporean organizations.

Multinational firms must recognize that while IS executives across the globe share many concerns, they also face different cultural, political and economic environments. The relative importance of the specific issues they face can vary from region to region. Forewarned, IS executives can tailor their policies to address regional differences, possibly through a combination of regional and international resources. Differences in growth stages might be bridged with leading edge strategies from other regions and by seeking the advice of executives who have successfully led the transition through a prior growth stage. In any event, IS executives will be required to manage their function cognizant of any varying perspectives inherent in a global economy.

IS executives with localized responsibilities should realize that their key issues can be strongly influenced by domestic conditions. For example, Australian IS executives should recognize that their high rating of human resources may be a product of a public policy that has reduced Australian universities' capacity to produce more IS graduates. Singaporean IS executives should understand that their business culture could play an important role in influencing their judgement on key issues. USA executives who face skill shortages in their department may find their views are more in accord with their Australian counterparts than those of the USA.

While the studies reviewed appear to be the best indicators of regional IS issues available at the time of writing, differences in timing and methods employed across studies limit the generalizations which can be drawn. The survey nature of the studies also limits the depth to which differences can be explained. Despite the talk of unification, portraying Europe as a homogeneous market may be inaccurate. In addition, Singapore is not necessarily representative of industrialized Asia. Thus, the reported findings should be generalized cautiously.

This study represents a first attempt to examine the key issues of IS executives on a worldwide basis. The study's shortcomings highlight the need for more consistent and detailed data. For example, extending key issues studies into less developed parts of the world might provide some elucidating glimpses into the ways that cultural, economic and structural differences impact the management of the IS function.

Because of the prevalent use of IS, it is recommended that future national studies adopt the issues and methods employed in the ongoing SIM/MISRC USA-based studies. This key issues framework has a history of use dating back to 1980. It provided the basis for three of the four studies reviewed. Use of a consistent issues framework assists interpretation of results across regions and over time. The Delphi format encourages tailoring of issues based on national differences in the early rounds of the study. This enhances the distinctiveness of national/regional data while retaining a degree of uniformity.

Future studies should continue to target the highest ranking IS executive in the organization. Consistency in respondent population assists in the analysis of data across studies and in the generalizability of findings. In addition, follow-up interviews or survey measures are recommended for improving understanding about why particular issues are important.

Given a more consistent and detailed analysis of issues, knowledge about IS executive behaviour worldwide can begin to accumulate. Understanding of the nature and extent of regional differences should be sharpened. Such understanding may prove invaluable to IS executives who find themselves increasingly following their peers in finance down the global road to a world economy.

6.5 POSTSCRIPT

The authors would be happy to assist researchers with national key issue studies detailed information on methods and instruments. They are currently working with researchers in several other countries.

6.6 ACKNOWLEDGEMENTS

The authors wish to thank Rudi Hirschheim, University of Houston (formerly of the Universities of Oxford and London); Tor Larsen,

Norwegian School of Management: K S Raman, National University of Singapore, and the anonymous referees for their contributions to this study.

Chapter 7

MIS Research Strategies

SCOTT HAMILTON

COMSERV Corporation, Minnesota,

AND

BLAKE IVES

Dartmouth University, New Hampshire

Different strategies for conducting empirical research in the management information systems (MIS) field are discussed. Strategies employed in 532 MIS articles published in 15 journals between 1970–79 are analysed. The trends are analysed over the ten year period with respect to the differences between articles authored by practitioners and academics, differences between articles that are cited frequently versus infrequently, and the relationship with the type of research conducted.

The analysis points out that more than two thirds of published MIS research by either academicians or practitioners has utilized non-empirical approaches and focussed on a single variable. Case studies are the most commonly employed empirical strategy and most studies do not measure the impact of independent variables on the process of using, developing or operating information systems. The analysis suggests that MIS journal articles employing empirical research strategies are cited more frequently than non-empirical ones.

7.1 INTRODUCTION

Research in Management Informations Systems (MIS) has been criticized as overly conceptual (Dickson *et al.* 1980), lacking in rigour (Turner 1980), and being non-cumulative (Keen 1980). To address these problems, different research strategies have been proposed. While each of these has contributed to the general body of MIS knowledge, they differ in their usefulness in answering particular questions. Discussions of empirical methods are typically illustrated by actual studies, but a comprehensive analysis of MIS research methods is lacking.

The purpose of this paper is to provide such an analysis. Answers to the following questions were sought:

(1) How frequently are various research strategies used in MIS research?
(2) Are there discernible trends in the use of these strategies?
(3) Have practitioner authors employed different research strategies from academic ones?
(4) Have articles which have made important contributions to MIS utilized different strategies from less important articles?
(5) What is the relationship between the research strategy and the type of research?

Chervany (1973) suggested the need to make a study of MIS research strategies with respect to the variables investigated (question 5). Cherns (1969) hypothesized that the choice of a strategy would influence diffusion of the results (question 4). The conflict between respectability in academia and relevance to management suggests that the researchers' affiliation (question 3) may influence the strategies. The maturation of the MIS field (question 2) and the development of firmer research paradigms (Kuhn 1961) may also influence the use of various strategies.

7.2 EMPIRICAL MIS RESEARCH STRATEGIES

Alternative strategies for conducting empirical MIS research have been defined, illustrated and compared by several authors. Van Horn (1973) examined four methods – case studies, field studies, field tests and laboratory studies – and presented numerous illustrations and arguments for each. Van Horn suggested that field tests and rigorous field studies are rare, that rigorous field studies are useful for studying MIS design, development and implementation, and that valid laboratory studies offer the most promise for MIS research.

Dickson, Senn & Chervany (1977) similarly note the paucity of empirical studies, especially field tests. They illustrate the four methods and emphasize the usefulness of man-machine experiments (one type of laboratory study) for assessing information support of the decision process. The usefulness of laboratory methods of studying information support of the decision process has also been discussed by Jenkins (1977) and Schneiderman (1978). Action research has been discussed and advocated by Gibson (1975) and Keen (1974) for studying MIS design and implementation. Action research methods ease participant learning and use, and may be combined with case studies, field studies and field tests.

The methodological foundations of each strategy have been discussed by authors in different disciplines. For example, discussions of strategies in organizational psychology include field tests (Cook & Campbell 1976), field studies (Bouchard 1976), and laboratory studies Fromkin & Streufert 1976). Trade-offs between alternative strategies have been compared in terms of internal and external validity (Kilman 1979) and in terms of diffusing research results (Van de Wall 1975).

Problems in the methodological foundations of empirical MIS research have been discussed by Turner (1980). The lack of empirical research is another problem. Authorities suggest that the published literature primarily reflects non-empirical research methods. For example, Van Horn (1973) characterized 78% of 27 papers presented at two MIS conferences as non-empirical. Approximately 33% of 430 MIS-related doctoral dissertations were non-empirical in nature (Hamilton *et al.* 1981).

7.3 ANALYSIS OF MIS RESEARCH STRATEGIES

This analysis dealt with relevant MIS articles published in fifteen journals. Table 7.1 identifies them within discipline area. For issues of each journal published between 1970 and 1979, articles within the MIS discipline were identified. A detailed discussion of the journals, the journal selection procedure, and the article selection procedure was previously published (Hamilton & Ives 1982). The article selection procedure identified 532 MIS articles published in the 15 journals over the 10 year period. The number of MIS articles appearing in each journal during the publication time period is also shown in Table 7.1.

Each article was classified as utilizing one of five MIS research strategies. The five are: case study, field study, field test, laboratory study and a non-empirical approach. Non-empirical approaches (e.g. tutorials and conceptual works) rely on secondary sources or the author's experience to support conclusions. Table 7.1 characterizes

Table 7.1 Characteristics of journals examined.

Discipline	Journal	Publication time period	Published MIS articles	
			Number	% empirical
MIS	*Data Base*	1970–79	98	12.2
	*Information and Management**	1970–79	129	27.1
	MIS Quarterly	1977–79	49	46.9
Accounting	*Accounting Review*	1970–79	10	60.0
	Journal of Accountancy	1970–79	13	30.8
Computer science	*ACM Transactions on Database Systems*	1976–79	5	0.0
	Communications of the ACM	1970–79	41	31.7
	Computing Surveys	1970–79	21	0.0
	IBM Systems Journal	1970–79	39	25.6
Management	*Academy of Management Journal*	1970–79	14	100.0
	Academy of Management Review	1970–79	5	0.0
	Harvard Business Review	1970–79	34	17.6
	*Sloan Management Review***	1970–79	25	40.0
Management science	*Decision Sciences*	1970–79	17	64.7
	Management Science	1970–79	32	53.1
Total			532	29.9

* *The IAG Journal* (1970–71). *Management informatics* (1972–74). *Management Datamatics* (1975–76) were utilized as predecessors to *Information and Management* (1977–79).
** *The Industrial Management Review* (1970) was used as the predecessor to *Sloan Management Review* (1971–79).

each journal in terms of the percentage of MIS articles which utilized an empirical research strategy.

7.3.1 Research strategy trends

MIS research published in journal articles employed a surprisingly high percentage (70.1) of non-empirical research strategies, as shown in Table 7.2. Empirical researchers favoured case studies (11.8%) of the 532 articles, while utilizing field studies (7.9%), field tests (4.9%), and laboratory studies (5.3%) less frequently. The trend data in

Table 7.2 Research strategies employed.

Research strategy	Overall data 1970–79		Trend data	
			1970–74 %	1975–79 %
	Count	%		
Empirical				
Case studies	63	11.8	11.8	11.9
Field studies	42	7.9	10.8	6.2
Field tests	26	4.9	2.6	6.2
Laboratory studies	28	5.3	4.6	5.6
Subtotal	159	29.9	29.7	30.0
			(58)	(101)
Non-empirical				
Conceptual	326	61.3	63.1	60.0
Tutorial, review, other	47	8.8	7.2	10.0
Subtotal	372	70.1	70.3	69.9
Total	532	100.0	(137)	(236)

Numbers in parentheses are counts.

Table 7.2, comparing data from 1970–74 with data from 1975–9, suggests that research strategy utilization has changed very little. The more recent period continues to reflect a high utilization of non-empirical strategies. In terms of empirical approaches, the use of field tests and laboratory studies increased while the reliance on field studies decreased.

7.3.2 Research strategy by author occupation

Practitioners and academics were expected to employ different research strategies. Articles were assigned to one occupational group on the basis of the occupational affiliation of the author. Table 7.3 displays the breakdown of research strategies for articles authored by academics (i.e. university affiliation) versus practitioners (i.e. non-university affiliation). Since multiple authors are typically from the same institution (Narin 1976), the occupational affiliation of the first author was used when more than one author was listed. Approximately two thirds (62.6%) of the articles were authored by academics.

Academics' articles utilized empirical research strategies more than

Table 7.3 Research strategies employed by academic versus practitioner authors.

Research strategies	Overall data 1970–79		Trend data			
	Academic author %	Practitioner author %	Academic author		Practitioner author	
			1970–74	1975–79	1970–74	1975–79
Empirical						
Case studies	10.6	14.1	9.7	11.1	15.7	13.3
Field studies	10.3	3.5	16.1	6.8	1.4	4.7
Field tests	7.2	1.0	3.2	9.7	1.4	0.8
Laboratory studies	7.9	1.0	6.5	8.7	1.4	0.8
Subtotal	36.0	19.6	35.4	36.2	20.0	19.5
	(119)	(39)	(44)	(75)	(14)	(25)
Non-empirical						
Conceptual	56.5	69.2	58.9	55.1	70.0	68.8
Tutorial, review, other	7.6	11.2	5.6	8.7	10.0	11.7
Subtotal	64.07	80.4	64.5	63.8	80.0	80.5
	(212)	(159)	(80)	(132)	(56)	(103)
Total	100	100				
	(333)	(198)				

Numbers in parentheses are counts.

articles authored by practitioners. One exception was the use of case studies, which were more commonly employed by practitioners.

The trend data in Table 7.3, comparing data from 1970–74 with data from 1975–9, suggests that practitioners and academics have continued primarily to rely on non-empirical approaches. One interesting trend among academics is the move away from field studies and towards field experimentation.

7.3.3 Research strategy and article importance

A rough indicator of article importance is citation frequency. The more an article is cited, the more the research community is expressing the fact that the article contains useful information. The threshold for defining important articles appears to be a citation rate of three or four times a year, a number which only a few percent of all articles ever achieve (Garfield 1972). Comparing the research strategies employed in frequently cited articles with those employed in less frequently cited articles provides a measure of the relative contribution of a particular research strategy to MIS research.

A subset of 370 articles, published between 1970 and 1977, were selected from the 532 articles published between 1970 and 1979. Articles from 1978 and 1979 would not yet have been commonly cited and were therefore excluded. Citation frequencies were calculated for the subset (370 MIS articles) based on an analysis of bibliographic references attached to the total set (532 MIS articles). The cited articles in the subset were broken into two groups: the first group contained articles cited two or more times, while the second group included articles that have not been cited or were cited only once. Table 7.4 summarizes the analysis of research strategies utilized in the two groups of articles.

The analysis suggests that important articles are more likely to employ an empirical strategy than less important articles (40% against 28.1%). The only exception is the case study, which is more commonly employed in less important articles. Conceptual approaches, though still the most frequently utilized in heavily cited works, are also more commonly employed in less important articles.

7.3.4 Research strategy by research type

The variables investigated in each article were characterized by mapping them into a comprehensive framework for MIS research

Table 7.4 Research strategies employed in articles frequently cited versus articles infrequently cited.

Research strategy	Citation frequency			
	Cited two or more times		Cited less than two times	
	Count	%	Count	%
Empirical				
Case studies	8	10.7	37	12.5
Field studies	9	12.0	25	8.5
Field tests	6	8.0	7	2.4
Laboratory studies	7	9.3	14	4.7
Subtotal	30	40.0	83	28.1
Non-empirical				
Conceptual	37	49.3	190	64.4
Tutorial, review, other	8	10.7	22	7.4
Subtotal	45	60.0	212	71.8

Citation frequencies were calculated for the 370 MIS articles published during the 1970 to 1977 period based on an analysis of bibliographic references attached to 531 MIS articles published between 1970 to 1979.

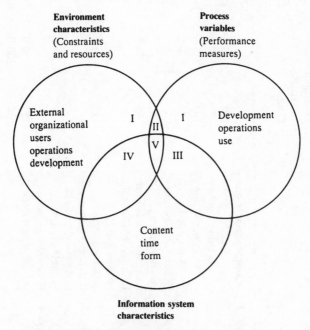

Fig. 7.1 Five categories of information systems research.

Table 7.5 Research strategies by research type.

Research type	Published MIS articles		Empirical research strategy				Non-empirical research strategy	
	Count	%	Case study	Field study	Field test	Lab study	Conceptual	Tutorial other
Type I A single variable group								
1a: A specific variable	252	47.4	17	3	4	1	200	27
1b: Relationship between variables within group	62	11.6	1	7	2	0	46	6
1c: A specific IS	85	16.0	34	5	0	0	40	6
Type II Relationship between environment and process variable groups	75	14.1	5	21	13	13	19	4
Type III Relationship between process and IS variable groups	10	1.9	2	1	1	3	2	1
Type IV Relationship between environment and IS variable groups	16	3.0	0	1	3	2	9	1
Type V Relationships among groups of variables	32	6.0	4	4	3	2	10	1
Total	532	100.0	63	42	26	28	326	47
%	100.0		11.8	7.9	4.9	5.3	61.3	8.8

developed by the authors (Ives *et al*. 1980). The framework defines three variable groups (environment, process and information system) and major variable classes within each group. This model permits an examination of MIS research from a number of alternative perspectives. The five different types of research derivable from the model are identified in Fig. 7.1 and briefly described in Table 7.5.

The authors previously published (Ives *et al*. 1980) a detailed analysis of research strategies by research types for 331 MIS-related doctoral dissertations completed between 1973 and 1979. Table 7.5 presents a replication of their analysis for MIS journal articles published between 1970 and 1979. Each type of research reflects different approaches in the research strategies taken, as summarized below:

(1) Type I articles generally employed case studies or used non-empirical research strategies, primarily conceptual studies relying on secondary sources or the author's experience.

(2) Type II articles employed field studies, field tests, and laboratory studies. In most cases, the Type II articles examined relationships between the user environment and the use process.

(3) Type III articles were uncommon and typically employed empirical strategies. In a few cases, laboratory studies were used to test the impact of information system characteristics (via simulation on the use process).

(4) Type IV articles were also uncommon but typically employed conceptual approaches. Lab and field tests were preferred when empirical strategies were used.

(5) Type V articles studied commonly employed empirical strategies. In many cases a laboratory study was used to test the impact of various information system characteristics (via simulation) and various user characteristics on the user process.

In comparison with the research types examined in the 331 MIS-related dissertations, the MIS journal articles focussed on a specific variable (Type Ia research) far more frequently (47.4% compared with 29.6%). In most of these cases, the article presented a development approach and relied on a conceptual analysis to support conclusions. The empirical studies typically failed to consider process measures as dependent variables. Only 46.5% of the 159 empirical studies

Table 7.6 Comparison of research strategies employed in MIS articles versus MIS-related dissertations.

Research strategy	Published MIS articles (1970–79)		MIS-related dissertations (1973–79)	
	Count	%	Count	%
Empirical				
Case studies	63	11.8	46	13.9
Field studies	42	7.9	102	30.8
Field tests	26	4.9	6	1.8
Laboratory studies	28	5.3	45	13.6
Subtotal	159	29.9	199	60.1
Non-empirical				
Conceptual	326	61.3	101	30.5
Tutorial, review, other	47	8.8	0	
Subtotal	373	70.1	101	30.5
Unknown	0	0.0	31	9.4
Total	532	100.0	331	100.0

measured the impact of independent variables on the process of using, developing, or operating information systems.

In comparison with research strategies employed in the 331 MIS-related doctoral dissertations, the MIS journal articles rely more heavily on non-empirical methods to support conclusions. Table 7.6 summarizes this. While 61.3% of MIS journal articles were of a conceptual nature, only 30.5% of MIS-related dissertations were conceptual. In terms of empirical approaches, the authors of MIS journal articles were less inclined to use field studies (7.9% compared with 30.8%) and laboratory studies (5.3% compared with 13.6%), and more inclined to use field tests (4.9% compared with 1.8%).

7.4 CONCLUSION

The analysis of MIS research strategies provides some empirical ammunition for those assessing the present state of MIS research. The majority (70.1%) of MIS research published in journals during the ten year period (1970–79) by either academicians or practitioners has been non-empirical in nature and has typically focussed on a single variable (e.g. a new development technique). Case studies are the most commonly employed empirical strategy and most empirical studies failed to consider process measures as dependent variables (e.g. the impact on user performance).

The analysis of the MIS journal articles does provide hope for future research. The analysis of article importance suggests that use of empirical research strategies should be rewarded by greater recognition. A need exists to establish a balance and integration between the research strategies in the MIS field. Past conceptual work and case studies have indicated important hypotheses which can now undergo more rigorous testing in laboratory settings. Field experimentation can serve as a testing ground for significant laboratory results. The key to good research, though, is not just in choosing the right research strategy, but in asking the right questions and picking the most powerful method(s) for answering the questions given the objectives, research setting and other salient factors.

Chapter 8

Choosing Information Systems Research Approaches

R.D. GALLIERS
Warwick Business School, University of Warwick

This chapter attempts to review the range of approaches that have been advocated as being suitable for research in the field of information systems. *Inter alia*, it assesses their strengths and weaknesses, divides the approaches into two categories, empirical and interpretive, and summarizes the arguments for rethinking the view that it is only the empirical approaches that produce usable and useful results. In addition, the approaches are placed in the context of the process of building and extending information systems theory.

As a result of this analysis, a revised taxonomy of information systems research methods is developed. This taxonomy attempts to identify the situations in which individual approaches appear to be best suited in relation to (a) the general topic area (i.e. the object) of the proposed research and (b) the process of theory development and extension in the specific topic area being researched.

The chapter concludes with some practical guidelines in the use of this revised taxonomy when choosing an appropriate research methodology for a particular information systems research project.

8.1 INTRODUCTION

A range of research approaches has been recommended for use in the general field of information systems. A particular approach is likely to have its adherents who, all too frequently, argue (often most cogently) for its *universal* applicability. 'All too frequently' because, as in most aspects of information systems, an approach with universal applicability is highly unlikely.

Examples of this behaviour can be found in the Proceedings of the

144

IFIP WG 8.2 Colloquium 'Information Systems Research – a doubtful science?' held in September 1984 (Mumford *et al.* 1985), which was the forerunner to ISRA-90 (Nissen *et al.* 1991). Perhaps it is enlightening to note the title – Information Systems Research Methods – given to the published version of the proceedings, as compared to the title of the colloquium itself.

In their introduction, the editors note the change and remark that the reason for it 'will have to remain a mystery'. My view has been that the change was brought about, in part at least, by the very nature of many of the papers presented. The colloquium was held to 'enable a concern about research methods in information systems to be aired' and to 'ask whether the scientific research methodology is the only relevant methodology for information systems research or indeed whether it is an appropriate one at all'. Many of the presenters at the colloquium interpreted these objectives as an invitation to argue for their particular approach to information systems research, rather than as an opportunity to review the range of approaches available, with each being more or less appropriate in different circumstances.

Additional evidence, from the other side of the Atlantic, which supports the view that the research approach adopted is likely to be affected more by the location of the research than by the object of that research, comes from the proceedings of a similar colloquium, held at the Harvard Business School at about the same time (McFarlan 1984), and from a paper by Vogel & Wetherbe (1984). Both sources analyse, *inter alia*, the research approaches adopted by a number of information systems faculties in the USA. While it would be an exaggeration to contend that each faculty utilizes a single approach only, it is possible to discern a particular house style in many instances. Given acceptance of the proposition that no one single approach is universally applicable, this fact gives some cause for concern. Given, too, the unfortunate preponderence of information systems discourse which does not adequately deal with the question of choice in research approach (both in terms of what is an appropriate choice, and of the likely effects of a particular choice on the results), one's level of concern becomes the greater. (Exceptions to the lack of discussion of choice are provided by Keys (1988) in respect of alternative problem solving methodologies, and Benbasat (1984) in respect of alternative research approaches in the field of Management Support Systems.)

In the light of the above, a means of identifying which approaches appear most suitable in particular circumstances would appear to be a useful contribution to a debate on information systems research methods. It is with this in mind that this chapter was written.

It sets out to use the 1984 colloquium as a base for:

(1) assessing the strengths and weaknesses of the various research approaches that have been, and are being, used in the information systems field;
(2) developing a revised taxonomy of research methods which takes into account their relative strengths and weaknesses in the context of the particular aspect of information systems under study, and of the process towards theory development and extension;
(3) using the taxonomy to assist the would-be researcher in choosing an appropriate information systems research approach.

Table 8.1 Approaches to information systems research: a summary.

Researchers' approaches	Van Horn (1973)[1]	Hamilton & Ives (1982) (Chapter 7)	Vogel & Wetherbe (1984)	Galliers (1985) Galliers & Land (1987)	Farhoomand (1987) (Chapter 5)
Laboratory experiments	*	*	*	*	*
Field experiments	*	*	*	*	*
Surveys	*	*	*	*	*
Case studies	*	*	*	*	*
Theorem proof				*	*
Subjective/argumentative[2]		*	*	*	*
Empirical[3]			*		
Engineering			*		
Reviews		*			
Action research				*	
Longitudinal				*	
Descriptive/interpretive				*	
Forecasting/futures research				*	
Simulation[4]				*	

[1] This list is confirmed by Ein-Dor & Segev (1981).

[2] The subjective/argumentative category used by Vogel & Wetherbe (1984) may reasonably be equated with the conceptual category of Hamilton & Ives (1982) and the non empirical category used by Farhoomand (1987).

[3] The empirical category used by Vogel & Wetherbe (1984) is seen as a more generic term by, e.g., Hamilton & Ives (1982) and Galliers & Land (1987). In the latter cases, the term incorporates the field and laboratory experiments categories, together with case studies and surveys.

[4] Includes game/role playing.

8.2 APPROACHES TO INFORMATION SYSTEMS RESEARCH

A number of taxonomies of information systems research approaches have been postulated over the years. Table 8.1 attempts to summarize the major approaches identified. In addition, several taxonomies of organization theory suggest suitable approaches to information systems research (e.g. Morgan 1980; Benson 1983).

In identifying alternative research styles, I have used the word approaches as opposed to methods. This is because I wish to differentiate between the two terms. As Weick (1984) argues: 'Methods are simply ways to systematize observation'. Different approaches, as the term is used in this chapter, are a way of going about one's research. They may embody a particular style and may employ different methods or techniques. Approaches are therefore a more generic concept than methods.

Weick (1984) goes on to list alternative ways of observing events when discussing alternative methods, to which I have added references to various approaches (the latter are themselves described in more detail in Section 8.4):

- *sustained*, *cf.* longitudinal research, as advocated by, e.g., Pettigrew (1983) and Vitalari (1985);
- *explicit*, i.e. 'procedures [that] are . . . open and contestable . . . and capable of reconstruction' (*cf.* experimental research);
- *methodical*, i.e. methods that adhere 'to an orderly sequence of data collection' (*cf.* survey research);
- *observing*, i.e. 'examining steadily and in detail the stream of events toward which attention is directed', e.g. Barton & Lazarsfeld (1969) (*cf.* case study research);
- *paraphrasing*, which might be likened to labelling events, *cf.* phenomenological research, as advocated by, e.g., Husserl (1936) and Boland (1985);
- *social situations*, i.e. observations of interactions 'among a place . . . , actors . . . , and activities', as opposed to solitary research;
- *naturally occurring contexts*, i.e. observations of uncontrived environments that allow 'one to ask how and why these things are going on'.

When reviewing Table 8.1, it is reasonable to divide the approaches into two categories which can be labelled scientific (empirical) and interpretivist. Scientific approaches may be defined as those that have arisen from the scientific tradition – characterized by repeatability, reductionism and refutability (*cf.* Checkland 1981) – and which assume that observations of the phenomena under investigation can be made objectively and rigorously (*cf.* Klein & Lyytinen 1985). Interpretivist approaches argue that the scientific ethos is misplaced in social scientific enquiry because of, *inter alia* (Galliers 1985, after Checkland 1981):

'• the possibility of many different interpretations of social phenonema;
• the impact of the social scientist on the social system being studied;
• the problems associated with forecasting future events concerned with human . . . activity [given the fact that] there will always be a mixture of intended and unintended effects and . . . the danger of self-fulfilling prophecies or the opposite.'

The argument of those who espouse the scientific approach may be summarized (somewhat tautologically) as follows (Bleicher 1982):

'The empirical-analytical method is the only valid approach to improve human knowledge. What can't be investigated using this approach, can't be investigated at all scientifically. Such research must be banned from the domain of science as "unresearchable".'

This leads a number of information systems researchers into the following 'illogic', according to Weick (1984):

'(1) every real phenomenon can be measured;
(2) if it can't be measured, it's not real;
(3) if it can be measured, it is real.'

There are others who argue for eclectic approaches, given that information systems is a 'fragmented field or, to put it in other words, an essentially pluralistic scientific field'. In view of this, Banville & Landry (1989) argue that the field of information systems can best 'be understood and analysed only with the help of pluralistic models' (see Chapter 4).

Returning to Table 8.1, it is possible to divide the approaches into two camps as shown in Table 8.2.

Table 8.2 Information systems research approaches in the context of the scientific and interpretivist philosophies.

Scientific	Interpretivist
Laboratory experiments	Subjective/argumentative
Field experiments	Reviews
Surveys	Action research
Case studies	Descriptive/interpretive
Theorem proof	
Forecasting	Futures research
Simulation	Role/game playing

I have split the forecasting-futures research approach and the simulation-role/game playing approach between the two camps according to their underlying ethos. In addition, I have excluded two of the Vogel & Wetherbe (1984) categories: empirical and engineering. The former term more reasonably describes the *range* of approaches of this type (*cf.* the argument of Hamilton & Ives 1982), and the latter term more reasonably describes the *focus* of the research (i.e. the application area) rather than the *approach* to that research. In addition, longitudinal research can be incorporated in other approaches (as will be argued below) and has, therefore, also been excluded.

An attempt has been made to keep the number of approaches in each category to a minimum while, at the same time, providing a useful summary of the range of approaches (i.e., I have applied the two criteria of comprehensiveness and parsimony against which Vogel & Wetherbe (1984) measure utility in this context).

8.3 INFORMATION SYSTEMS RESEARCH APPROACHES: STRENGTHS AND WEAKNESSES

In this section, the key features of each of the information systems research approaches identified in Table 8.2 will be considered in turn, followed by a consideration of its relative strengths and weaknesses. Table 8.3, which summarizes the key features, strengths and weaknesses, can be found overleaf.

Table 8.3 A summary of the key features, strengths and weaknesses of alternative information systems research approaches. (Amended and extended from Galliers, 1985, pp. 292–294.)

Approach	Key features	Strengths	Weaknesses
Laboratory experiments	Identification of precise relationships between chosen variables via a designed laboratory situation, using quantitative analytical techniques, with a view to making generalizable statements applicable to real-life situations.	The solution and control of a small number of variables which may then be studied intensively.	The limited extent to which identified relationships exist in the real world due to oversimplification of the experimental situation and the isolation of such situations from most of the variables that are found in the real world.
Field experiments	Extension of laboratory experiments into the real-life situations of organizations and/or society.	Greater realism; less artificial/sanitized than the laboratory situation.	Finding organizations prepared to be experimented on. Achieving sufficient control to enable replication, with only the study variables being altered.
Surveys	Obtaining snap shots of practices, situations or views at a particular point in time (via questionnaires or interviews) from which inferences are made (using quantitative analytical techniques) regarding the relationships that exist in the past, present and future.	Greater number of variables may be studied than in the case of experimental approaches. Description of real world situations. More easy/ appropriate generalizations.	Likely that little insight obtained re. the causes/processes behind the phenomena being studied. Possible bias in respondents (cf. self-selecting nature of questionnaire respondents); the researcher, and the moment in time which the research is undertaken.

Case studies	An attempt at describing the relationships which exist in reality, usually within a single organization or organizational grouping.	Capturing 'reality' in greater detail and analysing more variables than is possible using any of the above approaches.	Restriction to a single event/ organization. Difficulty in generalizing, given problems of acquiring similar data from a statistically meaningful number of cases. Lack of control of variables. Different interpretations of events by individual researchers/ stakeholders.
Forecasting, futures research	Use of such techniques as regression analysis and time series analysis, or the delphi method and change analysis, to extrapolate/deduce likely/future possible events or impacts.	Provision of insights into likely future occurrences in situations where existing relationships may not hold true in the future. Attempts to deal with the rapid changes taking place in IT and their impacts on individuals, organizations and society in general.	Complexity and changing relationship of variables under study. Lack of real knowledge of future events. Scenarios are not 'true' pictures of the future but enable decisions re. reactions in different 'futures'. Dependent on precision/relevance of past data and expertise of scenario builders. Possibility of self-fulfilling prophecies.
Simulation, game/role playing	An attempt at copying the behaviour of a system which would otherwise be difficult/ impossible to solve analytically, by the generation/introduction of random variables.	Provision of an opportunity to study situations that might otherwise be impossible to analyse.	Similar to experimental research in regard to the difficulties associated with devising a simulation that accurately reflects the real world situations.

Table 8.3 *Continued*

Approach	Key features	Strengths	Weaknesses
Subjective, argumentative (cf. phenomenology, hermeneutics)	Creative research based more on opinion/speculation than observation, thereby placing greater emphasis on the role/perspective of the researcher. Can be applied to existing body of knowledge (reviews) as well as actual/past events/situations.	Useful in building theory that can subsequently be tested. Creation of new ideas and insights. Recognition that the researcher will interpret what is being studied in a particular way. Contributes to cumulative knowledge.	Unstructured, subjective nature of research process. Despite making the prejudice of the researcher known, there is still the likelihood of biased interpretations, a problem which is compounded by the time at which the research is undertaken.
Action research	Applied research where there is an attempt to obtain results of practical value to groups with whom the researcher is allied, while at the same time adding to theoretical knowledge.	Practical as well as theoretical outcomes most often aimed at emancipatory outcomes. Biases of researcher made known.	Similar to case study research, but additionally places a considerable responsibility on the researcher when objectives are at odds with other groupings. The ethics of the particular research are a key issue.

8.3.1 Scientific approaches

Laboratory experiments

The key feature of the laboratory experiments approach is the identification of the precise relationships between variables in a designed, controlled environment (i.e. the laboratory) using quantitative analytical techniques. This is done with a view to making generalizable statements applicable to real world situations. The major strength of the approach rests in the ability of the researcher to isolate and control a small number of variables which may then be studied intensively. The major weakness of the approach is the limited extent to which identified relationships exist in the real world due to over-simplification of the experimental situation and the isolation of such situations from most of the variables that exist in the real world.

Essentially, the value given to those variables excluded from the experiment is zero, which is probably the one value they do not have! (For a debate on the appropriateness or otherwise of the laboratory experiments approach to informations systems research, see Jarvenpaa (1988) and Galliers & Land (1988).) In addition, much of the research undertaken using this approach utilizes students as surrogates for real decision makers, thus adding to the sanitized nature of the laboratory situation. (For a discussion of the pros and cons of using students as surrogates in behavioural research, see e.g., respectively Khera *et al.* (1970) and Copeland *et al.* (1973, 1974).)

Field experiments

Field experiments are an extension of laboratory experiments into the real world of organizations/society. The idea here is, of course, to attempt to construct an experiment in a more realistic environment than is possible in the artificial, sanitized laboratory situation. Strengths and weaknesses are as in the case of laboratory experiments, but an additional weakness is the difficulty in finding organizations prepared to be experimented on! In addition, replication is problematic, in that it is extremely difficult to achieve sufficient control to enable replication of the experiment with only the study variables being altered.

Surveys

Surveys are essentially snapshots of practices, situations or views at a particular point in time, undertaken using questionnaires or (structured) interviews, from which inferences may be made. Quantitative techniques are often used in analysing responses with a view to identifying significant results. (For a critique of the application of statistical techniques in information systems research, see Baroudi & Orlikowski (1989).) With careful design, surveys are a good means of looking at a far greater number of variables than is the case with the experimental approaches. They can therefore provide a reasonably accurate description of real world situations from a variety of viewpoints. Given large sample sizes, generalization of the results may be somewhat less of a concern too. However, little insight is usually gained regarding the causes or the processes behind the phenomena under study. In addition, there remains the likelihood of bias on the part of the respondents (especially those responding to questionnaires, since they will be self-selecting), in the researcher, and in the time that the research is undertaken.

Case studies

Another common approach to information systems research in the real world is the case study approach. In some respects, one could argue whether case studies are necessarily a particular form of research approach, given that they are essentially merely a means of describing the relationships that exist in a particular situation, usually in a single organization. However, given that case studies are generally considered to be a form of research, they have been included in this discussion.

There could also be some debate as to whether the case study approach should be listed under the scientific banner or should fall within the interpretivist category, especially given the particular 'appreciative system' (Vickers 1980) or 'cognitive filter' (Simon 1978) of the researcher. Again, however, I have decided to include it in the empirical/scientific category, since many of its exponents classify it thus (e.g. Lee 1989).

The strength of the case study approach is that it enables the capture of reality in considerably greater detail (and the analysis of a considerably greater number of variables), than is possible with any of the above approaches. Its weaknesses include the fact that its application is usually restricted to a single event/organization, and the difficulty in acquiring similar data from a statistically meaningful number of similar organizations – and hence, the problems associated with making generalizations from individual case studies (Spencer & Dale 1979). However, as argued in Lawler *et al.* (1985), single case studies are helpful in developing and refining generalizable concepts and frames of reference. Further, when multiple case studies are used, it is possible to relate variability in context to constants in processes and outcomes (*cf.* contextualist research, as advocated by, e.g., Lipset *et al.* 1956; Berg 1979; Pettigrew 1983).

Additional limitations of the approach include the different interpretations, as alluded to above, and the lack of control of individual variables – and hence the difficulties in distinguishing between cause and effect. The problems associated with the latter have been circumvented, to a degree at least, by undertaking longitudinal case study research (Pettigrew 1983; Vitalari 1985).

Theorem proof

The theorem proof category is defined by Vogel & Wetherbe (1984) as capturing 'application areas from fields such as computer science that otherwise would not be identified'. Given that I have excluded their engineering categorization from Table 8.2 for the very reason that it describes an application area of research and not an approach, it may seem inconsistent to retain theorem proof as a separate category. I have done so since it describes reasonably accurately that subset of information systems research approaches concerned with development and testing of theorems at the technical end of the socio-technical spectrum. The strengths of the approach equate closely to the strengths of the scientific method generally, *cf.* Checkland's (1981) repeatability, reductionism and refutability, and the precision of the results. The major weakness lies in the limited applicability of this style of research as one moves towards the social pole of the socio-technical spectrum.

Forecasting and futures research

Forecasting and futures research represent, respectively, the scientific and interpretivist aspects of this form of research. Forecasting (in the scientific context) relies on techniques such as regression analysis (Draper & Smith 1981) and time-series analysis (Chatfield 1984) to extrapolate likely future trends from past data. Conversely, futures research – in the interpretivist context of information systems research – is concerned with 'the emergence of new social forms and behaviours, and the development of the so-called information society or information age' (Vitalari 1985). It is therefore a particularly appropriate approach when investigating the future societal impacts of information technology.

In addition, however, it has also been successfully applied within organizations by, for example, Nilles and his colleagues (Nilles 1984; Nilles *et al.* 1983). 'In this kind of research, different scenarios, or futures, are postulated and the different aspects of information technology and information systems are identified given these different situations' (Galliers 1985). Techniques employed here include, for example, the delphi method (e.g. Delbecq *et al.* 1975) and change analysis (Land 1982).

Strengths of the forecasting approaches include the ability to provide insights into likely future occurences (clearly of significant benefit in the rapidly changing world of information systems), but these insights are dependent on the precision of past data in the one case and the expertise of the scenario builders on the other. Other limitations relate to the unpredictability of environmental factors and the problems associated with self-fulfilling prophesies identified by Checkland (1981): 'Predictions on the outcome of observed happenings in social systems may change the outcome. Physical systems cannot react to predictions made about them; social systems can.'

Simulation and game/role playing

Similarly, simulation and game/role playing represent respectively the scientific and interpretivist aspects of this form of research. Simulation is a method 'used to solve problems which are difficult or impossible to solve analytically by copying the behaviour of the system under study by generating appropriate random variables' (Chatfield 1988). Its particular strengths are associated with these situations. Its weaknesses relate, as in the case of laboratory and field experiments, to the difficulties associated with devising a simulation that accurately reflects the real world situation it is supposed to replicate.

8.3.2 Interpretivist approaches

Futures research and game/role playing

The futures research and game/role playing approaches have been covered in the above discussion but, as argued, these can also be placed in the interpretivist category of information systems research approaches. In addition, there are in this category the subjective/ argumentative, action research and descriptive/interpretive (including reviews) approaches. Each will be discussed in turn.

Subjective/argumentative research

The subjective/argumentative category captures (according to Vogel & Wetherbe 1984) 'creative MIS research based more on opinion and speculation than observation'. I have separated it from the futures research and game/role playing approaches because it tends to be more of a free-flowing process (i.e. less structured) than either of these approaches. In addition, it is more likely to be an individual, rather than group, activity.

Adherents to the scientific school would question whether this form of approach is genuinely research. However, it is included because, in the right hands, this kind of creative process makes a valuable contribution to the building of theories which can subsequently be tested by more formal means. Its strengths lie in the creation of new ideas and insights. Its weaknesses arise from the unstructured, subjective nature of the process.

Action research

The action research approach (Antill 1985; Wood-Harper 1985) might be seen as a subset of the case study and field experiment categories discussed above. However, it is included as a separate approach in view of its underlying philosophy which sets it apart from these scientific approaches. (For further discussion on the subject of action research as distinct from the more empirical forms of applied research see, e.g., Checkland (1981) and Clark (1972)). This relates to the fact that the action researcher knows that their very presence will affect the situation they are researching. Indeed, their role is to actively associate themselves with the practical outcomes of the research in addition to seeking to identify theoretical outcomes (Foster 1972). In addition, the roles of subject and researcher can easily be reversed at times during action research studies (Clark 1972).

The strengths of this form of research include the very practical benefits that are likely to accrue to client organizations as a result, and the fact that the researcher's biases are made overt in undertaking the research (White 1985). Weaknesses are similar to those already identified for the case study approach. In addition, however, this approach places a great deal of responsibility on the action researcher, who must be aware that in certain circumstances they could well align themselves with a particular grouping whose objectives are at odds with other groupings. The ethics of the research must therefore be an important consideration.

Descriptive/interpretive research

The descriptive/interpretive form of research may be equated with the phenonemonological school of thought (*cf.* Husserl 1936; Boland 1985). The argument goes something like this: all we can ever know are phenomena, since there is no such notion as a 'thing in itself'. However, once we have understood phenonema correctly, we know all that there is to be known. Phenonema are the essence of our experience. Essences are grasped intuitively (i.e. they are not verified empirically), since the proof of an essence is its self-evidence. (Paraphrased from Boland 1985; see also Chapter 3.)

The strengths of this form of research lie in its ability to represent reality following an in-depth self-validating process in which pre-suppositions are continually questioned and our understanding of the phenomena under study is refined. The weaknesses relate to the skills of the phenomenologist and their ability to identify their biases and unheralded assumptions. Despite the fact that the researcher's biases are identified, these could still cloud the interpretation of the phenomena under study.

Descriptive or interpretive research can be focussed on the literature or past developments, in addition to actual, current happenings. Significant advances in our knowledge, and our ability to develop theory, can be made through an in-depth review of this kind in a particular aspect of our subject matter. All too often, we fail to develop cumulative knowledge (Keen 1984) in the information systems field. A thorough review of past research/developments may not only lead to new insights but also is more likely to ensure that subsequent research builds on past endeavours. The approach's weaknesses include the problems the reviewer faces in interpreting the results of research with which they may be unfamiliar.

Table 8.4 Information systems research approaches: a revised taxonomy (amended from Galliers & Land, 1987, p. 901; Galliers, 1991, p. 339).

Object	Modes for newer approaches (interpretations)					Modes for traditional empirical approaches (observations)				
	Theorem proof	Laboratory experiment	Field experiment	Case study	Survey	Forecasting and futures research	Simulation and game/role playing	Subjective/argumentative	Descriptive/interpretive (including reviews)	Action research
Society	No	No	Possibly	Possibly	Yes	Yes	Possibly	Yes	Yes	Possibly
Organization/group	No	Possibly (small groups)	Yes	Yes	Yes	Yes	Yes	Yes	Yes	Yes
Individual	No	Yes	Yes	Possibly	Possibly	Possibly	Yes	Yes	Yes	Possibly
Technology	Yes	Yes	Yes	No	Possibly	Yes	Yes	Possibly	Possibly	No
Methodology	Yes	No	Yes	Yes	Yes	No	Yes	Yes	Yes	Yes
Theory building	No.	No	No	Yes	Yes	Yes	Yes	Yes	Yes	Yes
Theory testing	Yes	Yes	Yes	Yes	Possibly	No	Possibly	No	Possibly	Yes
Theory extension	Possibly	Possibly	Possibly	Possibly	Possibly	No	No	No	Possibly	Possibly

8.4 INFORMATION SYSTEMS RESEARCH APPROACHES: A REVISED TAXONOMY

Using Vogel & Wetherbe's (1984) criteria of parsimony and comprehensiveness, and ensuring that the information systems research approaches that are to be included are genuinely approaches and not methods (*cf*. Section 8.2) nor application areas (Galliers & Land 1987), Table 8.2 can be amended to provide a revised taxonomy, as shown in Table 8.4.

The revised taxonomy distinguishes between the scientific and interpretivist approaches and reflects the likely suitability of each approach in the context of the particular research topic under study. In the context of the latter, it is likely – as Vitalari (1985) has argued – that our research will focus on information technology as it impacts on society, on organizations or groups, or on the individual. It may also focus on the technology itself or on methodological considerations.

In addition, the taxonomy attempts to illustrate the likely applicability of each approach (in the context of a particular object or focus) in the process of theory building (Fig. 8.1).

Note that longitudinal studies (Pettigrew 1983; Vitalari 1985) have not been included in Table 8.4 as a separate category, since field experiments, case studies, descriptive/interpretive, action, and even survey research, can all be undertaken over time.

The use of different research approaches, in the context of building, testing and extending theory, is illustrated in Fig. 8.1. The two examples are taken from Jarvenpaa (1988) and Galliers & Land (1988).

The taxonomy does not include that form of information systems research concerned with research and development (R&D). While this is, of course, a perfectly valid research form, it is of a sufficiently different type not to be considered in the same context. By this I mean that the objective of the R&D form of research is usually concerned with the development of, e.g., a technology, as opposed to the development of theory. Having said that, I have included technology as one of the objects of our research attention, and in this context R&D could well be incorporated in the theorem proof and laboratory/field experiments categories, as shown in Table 8.4.

One final point relates to the general applicability of the research approaches. By studying the taxonomy, it is clear that – in my estimation – the survey, descriptive/interpretive and action research approaches appear to have the widest applicability in information systems research. Others may or may not agree with this analysis.

8.5 APPLICATION OF THE TAXONOMY: NOTES FOR GUIDANCE

The revised taxonomy shown in Table 8.4 may be used in a number of ways. First, by considering the object of one's research, it is possible to use it to identify those approaches most likely to be appropriate for one's study. Similarly, one can use it to identify the most likely approaches to adopt in the context of building, extending and testing theory (Fig. 8.1). The taxonomy should be interpreted as providing guidance only, however. It is not meant to be prescriptive. In other words, it provides a framework upon which to base questions as to the likely utility of alternative approaches in a given context. It does not provide the answers.

In both these contexts, it is useful to review previous research in one's particular field of study, from the perspective of the research approaches that have been employed as much as from the perspective of the results/conclusions of that research. If, as is often the case, previous research has employed one or two approaches only, it may prove useful to adopt another approach in order to look at one's

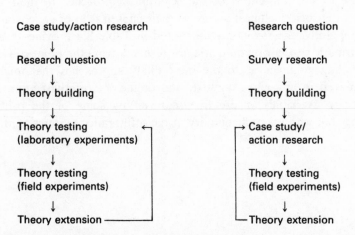

Fig. 8.1 The use of alternative information systems research approaches in the process of theory building, testing and extension (Jarvenpaa, 1988, p. 1504; Galliers & Land, 1988, p. 1505).

chosen topic in a different light. Similarly if, in reviewing previous research, it is apparent that most effort has been exerted on, e.g., building theory, it may prove worthwhile to focus one's research efforts on theory testing and extension – with consequent implications regarding the choice of approach.

It should be noted, however, that I have been somewhat more circumspect in identifying approaches that are likely to lead to theory extension. This is because I am inclined to the view that theory extension is the most difficult phase of research in a complex field such as information systems. Again, others may disagree.

8.6 CONCLUDING REMARKS

The state of much information systems research has been criticized from the perspective of the almost unthinking use of a particular approach that happens to have found favour in one's research institution. Additionally, it is fair to say that in a significant proportion of this research, considerable effort is exerted in arguing the importance of the research topic and, possibly, in addition, the particular research design that is to be adopted. Unfortunately, less attention is paid to the choice of the research approach that would appear suitable, given the object (or focus) of one's research and its place in the context of theory development.

Further, information systems researchers are becoming increasingly aware of the limitations of the scientific approaches to their work, given the socio-technical nature of their chosen field of endeavour.

Hopefully, the taxonomy illustrated in Table 8.4 provides a useful contribution to information systems research from the point of view of providing guidance as to the most likely approaches that might be employed in any given context, and of the interpretivist approaches that are available for use in circumventing some of the problems associated with scientific enquiry in the information systems field.

Part 3

Practical Guidelines

Introduction

Parts 1 and 2 of this book have concentrated on the nature of information systems; on the kind of issues requiring further research; and on the approaches best suited for these circumstances. The focus has been predominantly theoretical thus far but, as I say to my students, 'there's nothing so practical as a good theory!'

From this perspective, it is hoped that Parts 1 and 2 have provided not only food for thought but also some ideas that can be turned to practical use in conducting research. For example, the issues identified in Chapter 6 and the framework to aid in the choice of approach(es) introduced in Chapter 8, will hopefully be of considerable help in formulating research plans.

Part 3 concentrates its attention on these kinds of practical issues. The hope is that, once you have read through the whole of the book's contents, you will be in a much stronger position to undertake research in this fascinating field of study.

Part 3 commences with two chapters extracted from Larry Locke and colleagues' exceptionally useful book *Proposals that Work: A Guide for Planning Dissertations and Grant Proposals* (see the Further Reading section at the end of the book for full details of this book and others which will provide additional useful reading when planning a research project). Chapter 9 focusses on the function and content of research proposals, while Chapter 10 provides much sound advice in helping to surmount many of the problems often encountered in developing proposals.

Chapter 11, by Graham Pervan and Des Klass, looks at the question of the use and misuse of statistical analytical techniques when undertaking information systems research. In the quest for scientific respectability it is, I'm afraid, often the case that researchers go to very great lengths to apply statistical techniques when their data is not of the kind that is amenable to such analysis. Far from strengthening their analysis, this common fault actually weakens their argument and is a trap to be avoided. The do's and don'ts of statistical analysis in our context are explained – in layman's terms – in Chapter 11.

The book closes with Chapter 12, by Gordon Davis, taken from a paper he presented at an information systems research conference held at the National University of Singapore in 1987. In it, he widens our perspective somewhat away from matters concerned with research *per se* to matters associated with publishing research findings – and with academic career development, bearing in mind the well-known expression 'publish or perish'! Intended as a tutorial for those considering an academic career or for recently appointed faculty members, this Chapter can also usefully serve as a kind of checklist or *aide memoire* for the more established information systems faculty.

In it, Davis covers such useful points as knowing one's research strengths (and weaknesses); establishing a network of colleagues, and establishing a personal and group research strategy. Other areas covered include means of developing relevant research ideas and deciding on an appropriate research approach. In this way he builds on the issues covered in Part 2 by providing a number of practical hints to assist in establishing a clear research direction, which will not only cover one's own personal interests but will improve one's chances of research success.

I hope you will find Part 3 of real practical use, and that you have enjoyed the book as a whole. Hopefully it will have equipped you with some of the tools necessary to undertake quality research in information systems. Hopefully, too, it will have whetted your appetite for information systems research. Good luck!

Chapter 9

Research Proposals: Function and Content

L.F. LOCKE
University of Massachusetts
AND
W.W. SPIRDUSO and S.J. SILVERMAN
University of Texas, Austin

A research proposal sets forth both the exact nature of the matter to be investigated and a detailed account of the methods to be employed. In addition, the proposal usually contains material supporting the importance of the topic selected and the appropriateness of the research methods to be employed. This chapter sets out the role and function of research proposals. Further, while there is no universally applicable and correct format for every proposal, the kind of topics that need to be considered are introduced, and guidelines regarding desirable and undesirable proposal features are also included.

9.1 FUNCTION

A research proposal may serve at least three functions:

(1) *Communication* The proposal serves to communicate the student's research plans to those who give consultation and advice. The proposal is the primary instrument on which supervisors base their advice and guidance, and on which those overseeing the research programme must base the decision whether or not to approve the proposed research. Both the quality of assistance obtained and the economy of

consultation depend directly on the clarity and thoroughness of the proposal.

(2) *Plan* The proposal serves as a plan for action. All empirical research consists of careful, systematic, and preplanned observations of some restricted set of phenomena. The acceptability of results is judged exclusively in terms of the adequacy of the methods employed in making, recording, and interpreting the planned observations. The plan for observations, with its supporting arguments and explications, is the qualitative basis on which the thesis or dissertation will be judged.

A thesis or dissertation can be no better than the plan of investigation – methodology or procedures – employed. Hence, an adequate proposal sets forth the plan in step-by-step detail. The existence of a detailed plan that incorporates the most careful anticipation of problems to be confronted and contingent courses of action is the most powerful insurance against oversight or ill-considered choices during the execution phase of the investigation. The hallmark of a good proposal is a level of thoroughness and detail sufficient to permit another investigator to replicate the study, that is, to perform the same planned observations with results not substantially different from those the author might obtain.

In the case of interpretative approaches, it is still necessary to set out as clearly as possible the research methodology. For example, where 'grounded theory' (Glaser & Strauss 1967) forms the basis of the research approach that is intended to be adopted, a clear statement is required regarding the data to be analysed and from which, it is hoped, theory will be generated.

(3) *Contract* A completed proposal approved for execution by the Graduate Studies Committee, constitutes a bond of agreement between the researcher and their supervisor(s). The approved proposal describes a study that, if conducted competently and completely, should provide the basis for a report that would meet all standards for acceptability. Subsequent changes, introduced either by the student or by the supervisor, should be made only with the full knowledge and concurrence of all parties. Substantial changes should be supported by arguments for absolute necessity or compelling desirability. In all but rare instances, revision of the proposal should be completed prior to the collection of data.

9.2 REGULATIONS GOVERNING PROPOSALS

No set of universal rules or guidelines exists to govern the form or content of the research proposal. There are, however, several sources of regulations governing the form and content of the final research document. In as much as the proposal sets forth a plan of action that must eventuate in a thesis or dissertation conforming to these latter regulations, it is important to consider them in writing the proposal.

Although it is evident that particular traditions have evolved within individual departments, it is (thankfully) rare to find the imposition of any formal limitation on the selection of either topic or method of investigation, although there is some evidence of house styles (see Vogel & Wetherbe 1984). The factors that normally circumscribe the planning and execution of student research are existing departmental policy on format for the final report, university regulations concerning theses and dissertation reports, and informal standards exercised by individual supervisors.

9.2.1 The function of the proposal

In most cases, departmental and university regulations are either so explicit as to be perfectly clear, for example, 'The proposal may not exceed 25 typewritten pages' or 'The proposal will conform to the style established in Campbell 1969'; or so general as to impose no specific or useful standard, for example, 'The research topic must be of suitable proportions' or 'The proposal must reflect a thorough knowledge of the problem area'. The student, therefore, should find no serious difficulty in developing a proposal that conforms to departmental and university regulations.

There is a third potential source of regulation: the individual thesis or dissertation committee or the individual supervisor. Individuals serving on such committees, or individual supervisors, may have strong personal commitments concerning particular working procedures, writing styles and proposal format. Research students must confront these as a unique constellation of demands that will influence the form of their proposal. It is wise to anticipate conflicting demands and to attempt their resolution before the collection of data and the preparation of a final report.

Research committees and/or supervisors are likely to make style and format demands that differ substantially from commonly accepted modes of research writing. As a general rule, most advisers subscribe to the broad guidelines outlined in this document. Where differences occur, they are likely to be matters of emphasis or largely mechancial items.

9.3 GENERAL CONSIDERATIONS

Most problems in preparing a proposal are straightforward and relatively obvious. The common difficulties do not involve the subtle and complex problems of design and data management. They arise instead from the most basic elements of the research process:

- What is the proper question to ask?
- Where is the best place to look for the answer?
- Which research methodologies would best serve my intended purpose?
- How best to standardize, quantify and record observations?

Determining the answers to these questions remains the most common obstacle to the development of adequate proposals.

Simplicity, clarity and parsimony are the standards of writing that reflect adequate thinking about the research problem. A proposal helps researchers solicit prompt and accurate advice to the degree that the document is easily and correctly understood by their advisors. Complicated matters are best communicated when they are the clear objects of terse, well-edited prose. In the mass of details and intellectual efforts that go into the planning of a research study, the researcher must not forget that the proposal's most immediate function is to inform its readers quickly and accurately.

The problem in writing a proposal is essentially the same as in writing the final report. When the task of preparing a proposal is well executed, the task of preparing the final report is more than half done. Under ideal conditions, such minor changes as altering the tense of verbs converts the proposal into the opening chapters of the final report. This is not to be underestimated. Given the limited time available for the research, and what seems like a mountain of a task facing all research students in writing the dissertation or thesis, to have the opening chapters practically written before the research proper begins is a significant accomplishment and a major moral booster!

Most, although not necessarily all, proposals evolve through a series of steps from preliminary discussions with colleagues and faculty members, to a final document which will form the basis for a decision to allow the research to go ahead or not. Sometimes, (for example, in most North American universities) this will be presented at a formal meeting of the full dissertation or thesis committee, and sometimes (for example, in British and Australian universities) the decision will be based on a reading of the document itself. This process can be accelerated and made more productive if the student follows these simple rules:

(1) Prepare clean, updated copies of the evolving proposal and submit them to advisers in advance of scheduled consultation.
(2) Prepare an agenda of questions and problems to be discussed and submit them to advisors in advance of scheduled consultations.
(3) Keep a carefully written record of the discussion and decisions that occur with regard to each item on the consultation agendum.

A number of research textbooks and form guides are available to help in developing an adequate proposal. In addition, checklists now exist for reviewing the adequacy of proposals for several specific types of research.

A list of general standards for judging the acceptability of a thesis or dissertation proposal is given in Table 9.1 overleaf. This list can serve both as a preliminary guide for anticipating problems in development of the proposal and as a checklist to use in revising and refining the final document.

9.4 GENERAL FORMAT

Guidelines for the format of proposals, even when intended only as general suggestions, often have an unfortunate influence on the writing process. Once committed to paper, such guidelines quickly tend to acquire the status of mandatory prescription. In an attempt to conform to what they perceive as an invariate format, students produce proposal documents that are awkward and illogical as plans for action, as well as stilted and tasteless as prose writing.

There is no universally applicable and correct format for the research proposal. Nonetheless, there are certain communication tasks

Table 9.1 Some general standards for judging the acceptability of a thesis or project proposal. Extracted from Locke & Spirduso (1970).

	Desirable	Undesirable
(1) Topic		
(a) Importance		
(i) Basic research	Topic is articulated to a body of knowledge recognized as broadly relevant to professional concerns. There is a clear relation between the topic and existing information in related areas of knowledge. Topic is recognized as substantial by people who are knowledgeable in the area.	Proposal does not support the importance of the study. Topic seems unrelated to existing facts and theoretical constructs. Proposed study is not inserted into a line of inquiry.
(ii) Applied research (projects)	Topic is relevant to professional needs and recognized as substantial by competent individuals engaged in professional practice. There is a close relation between the topic and existing problems in practice.	Topic seems unrelated to realistic professional concerns and divorced from matters of practice.
(b) Scope	The extent of the proposed study is reasonable in terms of the time and resources available to the candidate. There is clear indication that the student has considered and made provision for each of the demands implicit within the study.	Projected study is grandiose and unreasonable in terms of time and resources. Or, the study is so small or limited in its concern as to provide little useful information and to involve less than a reasonable exposure to scholarly inquiry for the candidate.
(c) Advisement	At least one faculty member possessing scholarly competence in the domain of the topic is both interested and available. Resources for developing or obtaining needed technical skills are available and specifically identified.	Faculty members available for substantial assistance lack special competence in the domain of the topic. Needed sources of technical assistance are not specified or identified.

(2) Scholarship

(a) Originality

The proposal provides in the definition of the problem, the methodology employed, or the mode of interpretation, some contribution that is different from work previously done, and that distinctly is the product of the candidate's own thinking. In replicative studies special attention is given either to deliberate alteration in method and design or to the unique problems of maintaining equivalent conditions for all critical variables.

Proposed study paraphrases and collects opinions, results or conclusions of others without criticism, synthesis or the creative development of an organizing structure. Replicates without intentional and appropriate variation in method or special attention to the problems of creating a satisfactory level of experimental equivalence.

(b) Perspective

Student reveals that he is able to relate his topic to a large framework of knowledge and theory.

Student treats the problem in isolation from previous work, related disciplines, and relevant theoretical structures.

(c) Logic

Design of the proposed study is appropriate to the nature of the topic, being no more elaborate than demanded by the question asked. There is congruence among title, problem and procedures. Student makes explicit the rationale and assumptions that underlie the form of the question and the procedures that might have been followed and makes visible the reasoning for his choices.

Proposed design is more complex than demanded by the question and the present level of knowledge. Design fails to confront important complexities in the topic through the use of methods leading to multi-variate analysis. Title does not exactly reflect the central problem. Procedures are not designed to deal with the problem identified as central to the study. Student does not make clear the procedural alternatives that might have been followed.

(d) Objectivity

Student clearly delineates the limits, weaknesses, and strengths of his study, and maintains objectivity. He restricts his language to a level made justifiable by previous findings and a conservative appraisal of current knowledge and practice.

Student overgeneralizes from an inadequate body of knowledge or suggests applications that seem unwarranted by the evidence he presents. He seems unaware of the limitations imposed by his selection of sample or methodology.

Table 9.1 *Continued*

	Desirable	Undesirable
(e) Depth of preparation	Student demonstrates familiarity with the major sources of information that relate to his problem, and makes apt and ready application of these to the development of his study. Includes pilot study data, tests for determining sample size, and relevant sample applications of the methods to be employed. Student makes clear that he has considered the feasibility factors of time, cost and the availability of data. Student indicates how he plans to obtain special competence demanded by his procedures.	Student has not completed a thorough search of relevant literature, or has not digested it to the point of understanding the major concepts involved and their application to his problem. Proposal includes no pilot study data or relevant sample applications of methods to be employed. He fails to recognize the sophisticated scholarship needed for the use of such procedures as sampling, use of demographic data, test and questionnaire construction, interviewing, or the selection and use of psychometric instruments.
(3) Presentation (a) Mechanics	Proposal is well edited, with adequate attention to grammar, sentence structure, spelling, and all matters of mechanical accuracy. The style is terse, with a minimum of unnecessary words and irrelevant commentary.	Obvious failure to proof read as revealed by mechanical errors. Unnecessary use of descriptive words and phrases. Rambling style, introduction of peripheral commentary, and use of trite jargon.

(b) Documentation	Citations are limited to and consistently provided for (a) concepts, procedures, or materials (including quoted materials) that are the unique products of particular individuals and fall under the broad canon of 'credit due', and (b) positions, interpretations, or methodological alternatives elected by the author that might require the support of further argument and explication as developed in supplementary references.	Inadequate reference to the relevant literature, failure to give credit where due, or failure to indicate sources likely to be needed by the interested and critical reader. Over-abundance of documentation in which citations are irrelevant, needlessly repetitious, or refer to matters clearly within the public domain. Extensive use of direct quotations that are not justified by their contribution to the main tasks of the proposal.
(c) Organization	Proposal has logical, easily understandable sequence from initial statement of the problem through last appendix. Major topics are separated under appropriately devised sub-headings. Format tailored to meet demands peculiar to the topic.	Order of topics violates logic and causes reader to skip forward and back to make sense of the presentation. Words used to indicate systematic meanings, prior to their definition. Arbitrary format followed even when inappropriate to topic.
(d) Clarity	Proposal makes explicit each step of the project. Procedures are described in terms of specific operations. Copies of such relevant materials as test instruments, interview schedules, directions to subjects, criteria for selection of experts, and pilot test data are appended to the main proposal document. Given the level of detail contained in the proposal, any appropriately trained researcher could carry out the study with results not differing substantially from those that would be obtained by the author. Explicit, step-by-step sequence of operations presented.	Report makes vague references to unspecified procedures that are described only in general terms or that are linked together by relationships that leave their purpose unclear. Such important operations as 'a structured interview', 'an analysis of literature', 'an evaluation of materials', or 'a test of attitudes' are not presented in explicit forms such as particular test instruments, lists of criteria, procedures for analysis, or experimental operations. Exact temporal sequence of individual parts of the investigation not made clear.

to be accomplished. A few of these tasks are common to all proposals, whereas other tasks are unique to particular research topics. Taken together, the tasks encompassed by the proposal demand the creation of a format designed to fit the real topic at hand, not some preconceived ideal.

9.5 SPECIFIC TASKS

The following paragraphs specify communication tasks that are present in nearly all proposals for empirical research. Within a given proposal the tasks may or may not be identified by such traditional section designations as background, definitions, importance, purpose, review of literature, choice of methodology, research design or limitations. Particular proposals are sure to demand changes in the order of presentation or attention to yet other tasks not specified below. It is particularly important to note that adjacent tasks in the following paragraphs most often may be conveniently merged into single sections.

9.5.1 Introducing the research/abstract

Proposals, like other forms of written communications, are best introduced by a short, meticulously devised statement that establishes the overall area of concern, arouses interest, and communicates information essential to the reader's comprehension of what follows. The standard here is 'gentle introduction' that avoids both tedious length and the shock of technical details or abstruse argument. A careful and artful introductory statement is the precursor of task 3 (background) and may, in fact, simply be written as the opening portion of that later task.

9.5.2 Establishing the research focus

Early in the proposal it is wise to set forth an explicit statement of the issue about which the investigation will be directed. This statement need not include all the sub-topics, nor need it be stated in the formal language of research questions of hypotheses. It should, however, provide a specific and accurate synopsis of the overall purpose of the study. An early and specific announcement of the research focus satisfies the most pressing of the reader's needs. Such information leaves the reader free to attend to the author's subsequent exposition and development of the topic without the nagging sense of having to hunt for the main object of study. Consequently, it is useful to give this problem high visibility.

9.5.3 Discussing the background of the problem

Any research problem must show its lineage from the background of existing knowledge or previous investigation.

(1) What do we already know or do? (The purpose here is to supply the legitimacy and importance of the question).
(2) How does this particular proposal relate to what we already know or do? (The purpose here is to explain and support the focus for the study.)
(3) Why select this particular method of investigation? (The purpose here is to explain and support the selections made from among alternative methods of investigation e.g. what are the most appropriate approaches? What approaches have been used in researching this topic area in the past?)

In reviewing the research literature that often forms the background for the study, the author's task is to indicate the main directions taken by workers in the area and the main issues of methodology and interpretation that have arisen. Particular attention must be given to a critical analysis of previous methodology and the exposition of the advantages and limitations inherent in various alternatives. Close attention must be given to conceptual and theoretical formulations that are explicit or implicit within the selected studies.

By making the selection of method contingent upon previous results; by making the questions or hypotheses emerge from the total matrix of answered and unanswered questions; by devising, when appropriate, a theoretical basis for the study that emerges from the structure of existing knowledge, the researcher inserts their proposed study into a line of inquiry and a developing body of knowledge. Such careful attention to background is the first step in entering the continuing conversation that is science – the pursuit of systematic and formulated knowledge.

The researcher should select those studies that provide a foundation for the proposed investigation, discuss these studies in sufficient detail to make their relevance entirely clear, note explicitly the ways in which they contribute to the proposed research, and give some indication of how the proposal is designed to move beyond earlier work.

It is important for the student to resist the impulse to display both the extent of their personal labours in achieving what they know and the volume of interesting but presently irrelevant information they have accumulated in the process. The rule in selecting studies for review is exactly the same as that used throughout the proposal – limit discussion to what is essential to the main topic. A complete list of all references used in developing the proposal – properly called a bibliography as distinct from the list of references – may be placed in an appendix, thereby providing both a service to the interested reader and some psychological relief to the student!

Whenever possible, the researcher should provide conceptual or theoretical clarity by creating organizing frameworks that encompass both the reviewed studies and the proposed research. This may take the form of something as obvious and practical as grouping studies according to certain methodological features (often for the purpose of examining divergent results), or something as esoteric as identifying and grouping the implicit assumptions made by various researchers in formatting their statement of the problem (often for the purpose of clarifying the problem elected in the present proposal).

In many proposals, the creation of an organizing framework represents the most important single opportunity for the application of original thought. In one sense, the organizing task is an extension of the need to achieve clarity in communication. A category system that allows division of diverse ideas or recondite events into easily perceived and remembered subsets is an organizational convenience for the author, as well as for the reader.

Beyond convenience, however, the development of organizing frameworks involves identifying distinctive threads of thought. The task here is to isolate the common ways by which researchers, working at different times and in varying degrees of intellectual isolation, have conceived of reality. In creating a scheme that deals meaningfully with similarities and dissimilarities in the work of others, the author of the proposal can serve both their own needs and the developing body of knowledge.

Even relatively simple organizing or integrating systems demand the development of underlying conceptual plans and, often, new ways of interpreting old results and presumed relationships. The sequence of variables in the study may provide a simple and generally adequate place to begin arranging the review. In turn, such conceptual schemata often contain useful assumptions about casual relationships and thus can serve as effective precursors to explanatory theory. The most elegant kind of research proposals achieve exactly that kind of linkage, using the framework for organizing the review of literature as a bridge connecting existing knowledge, a proposed theory, and the specific, theory-based hypotheses to be given empirical test, or questions to which answers are sought, in the proposed study.

9.5.4 Formulating questions or hypotheses

Those proposals that are not basing the intended research on grounded theory should arrive at a formal statement of questions or hypotheses. These may be set aside as a separate section or simply included in the course of other discussion. Such statements differ from the earlier statement of the research focus in that:

(1) they are normally stated in formal terms appropriate to the design and analysis of data to be employed;
(2) they display, in logical order, all sub-parts of the research topic.

The question form is most appropriate where the research is exploratory. Researchers should indicate by the specificity of questions, however, how carefully they have thought through the problem. By careful formulation of questions, the proposed study should be directed toward suspected alternatives rather than toward a scanning of interesting findings.

Hypotheses must be related to a theoretical base and should be employed whenever the state of existing knowledge permits the formulation of intelligent suppositions about the relationship of elements in the topic area. Even if the theoretical framework has been introduced in a previous section, it is often useful to provide a succinct restatement at a point contiguous to the formal presentation of hypotheses.

The proposal must provide a clear bridge connecting knowledge, theory and the proposed study. The process of translating the relationships expressed in theory into the form of testable hypotheses or researchers' questions involves logical operations that will be critical to the reader's understanding. For that reason, the author must make every effort to present a clear account of the linkages between knowledge, theory, hypotheses, questions and methodology.

9.5.5 Explaining procedures

Proposals should embody a plan for the careful and systematic observation (interpretation) of events. The methods selected for such observations determine the quality of data obtained. For this reason, the portion of the proposal dealing with procedures the researcher intends to employ will be subject to the closest critical scrutiny. Correspondingly, the presentation of methodology requires great attention to detail. The discussion of method should include at one level the choice of approach, and at another the sources of data and the means by which data are to be collected and analysed. In addition the discussion must show that the specific techniques selected will not fall short of the claims established in previous sections of the proposal.

The section or sections dealing with methodology must be freely adapted to the purpose of the study. Whatever the format, however, the proposal must provide a step-by-step set of instructions for conducting the investigation. For example, many studies demand explication of the following items:

(1) identification and description of a target population and sampling methods to be used;
(2) presentation of instruments and techniques for measurement;
(3) presentation of a design for the collection of data;
(4) presentation of procedures for collecting and recording data;
(5) development of plans for contingencies;
(6) presentation of plans for the analysis of data.

Many of the justifications for particular selections of method will emerge in the discussion of the project background. The rationale for some choices, however, will most conveniently be presented when the method is introduced as part of the plan for investigation.

9.5.6 Providing supplementary material

For the purpose of clarity and economical presentation, many items may be placed in appendices keyed to appropriate references in the main text. So placed, such materials become options available to the reader as needed, rather than distractions or impediments to under-standing the main themes of the proposal. Included in the appendices may be such items as the following:

(1) letters and other relevant documents;
(2) raw data or tabular material from pilot studies;
(3) interview schedules;
(4) diagrammatic models of the search design;
(5) diagrammatic models of any statistical analysis;
(6) tabular materials from related research;
(7) chapter outline for the final report;
(8) proposed time schedule for executing the study;
(9) supplementary bibliographies.

Chapter 10

Developing Proposals:
Some Common Problems

L.F. LOCKE,
University of Massachusetts
AND
W.W. SPIRDUSO and S.J. SILVERMAN
University of Texas, Austin

This chapter focusses on some of the common problems encountered in producing a research proposal. These are dealt with
in terms of the set of steps that are normally followed in the lead
up to formally presenting a proposal to one's research/thesis committee, supervisor, and the appropriate style and form for research
proposals. The chapter concludes by taking a further look at the
proposal's content. By raising some of the problems that are commonly encountered, it is hoped that many of these pitfalls may be
avoided.

The general purposes and broad format of the proposal document
were presented in Chapter 9. There remain, however, a number of
particular issues that cause a disproportionate amount of difficulty in
preparing proposals for student-conducted research. These issues are
the subject of this chapter.

In some cases the problems arise because of real difficulty in the
subtle and complex nature of the writing task. In other cases, the
problems are a consequence of confusion, conflicting opinions, and
ambiguous standards among research workers themselves and, more
particularly, among university research advisors.

As with many tasks involving an element of art, it is possible to
establish a few general rules to which most practitioners subscribe.
Success in terms of real mastery, however, lies not in knowing or even
following the rules, but in what the student learns to do within the
rules.

Each student will discover their own set of special problems. Some will be solved only through practice and the accumulation of experience. While wrestling with the frustrations of their proposal, the student should remember that the fascination of research lies in its problematic nature; in the tortuous search for more serviceable hypotheses; in the creative tasks of design, and in the stringent demand for clear, concise expression.

The aim here is to warn the student about the most common pitfalls; to provide some general suggestions for resolution of the problems; and to sound one encouraging note: consultation with colleagues and advisers, patience with the often slow process of 'figuring out', and scrupulous care in writing will overcome or circumvent most of the problems encountered in preparing a research proposal. In the midst of difficulty, it is useful to remember that problems are better encountered when developing the proposal than when facing a deadline for the final copy of the thesis.

The problems have been grouped into three broad categories:

(1) the sequence of proposing, from selecting a topic to oral presentation;
(2) style and form in writing the proposal;
(3) content of the proposal: important considerations.

Each section contains a number of specific issues that may confront the student researcher, and provides some rules of thumb for use in avoiding or resolving the attendant difficulties. Students should skim through the three sections and read selectively, since not all of the discussions will be relevant to their particular needs.

10.1 THE SEQUENCE OF PROPOSING, FROM SELECTING A TOPIC TO ORAL PRESENTATION

10.1.1 A plan of action – what follows what?

Fig. 10.1 can be useful for the novice if one central point is understood. A tidy, linear sequence of steps is *not* an accurate picture of what happens in the development of most research proposals. The peculiar qualities of human thought processes and the serendipity of retrieving knowledge serve to guarantee that development of a proposal will be anything but tidy. Dizzying leaps, periods of no

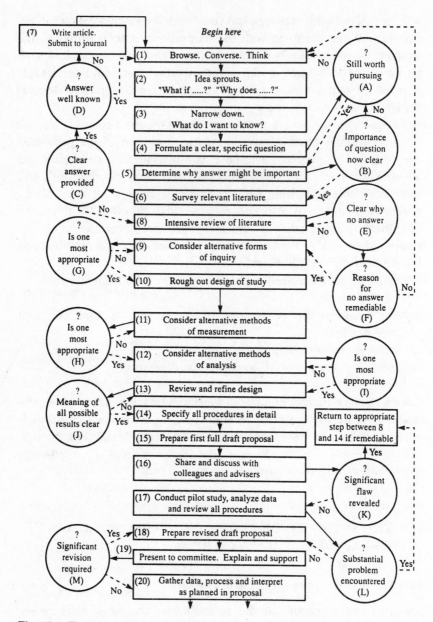

Fig. 10.1 Twenty steps to a proposal.

Note: Boxes represent major procedural steps; unbroken lines trace the main sequence of those steps. Circles represent the major questions to be confronted; the broken lines lead to the procedural consequences of the alternative *Yes* or *No* answers.

progress, and agonizing backtracking are more typical than is a continuous, unidirectional flow of events. The diagram may be used to obtain an overview of the task, to establish a rough time schedule, or to check retrospectively for possible omissions, but it is not to be taken as a literal representation of what should or will happen.

To say that development of a proposal is not a perfectly predictable sequence is not to say, however, that it is entirely devoid of order. When the proposal has been completed, a backward glance often indicates that an orderly progression through the steps would have saved time and effort. It is more important to complete some steps in sequence than others. For instance, although the mind may skip ahead and visualize a specific type of measure to be used, Step 11, Consider alternative methods of measurement, should not be undertaken until Step 6, Surveying relevant literature, is completed.

Many methods of measurement may be revealed and noted while perusing the literature. Sometimes suggestions for instrumentation materialize in unlikely places, or in studies that have been placed by the student into categories that seem unlikely to yield information concerning measurement. In addition, reported reliabilities and validities of alternative procedures will be needed before any final selection can be made. Thus, a large commitment of effort to consideration of alternative methods can be a waste of time if it precedes a careful survey of the literature, or if the issues raised in Chapter 8 have not been taken on board.

For simplicity, many important elements have been omitted from Fig. 10.1. No reference is made to such pivotal processes as developing a theoretical framework, categorizing literature or stating hypotheses. Further, the detailed demands that are intrinsic to the writing process itself, such as establishing a systematic language, receive no mention. What are presented are the obvious steps of logic and procedure – the operations and questions that mark development toward a plan for action. The following points within the diagram are the most frequent causes of difficulty.

Step 3. Narrow down. What do I want to know?

Moving from general to specific is always more difficult for the beginner than is anticipated. It is here that student researchers have their first encounter with two of the hard facts of life: logistic practicality and the perverse inscrutability of seemingly simple events.

Inevitably, they must learn to take one small step, one manageable question, at a time. In other words, the proposal must conform in scope to the realistic limitations of the research process itself. At their best, the tools of research can encompass only limited bits of reality, and stretched too far they produce illusion rather than understanding.

It is important to think big at first, to puzzle without considering practicality, and to allow speculation to soar beyond the confines of the sure knowledge base. From such creative conceptual exercises, however, the researcher must return to the question, Where, given my resources and the nature of the problem, can I begin?

Delimiting questions such as: Under what conditions? At what time? In what location? By observing which events? By manipulating which variables? serve the necessary pruning function.

Question A.   Still worth pursuing?

A question's worth may be viewed from two dimensions: that of its worth to the individual contemplating the answer, and that of its worth to information system practitioners, to the academic community, and ultimately to society. Question A, Still worth pursuing?, is the question that the researcher must answer in terms of their own interests and needs. The world is full of clearly formulated and specific questions that may not, once seen in their formal dress, seem worth the effort of answering.

Because researchers are human, perfectly legitimate questions may seem dull; interesting veins of inquiry may peter out into triviality, and well-defined issues may fail to suit for no better reason than a clash with personal style. On the other hand, the research topic has to be seen to be important by others who share an interest in the field of information systems. Chapter 6 may be useful here. It is not sufficient to pursue a research topic simply because it is of personal interest designed to quench one's curiosity about a long-held hunch.

The basic rule is to be honest before proceeding. If you really do not care about answering the question, it may be better to start again, while the investment still is relatively small. Enthusiasm may well be at its peak in the early stages of the project. To start off being less than enthusiastic for one's topic is a likely recipe for disaster.

Step 5.   Determine why answer might be important

This step places the proposed research in scientific-societal perspective. The study should contribute to the generation or validation of a theoretical structure or sub-component, or relate to one of the several processes by which knowledge is used to enhance practice. The trick here is to justify the question in terms appropriate to the nature of the question. Inquiry that is directed towards filling a gap in the structure of knowledge need not be supported by appeals to practical application (even though later events may yield just such return). Inquiry that arises directly from problems in the world of practice need not be supported by appeals to improve understanding of basic phenomena (even though later events may yield just such return). Each kind of question has its own correct measure of importance. The task of distinguishing the trivial from the substantive is not always easy; do not make it even more difficult by attempting to apply the wrong standard.

Step 6.   Survey relevant literature

A preliminary scanning of the most obvious, pertinent resources, particularly reviews of the literature, is a way of husbanding time. It is far better to abandon a line of thought after several weeks of selective skimming than to work one's way via slow, thorough digestion of each document to the same conclusion after several months of effort.

Conscientious students sometimes feel vaguely guilty about such quick surveys. Keeping in mind the real purpose, which is to identify questions that already have satisfactory answers, is one way of easing such discomfort.

Question F.   Reason for no answer remediable?

In some cases the literature contains an empty area because that state of technology, the available knowledge framework, or the logistic demands peculiar to the question have made it impossible or unreasonable to conduct appropriate forms of inquiry. So long as the gap in knowledge seems to exist because no one has yet defined the question or become interested in pursuing the answer, it is reasonable to proceed. There are other reasons for empty or ambiguous areas in the literature, however, and they signal caution before proceeding. For example, one should ask how feasible it is for your research to be undertaken; is a gap in the literature simply due to the problem being insurmountable?

Question J.   Meaning of all possible results clear?

The tighter the logic, the more elegant the theoretical framework, and the more closely the design is tailored to produce clarity along one dimension; in short, the better the quality of the proposal, the greater the risk that the proposer will be lured into an unfortunate presumption – that the result of the study is presumed before the data are in hand.

That student researchers sometimes are confronted by the stunning news that their treatment produced a reverse effect is in itself neither surprising nor harmful. Being unable to make an intelligent interpretation of such a situation is, however, unfortunate and in some cases unnecessary.

By serious consideration of every possible result at the time of constructing the proposal, it often becomes possible to include elements of the study that will give substance to any of several possible results. One method of anticipating the unexpected is to follow through the consequences of rejecting or failing to reject each hypothesis of the study. If the hypothesis were to be rejected, what is the explanation? How is the explanation justified by the rationale for the study? What findings would support the explanation?

Conversely, if the findings of the study fail to provide a basis for rejection, what explanations are to be proposed? What are alternative explanations? At least, some careful preliminary thought about alternative explanations for each possible result will serve as a shield against the panic that produces such awkward *post hoc* interpretations as 'no significant differences were observed because the instruments employed were inadequate'.

Step 16.   Share and discuss with colleagues and advisers

There is a well-known syndrome displayed by some who attempt research, symptomized by the inclination to prolong the period of writing the final report – indefinitely. Some people simply cannot face what they perceive to be the personal threat implied in opening their work to challenge in the public arena. These individuals are terribly handicapped and only rarely can become mature, productive researchers. An early sign of this syndrome is seen in students who cannot bring themselves to solicit advice and criticism for their proposals.

Sometimes a student experiences severe criticism because their ideas have been presented before they have been sufficiently developed into a conceptual framework that represents careful and critical preparation. Many professors avoid speculative conversations about 'half-baked' ideas that have just arrived in a blinding flash of revelation to the student. Few professors, though, refuse a request for advice concerning a proposal that has been drafted as the culmination of several weeks of hard thought, research and development. Even at that, having one's best effort devastated by pointed criticism can be an agonizing experience. The only alternative, however, is to persist in error or ignorance, and that is untenable in research.

If the student is fortunate enough to be in a department that contains a vigorous community of inquiring minds, with the constant give and take of intellectual disputation, they will soon learn to regard this kind of rough and tumble as an integral part of producing good research. They will solicit, if not enjoy, the best criticism that can be found. Dummy runs among colleagues in research seminars can be a very helpful experience, once ideas have begun to form.

The notion that it is vaguely immoral to seek assistance in preparing a proposal is at best a parody of real research and at worst, as in the form of an institutional rule, it is a serious perversion arising from ignorance. Research may have some game-like qualities, but a system of handicaps is not one of them. The object of every inquiry is to get the best possible answer under the circumstances, and that presumes obtaining the best advice available. Hopefully, the student will not be held to any lesser standard.

It should be obvious that the student, after digesting and weighing all the criticism received, must still make their own choices. Not all advice is good and not all criticism is valid. There is only one way to find out, however, and that is to share the proposal with colleagues whose judgements one can respect, if not always accept.

Step 20. *Gather data, process and interpret as in proposal*

This is the pay-off. A good proposal is more than a guide to action, it is a framework for intelligent interpretation of results and the heart of a sound final report. The proposal cannot guarantee significant results, but it will provide some assurance that, whatever the result, the student can wind up the project with reasonable dispatch and at least a minimum of intellectual grace. If that sounds too small a recompense for all the effort, consider the alternative of having to write a report about an inconsequential question, pursued through inadequate methods of inquiry, and resulting in a heap of unanalysable data.

10.1.2 Originality and replication – what is a contribution to knowledge?

In this brief chapter, the authors have not attempted to discuss events that precede the proposal, the critical and difficult steps of identifying and delimiting a research topic, but at least one such preliminary problem, the question of originality, has important ramifications for the proposal and thus must receive comment here.

Some advisers regard student-conducted research primarily as an arena for training – practising the art of research but not the real thing. Whatever may be the logic of such an assumption, it goes without saying that students generally do not take the same attitude. Their expectations are more likely to resemble the classic dictum for scholarly research: to make an original contribution to the body of knowledge.

An all-too-common problem in selecting topics for research proposals occurs when either the student or an adviser gives literal interpretation to the word original, defining it as 'initial, first, never having existing or occurred before'. This is a serious misinterpretation of the word as it is used in scholarly research. In research, 'original' clearly includes all studies deliberately employed to test the accuracy of results or the applicability of conclusions developed in previous studies. What are not included under the rubric of original are studies that proceed mindlessly to repeat an existing work either in foolish ignorance of its existence or without appropriate attention to its defects or limitations.

One consequence of the confusion surrounding the phrase 'original contribution' is that misguided students and advisers are led to ignore one of the most important areas of research activity and one of the most useful forms of training for the novice researcher: building on previous studies. That this kind of cumulative research is sometimes regarded simply as pure replication rote imitation, lacking sufficient opportunity for the student to apply and develop their own skills, is an indication of how badly some students and advisers misunderstand both the operation of a research enterprise and the concept of a body of knowledge.

The essential role of replication in scientific research has been argued elsewhere with great cogency, along with the inherent problems of replicating research in organisations (Checkland 1981). What has perhaps not been made sufficiently clear, however, is that replication (in the form of cumulative research) has a place in the social sciences, despite the problems involved (Keen 1984). Indeed, replication studies can involve challenging problems that demand creative resolution. Further, as a consequence of inexperience, some advisers do not appreciate the degree to which writing proposals for replicative studies can constitute an ideal learning opportunity for research trainees.

In writing a proposal for this kind of replicative study, the student should introduce the original with appropriate citation, make the comments that are needed, and proceed without equivocation or apology to propose their own work. Cumulative research is not, as unfortunate tradition has it in some departments, slightly improper or something less than genuine research.

Given the limitations of research reports, it is often useful to discuss the source study for the proposed replication or extension with the original author, directly or by mail. Most research workers are happy to provide greater detail and in some instances raw data for inspection or reanalysis. In a healthy science, replication is the most sincere form of flattery.

A proposal appendix containing correspondence with the author of the original report, or data not provided in that report, can often serve to interest and reassure a hesitant adviser.

10.1.3 Getting started – putting pen to paper

It is quite common for the student who has never written a research proposal to sit in front of their word processor and stare at a blank screen for hours. In short their mind is brimming with knowledge gleaned from the literature, but how do you actually get it down on paper? It is true, too, that the concept of 'research proposal' conjures up ideas of accuracy, precision, meticulous form, and the use of language that is quite foreign to the neophyte researcher. If the student is overwhelmed by such demands, the following suggestions may be helpful.

Make an outline that is compatible with the format selected to present the communication tasks. An initial approval of the outline by the adviser may save later revision time. Gather the source materials, notes and references and organize them into groups that correspond to the outline topics. For instance, notes supporting the rationale of the study would be in one group, and notes relating to the reliability of an instrument to be used would be in another group.

Once the outline is made and the materials gathered, tackle one of the topics in the outline (preferably the first) and start writing. If the topic to be written is labelled 'The Problem', assume someone has asked the question, What is the problem of this study? Your task is to answer that question. Start writing. Do not worry about grammer, syntax or writing in a particular style. Just write. In this way you can avoid one of the greatest inhibitions to creativity – an inward criticism that is so severe that each idea is rejected before it becomes reality.

Remember, it is easier to correct than to create. If all the essential parts of the topic are displayed in some fashion, they can later be rearranged, edited, and couched within the required style/language. With experience, students find themselves thinking in the accepted language, style and forms of the proposal. Until that time, the essential problem is to begin. Awkward or elegant, laborious or swift, there is no substitute for writing the first draft.

10.1.4 Prologue to action – the oral presentation

Many graduate schools (particularly in North America and parts of continental Europe) require a formal oral presentation of research plans before the student's committee (or a special seminar group designed for screening proposals). Master's and Doctoral thesis committees vary in number from one professor to a committee of five or six faculty members. In some instances, all committee members are from within the student's department. In other instances, the committee may be multi-disciplinary, with faculty representing other departments on the campus.

In preparing for the oral presentation, students should identify in advance the individuals who will hear their presentation, particularly as the presence of scholars from outside their discipline may impose special demands on both the presentation and the period of discussion and questions that normally follows. A multi-disciplinary committee certainly makes it imperative to refrain, at least in the oral summary, from technical detail of jargon specific to the area of the study.

The type of oral presentation demanded of the student will vary from committee to committee and university to university. Some universities (particularly in the United Kingdom and Australia for example) will carefully study the proposal and not expect a verbal recitation of what has been written. Rather, they may request a brief review of the student's past experiences that led to the choice of topic, some discussion of their skills and abilities within the area of the proposed research, and some commentary about their ultimate purpose in choosing the specific topic proposed.

The major purpose of the oral presentation and discussion with a committee (or in a research seminar) is to bring critical analysis and fresh ideas representing substantial research experience to bear upon the student's topic of study. The exposure of major flaws in design or inappropriate analyses may be discussed, with the result that a more elegant proposal is identified. Research students should anticipate that the oral presentation is a co-operative effort towards excellence by faculty and student, and should, therefore, look forward to the experience as one that will add substantially to the probability of success in their endeavours.

The oral presentation is the time when the student's knowledge of this area of interest will serve him well. Although a large percentage of his knowledge regarding the study is not directly appropriate for insertion in the proposal, the questions of the committee and the following discussion will test the extent and depth of the student's knowledge in the area. Students should, therefore, review their working notes prior to the oral presentation and should have the major items of pertinent literature fresh in their memory. A thorough review of any statistical techniques involved in the proposed study will avoid confusion and possible embarrassment.

In preparation for the oral presentation, the student should practise before several other graduate students, presenting their work just as they intend to present it and then entertaining a substantial period of questioning. Practise in fielding questions is sound preparation for the oral. It is wise to hold a practice session before the final draft of the proposal is prepared, as questions often point to needed clarifications or revisions in the document. This advice applies equally to the viva voce or defence of the final thesis.

10.2 STYLE AND FORM IN WRITING THE PROPOSAL

10.2.1 Praising, exhorting, and polemicising – don't

For a variety of motives arising pricipally from the reward system governing other writing tasks, many students use their proposal as an opportunity to praise the importance of information systems. Some use exhortative language to urge such particular points of view as the supposed importance of empirical research in designing professional practice. Others use the proposed research as the basis for arguments suggesting the use of a particular methodology or technology, for instance.

There is no need or proper place in a research proposal for such subjective side excursions. The purpose of a proposal is to set forth for a reader the nature of the matter to be investigated and an account of the methods to be employed. Anything else distracts and serves as an impediment to clear communication.

As a general rule, it is best to stick to the topic and resist the temptation to sound 'properly positive and enthusiastic'. Do not attempt to manipulate the opinions of the reader in areas other than those essential to the investigation. The simple test is to ask yourself this question: Does the reader really need to consider this point in order to judge the adequacy of my thinking? If the answer is no, then the decision to delete is clear, if not always easy, for the author.

10.2.2 Quotations – how to pick fruit from the knowledge tree

Too often, inexperienced students are inclined to equate the number of citations in a paper with the weight of the argument being presented. This, of course, is an error. 'Enough is enough' should be the catch phrase.

The proper uses of direct quotation are even more stringently limited than the use of general citations for paraphrased material. The practice of liberally sprinkling the proposal with quoted material – particularly lengthy quotes – is more than pointless. It is self-defeating. Few will read them and most readers find the presence of unessential quotes irritating and a distraction from the line of thought being presented for examination. When quotations are introduced at points for which even general citations are unnecessary, the writer has reached the limit of disregard for the reader.

There are two legitimate motives for direct use of another scholar's words:

(1) the weight of authoritative judgement, in which who said it is of critical importance;
(2) the nature of expression, in which how it was said is the important element.

In the former instance, when unexpected, unusual or genuinely pivotal points are to be presented, it is reasonable to show the reader that another competent craftsman has reached exactly the desired conclusion, or observed exactly the event at issue. In the latter instance, when another writer has hit upon the precise, perfect phrasing to express a difficult point, it is proper to employ their talent on behalf of your own argument. The rule to follow is simple. If the substance of a quotation can be conveyed by a careful paraphrase, followed of course by the appropriate citation, with all the clarity and persuasive impact of the original, *then don't quote*.

In almost all instances it is best for the proposer to speak directly to the reader. The intervention of words from a third party should be reserved for those rare instances when the targets are specific and truly critical to the outcome of the contest.

A technique that is beneficial to the student who recognises their propensity towards excessive quotation is to use the critical summary form of note taking. In this format, each article or book – after careful citation – is critically examined and then paraphrased on reference cards in the student's own words. During note-taking, a decision is made on whether the aesthetics of the author's phrasing or their importance in terms of authority justify the use of direct quotation. Except in rare instances, quoted material is not transferred to the note cards; thus, direct quoting becomes less tempting during the subsequent writing phase when the student has recourse to the notes.

Obviously the technique of making photocopies of stacks of articles and then writing with them directly at hand invites excessive quoting.

10.2.3 Clarity and precison – speaking in system language

The language we use in the commerce of our everyday lives is common language. We acquired our common language vocabulary and grammar by a process that was gradual, unsystematic and mostly unconscious. Our everyday language serves us well, at least as long as the inevitable differences in word meanings assigned by different people do not produce serious failures of communication.

The language of science, specifically the language of research, is uncommon. The ongoing conversation of science, for which a research proposal is a plan of entry, is carried on in system languages in which each word must mean one thing to both writer and reader. Where small differences may matter a great deal, as in research, there must be a minimum of slippage between the relevent object, the word used to stand for the object, and the images called forth by the word in the minds of listeners and readers.

The rules of invariate word usage give system languages a high order of precision. Minute or subtle distinctions can be made with relative ease. Evaluative language can be eliminated or clearly segregated from empirical discriptive language. More important, however, the language or research affords the reliability of commmunication that permits researchers to create a powerful interdependent research enterprise rather than limited independent investigations. When a chemist uses the system language of chemistry to communicate with another chemist, the word 'element' has one and only one referent, is assigned to the referent on all occasions, is used for no other purpose within the language system, and consistently evokes the same image in the minds of everyone everywhere who has mastered the language.

Various domains of knowledge and various research enterprises are characterized by differing levels of language development. Some disciplines, such as anatomy or entomology, have highly developed and completely regularized language systems, whereas others – and this is particularly so in the field of information systems – employ languages still in the process of development. Irrespective of the area of investigation, however, the language of any research proposal must, as a minimum requirement, be systematic within itself. The words used in the proposal must have referents that are clear to the reader and must be used consistently to designate only one referent. When the investigation lies within a subject area with an existing language system, then, of course, the author is bound to the conventions of that system.

Obviously student researchers should be familiar with the system languages that function in the area of proposed investigation. They must read and write both the specific language of the subject matter area and the more general languages common to the proposed methodology (statistics, experimental design, computer languages, etc.). Less obvious, however, is the fact that research proposals, by their exploratory nature, often demand the extension of existing language into new territory. Operations, observations, concepts and relationships not previously specified within a language system must be assigned invariate word symbols by the investigator. More important, the reader must carefully be drawn into the agreement to make these same assignments.

Advisers misunderstand student proposals far more often than they disagree with what is proposed. The failure of communication often occurs precisely at the point where the proposal moves beyond the use of the existing system language. This problem involves a failure of careful invention rather than a failure of mastering technique or subject matter. The following rules may be of some help as the student attempts to translate their personal vision of the unknown into the form of a carefully specified public record.

(1) Never invent new words when existing system language is adequate. If the referent has a label that, in established use, excludes what you do not want and includes all that you do want, then it needs no new name.

(2) If there is reasonable doubt as to whether the word is in the system or the common domain, give the system definition as that obtaining for the proposal. Those reading the proposal may give time and attention to the same question unless you put their mind at ease.

(3) Words that have been assigned system meaning should not be used in their common language form. For example, the word significant should not be used to denote its common language meaning of important in a proposal involving the use of statistical analysis. The system language of inferential statistics assigns invariant meaning to the word significant; any other use invites confusion.

(4) Where a system language word is to be used in either a more limited or a more expanded sense, make this clear when the word is first introduced in the proposal. If the norms for local style requirements permit, this is one of the legitimate uses of good notes to the text.

(5) Where it is necessary to assign invariant meaning to a common language word in order to communicate about something not already accommodated within the system language, the author should choose with great care. Words with strong evaluative overtones, words with a long history of ambiguity, and words that have well entrenched usage in common language, make poor candidates for elevation to system status. No matter how carefully the author operationalizes the new definition, it is always difficult for the reader to make new responses to familiar stimuli.

(6) A specific definition is the best way to assign invariant meaning to a

word. When only one or two words require such treatment, this can be accomplished in the test. Larger numbers may be set aside in a section of the proposal devoted to definitions. The best definition is one that describes the operations that are required to produce or observe the event or object.

This may be seen to be over-emphasising the point. However, communication *is* crucial in producing an acceptable proposal and in the field of information systems there is already too much evidence of terms meaning different things to different people, and different terms being used to mean the same thing!

10.2.4 Editing – the care and nurture of a document

A proposal is a working document. As a primary vehicle for communication with advisers, as a plan for action, and as a contract with the university, the student's proposal performs functions that are immediate and practical, not symbolic or aesthetic. Precisely because of these important functions, the proposal, in all its public appearances at least, should be free from distracting mechanical errors and the irritating confusion of shoddy format.

At the privacy of their own desks, students may use cross-outs and rough drafts as part of the intellectual process through which a proposal evolves toward final form. When, however, the proposal is given to an adviser or presented to a seminar, the occasion is public and calls for an edited, formally prepared document. Every sentence must be examined and re-examined in terms of its clarity, grammar and relationship with surrounding sentences. A mark of the neophyte writer is the tendency to resist changing a sentence once it is written. A sentence may be grammatically correct and still be awkward within its surroundings. If, in reading the sentence, a colleague, reviewer or friend stumbles, or has to reread it to understand its content, it needs to be rewritten.

Aside from meticulous care in writing and rewriting, the most helpful procedure in undertaking editorial revision is to obtain the assistance of colleagues in reading the proposal for mechnical errors, lack of clarity and inadequacies of content. An author can read the same error over and over without recognising it – and the probability of discovery declines with each review. The same error may leap at once to the attention of even the most casual external reader.

Although format will be a matter of individual taste or departmental regulation, several general rules may be used in designing the layout of the document.

(1) Use double spacing, substantial margins, and ample separation for major subsections. Crowding makes reading both difficult and unpleasant.
(2) Make ample use of graphic illustration. A chart or simple diagram can improve clarity and ease the difficult task of critical appraisal and advisement.
(3) Make careful and systematic use of headings. The system of headings recommended in the *Publication Manual of the American Psychological Association* (1974) is particularly useful for the design of proposals.
(4) Place in an appendix everything that is not immediately essential to the main tasks of the proposal. Allowing readers to decide whether they will read supplementary material is both courtesy and good strategy.

10.2.5 In search of a title – first impressions and the route to retrieval

The title of the proposal is the first contact readers have with the proposed research. First impressions, be they about people, music, food or potential thesis topics, generate powerful anticipatory concepts of what is to follow. Shocking the reader by implying one content domain in the title and following with a different one in the body of the proposal is certain to evoke a strong negative response. Thus, the first rule in composing a title is to achieve reasonable parity between the images evoked by the title and the opening pages of the proposal.

The proposal title is likely to become the thesis title and therefore calls for careful consideration of all the functions it must serve and the standard by which it will be judged. The first function of the title is to identify content for the purpose of retrieval. Theses and dissertations have become a part of the public domain of the scholar. The increasing incidence of microfilming has made the circulation of unpublished documents many times faster and far broader in geographic scope. Titling research has become, thereby, an important factor in sharing research.

In less sophisticated times, thesis titles could be carelessly constructed and the documents still discovered by diligent researchers who could take the time to investigate items that appeared no more than remotely related to their interests. Today, scholars stagger under the burden of sifting through enormous and constantly increasing quantities of material apparently pertinent to their domain. There is no recourse other than to be increasingly selective in documents actually retrieved and inspected.

Hence, each title the researcher scans must present at least a moderate probability of being pertinent – on the basis of the title alone – or it will not be included on the reading list for review. In short, the degree to which the title communicates a concise, thorough and unambiguous picture of the contents is the first factor governing whether a given report will enter the ongoing dialogue of the academic community.

The title should describe as accurately as possible the exact nature of the main elements in the study. Although such accuracy demands the use of specific language, the title should be free of obscure technical terms or jargon that will be recognized only by small groups of researchers who happen to pursue similar questions within a narrow band of the knowledge domain.

The mechanics of titling

Mechanically, the title should be concise and should provide comfortable reading, free from elaborate or jarring constructions. Excessive length should be avoided because it dilutes the impact of the key elements presented; two lines generally should be adequate. Some retrieval systems place a word limitation on titles, thus enforcing brevity. Redundancies such as Aspect of . . . , Comments on . . . , Study of . . . , Investigation of . . . , Inquiry into . . . and An analysis of . . . are expendable. It is obvious that a careful investigation of a topic will include aspects of the topic, whereas the research report has as its entire purpose the communication of comments on the findings of the study. It is pointless to state the obvious in a title.

Attempts to include all subtopics of a study in the title sometimes result in elephantine rubrics. The decision to include or exclude mention of a subtopic should be made less in terms of an abstraction, such as 'complete coverage', and more in terms of whether inclusion actually will facilitate appropriate retrieval.

One useful way to construct a title is to list all the elements that seem appropriate for inclusion, and then to weave them into various permutations until a title appears that satisfies both technical and aesthetic standards.

10.3 CONTENT OF THE PROPOSAL: IMPORTANT CONSIDERATIONS

10.3.1 Spadework – the proper use of pilot studies

The pilot study is an especially useful form of anticipation, and one too much neglected in student proposals. When it comes to convincing the sceptical reader (often your own adviser), no argument can be so effective as to write, 'I tried it and here is how it worked'.

It is difficult to imagine any proposal that could not be improved by the reporting of actual preliminary work. However used, the modest pilot study is the best possible basis for making wise decisions in designing research.

The use of even a small sample in an informal pilot can reveal a fatal flaw or misinterpretation before it can destroy months of work. The pilot may even provide an opportunity to improve the precision of the investigation or to streamline cumbersome methods. For all these reasons, students and advisers should not insist on holding stringent, formal standards for exploratory studies. A pilot study is a *pilot* study; its target is the practicality of the proposed research, not the creation of empirical truth.

The presentation of results from pilot studies sometimes does create a troublesome problem. The general rule is to make no more of the pilot study than it is honestly worth; most are no more than a report of experience under less than perfect conditions.

Brief reference to pilot work may be made in supporting the broad research strategies selected consequent to the review of research. Some pilot studies may, in fact, be treated as one of the works worthy of review. More commonly, however, the results of exploratory studies are used in supporting specific methods proposed in the section dealing with research design.

When the pilot study represents a formal and relatively complete research effort, it is proper to cite the work in some detail, including actual data. When the preliminary work has been informal or limited, it may be introduced as a footnote to the main text. In the latter case, it may be desirable to provide a more detailed account of the work in a section of the appendix, leaving readers the choice of pursuing the matter further if they wish.

10.3.2 Murphy's Law – anticipating the unexpected

Murphy's Law dictates that, in the conduct of research, if there is anything that can go wrong, it probably will. This is accepted by experienced researchers and research advisers but rarely considered by the novice.

Within reasonable limits, the proposal is the place to provide for confrontation with the inexorable operation of Murphy's Law. Subject attrition cannot be presented, but its effects can be circumscribed by careful planning. The potentially biasing effects created by non-returns in questionnaire studies can be examined and, to some degree, mitigated by plans laid carefully in the proposal. The handling of subjects in the event of equipment failure (such as in laboratory based experimentation) is far better considered at leisure, in writing the proposal, than in the face of an unanticipated emergency.

Equipment failure may interrupt carefully timed data collection sequence, or temporary computer breakdowns may delay data processing and analysis. At best these contingencies may place constraints on the time schedule of the study, and at worst may demand substitutions or substantive changes in procedure. Each step of the process should be studied with regard to potential difficulty, and plans in the event of a problem should be stated in the appropriate place within the proposal.

It is impossible to anticipate everything that can happen. A good proposal, however, provides contingency plans for the most important problems that may arise in the course of conducting the study.

10.3.3 Anticipating the analysis – do it now

The proposal is the proper place to reveal the exact nature of the analysis, as well as anticipated plans in the event of emergency. For many students, especially master's candidates, the analysis – if statistical – may represent new knowledge, recently acquired and not fully digested. In addition, the customary time limit of perhaps less than two years, by which master's candidates are themselves bound, adds to the difficulty.

Candidates may even be in the middle of their first formal course in techniques of data reduction and analysis, while they are constructing their proposal. Consequently, students find themselves in the awkward position of having to write lucidly about the nature of their analytic tools without yet knowing the entire armamentarium available. As untenable as this position is, and much as sympathy may be generated by students' advisers or friends, the omission of a full consideration of the analysis in the proposal may prove to be fatal. Countless unfortunates have found themselves in possession of shoe boxes heaped with unanalysable data, all because the analysis was supposed to take care of itself. A step-by-step anticipation of the analysis to be used is also a double check research design.

Descriptive, survey and normative studies require extensive data reduction to produce meaningful quantitive descriptions and summaries of the phenomena of interest. Techniques of determining sample characteristics may be different from those anticipated on the basis of pilot results; or the study sample may be skewed, resulting in the need to discuss techniques for normalizing the data.

The analysis segment of the proposal should be outlined to correspond to the objectives of the study, so that each analysis will yield evidence relating to a corresponding hypothesis or question. In addition, the reader should be able to determine how all data collected are to be analysed. If data are to be presented in tabular or graphic form, an example of one such table, including predicted figures, often will be helpful to the reader. The purpose of a table or figure in a research report is to summarize material and to supplement the text in making it clearly understandable. Tables and graphic presentation may serve the same purpose in a proposal.

Because of their display quality, the inclusion of tables in the proposal may expose errors of research design. For instance, some readers may not detect the use of an incorrect error term from a reading of the text, but one glance at the degrees of freedom column in an analysis of variance table may reveal the error. If several tables are listed and proposed, analysis of variance comparisons of non-independent variables may be exposed.

If the analysis activity of the project is studied carefully in advance, many headaches – as well as heartaches – may be avoided. It may seem to take an inordinate amount of time to plan the analysis, but it is time that will not have to be spent again. As the analyses are completed, the results can immediately be inserted in the prepared tables, and the researcher can complete his project with a feeling of fulfillment rather than a frantic scramble to make sense out of a puzzle for which some of the pieces may prove to be missing.

10.3.4 The statistical well – drinking the greatest draught

Students can usually expect help from their advisers with the design of statistical analysis. At minimum, an experienced adviser will have some suggestions about the type of analysis that would be most appropriate for the proposed investigation.

The student should not, however, operate under the faulty impression that when the data are collected, they can be turned over to a handy statistical expert who will magically return raw data in the finished form of findings and conclusions. Just as the student cannot expect the analysis of data to take care of itself, neither can the student expect a statistics consultant to take care of it.

The assistance of a statistician, invaluable though it may be, ordinarily is limited to the technology of design and data analysis. The conceptual demands of the study and the particular form and characteristics of the data generated are the investigator's province – to be explained to the consultant, not vice versa. Likewise, the interpretation of results is a logical, not a technical, operation and thus is a responsibility for which only the investigator is properly prepared. So make sure you read Chapter 11 thoroughly.

In undertaking empirical research, the student should be ready to provide answers to each of the following questions:

(1) What are the independent variables of the study?
(2) What are the dependent variables of the study?
(3) What are the organismic variables of the study?
(4) What is the measurement scale of each variable (nominal, ordinal, interval or ratio)?
(5) What are the reliability and validity of the instruments used to produce the score for each variable?
(6) What are the population distribution characteristics for each of the variables?
(7) What difference value between dependent variables would be of *practical* significance?

In summary, before consulting with a technical specialist research students must be able to express what they want the study to be designed to accomplish, identify the help they need in producing such a design, and provide all the explicit details the consultant will need in formulating advice.

10.3.5 The scientific state of mind – proof, truth, and rationalized choices

Scientific inquiry is not so much a matter of elaborate technology or even rigorous method, as a particular state of mind. The processes of research rest, in the end, on how researchers regard the world and their work. Although some aspects of scientific thinking are subtle and elusive, others are not. The latter, the basic attitudinal prerequisites for the conduct of scientific inquiry, are reflected in the way a novice speaks and writes about their proposed research. More directly their proposal will reflect the degree to which they have internalized critical attitudes towards such matters as proof, truth, and publicly rationalized choices.

What matters is not the observance of particular conventions concerning phrasing, but fundamental ways of thinking that are reflected in the selected words. When, for example, a student writes, 'The purpose of this study is to prove (or to demonstrate) that . . .', there is always the dangerous possiblity that they mean to do just that – to prove what they have decided must be true!

Such phrasing cannot be dismissed simply as awkward or naive. A student capable of writing such a sentence without hearing at once its dangerous implications is a student with a fundamental defect in their preparation. They should be allowed to go no further until they have understood both the nature of proof and the purpose of research, for clearly they understand neither.

Proof, if it exists at all in any useful sense, is a probabilistic judgement based on an accumulation of observations. Ordinarily, only a series of careful replications can lead to the level of confidence implied by the word proved. Research is not an attempt to prove or demonstrate, it is an attempt to ask a careful question and to allow the nature of things to dictate the answer. The difference between 'attempting to prove' and 'seeking proof' is subtle but critical, and a scientist must never confuse the two. Proof is even more problematic in the social scientific world of information systems.

If scientists have no illusions about proof, it is wrong nonetheless to believe that they never care about the direction of results obtained from their research. As humans, they are often painfully aware of the distinction between results that will be fortunate or unfortunate for their developing line of thought. As scientists, however, they recognise the irrelevance (and even the danger) of allowing personal feelings to intrude into the business of seeking knowledge. In the end, researchers must sit down before the data like children and allow themselves to be instructed. Their task lies in arranging the context for instruction, so that the answers to questions will be clear but the content of the lesson lies in the nature of the world.

A second critical sign of students' abilities to adopt this viewpoint is the general way the matter of truth is treated in proposals. When students write, 'The purpose of the study to is discover the actual cause of . . .', there is a danger that they think it possible to do just that – to discern the ultimate fact of reality at a single glance. The most fundamental remediation will be required if they are ever to understand, much less conduct, scientific inquiry.

Experienced researchers seek and revere veridical knowledge; they may even choose to think of research as a search for truth, but they understand the elusive, fragile and probabilistic nature of scientific truth. Knowledge is regarded as a tentative decision about the world, always held contingent upon the content of the future.

The business of researchers is striving to understand. Correspondingly, they place a high value on hard-won knowledge. They hold truths gently, however, and speak and write accordingly. It is not necessary to lard a proposal with reservations, provisos, and disclaimers such as 'it seems'. It *is* necessary to write with respect for the complexity of things and with modesty for what can be accomplished. The researcher's highest expectation for any study is a small but perceptible shift in the scale of evidence. We deal not in the heady stuff of truth, 'establishing actual causes', but in hard-won increments of probability.

A third sign by which to estimate a students' readiness for research is their ability (and willingness) to examine alternative interpretations of evidence; plausible rival hypotheses; facts that bid to discomfort their theoretical framework; and considerations that reveal the limitations of their methodology. It is important not only to lay out the alternatives for the reader but to explain the grounds for choice among them. The student who neither acknowledges alternatives nor rationalizes their choices simply does not understand research well enough to bother with a proposal.

The mature researcher feels no compulsion to provide perfect interpretations or to make unassailably correct choices. They do the best they can within the limits of existing knowledge and their present situation. They do feel compelled, however, to make clearly rationalized choices from among carefully defined alternatives; this is one reason readers outside the research community find research reports tedious in their attention to detail and explanation. It is the public quality of the researcher's reasoning that makes a community of scientific enterprise possible, not the construction of a facade of uniform certainty and perfection.

Student-conducted research often contains choices that must be rationalized less by the shape of existing knowledge and the dictates of logic, and more by the homely facts of logistics – time, costs, skills achieved and available facilities. The habit of public clarity in describing and rationalizing choices must begin there – with the way things are. An honest accounting of hard and often imperfect choices is a firm step for the student towards achieving the habits of a good researcher. Hopefully, this chapter will have helped a little in this regard.

Chapter 11

The Use and Misuse of Statistical Methods in Information Systems Research

GRAHAM P. PERVAN

AND

DESMOND J. KLASS

School of Information Systems, Curtin University of Technology

Though the field of information systems research requires a diversity of research approaches, the authors argue that all information systems researchers need a reasonable level of statistical knowledge. They discuss the need to understand the different data types and measurement scales and to assess the appropriateness of these scales in IS research. Several uni-variate, non-parametric and multi-variate methods are described and readers are alerted to the potential pitfalls in interpreting the results of tests of significance. The paper ends with a framework for choosing the most appropriate statistical test given the various circumstances in an IS study.

11.1 INTRODUCTION

It has long been argued that the field of information systems requires a diversity of research approaches in tackling the variety of problems that are worthy of study. Since IS is a field which spans a range of disciplines, from social sciences to business and management to the natural sciences, it is likely that different research approaches will be found suitable for different problems.

Past research in information systems *has* used a variety of approaches. A comprehensive list divided into scientific and interpretivist is given in Table 11.1. Many of these research approaches, particularly those in the scientific category, are empirically based and require knowledge of statistical methods. At the more sophisticated level of statistical knowledge, laboratory and field experiments require a sound capability in experimental design and, by controlling variables in

Table 11.1 IS research approaches (Galliers 1991)

Scientific	Interpretivist
Laboratory experiments	Subjective/argumentative
Field experiments	Reviews
Survey	Action research
Case studies	Descriptive/interpretive
Theorem proof	
Forecasting	Futures research
Simulation	Role/game playing

the problem under study, are amenable to collection of observed numerical data which can be analysed statistically.

By taking snapshots of a particular situation, usually through a questionnaire, surveys provide a rich base of numerical data responsive to statistical analysis. Frequently, these surveys act as a stand-alone research approach testing particular hypotheses via the information in the questionnaire. However, the survey approach is more often used in association with other research approaches. In conducting action research, descriptive and interpretive research, case studies, games and role playing, and simulation, surveys are often also used to complete the necessary collection of data relevant to the factor(s) being studied. The statistical skills required in undertaking a survey may vary, but even a fairly simplistic questionnaire needs some basic statistical knowledge relating both to design of the instrument and analysis of the data.

In this chapter we begin by discussing the reasons for *any* IS researcher to require statistical knowledge (Section 11.2). Section 11.3 covers the types of statistical data which may be used, and how it may be measured and validated. Section 11.4 summarizes the range of applicable statistical methods, with particular emphasis on multivariate approaches. Section 11.5 then discusses some of the major pitfalls in the application of these approaches. In Section 11.6 advice is given on how to select the appropriate statistical methods. A few references are suggested in Section 11.7 including a brief synopsis of each publication.

11.2 THE NEED FOR STATISTICAL KNOWLEDGE

As discussed above, many research projects in the information systems field will adopt a research approach which is empirically-based and will require the use of statistical methods. For such projects, therefore, it is imperative that the researcher has a reasonable skill in statistics in order to be able to carry out effectively the actual research.

Examination of past research indicates, however, that many research projects do *not* involve the collection of any quantitative data and so have no need for statistical analysis. As the question was posed by a student in a recent research methods for IS class: 'My project won't involve collecting any numerical data so why do I have to bother learning this statistics stuff?'.

An important point which the above student had overlooked (and which was forcibly made in response to the question), is that without some statistical knowledge he would not be in a position to make the judgement that no numerical data should be collected for his research problem. How can he argue against the use of any empirical approaches if he has no knowledge of those approaches? Furthermore, how can researchers (such as the above student) argue *for* the use of another (non-empirical) approach to their research if they do not have a sound understanding of all the alternative approaches available to them? One has to understand why an approach will not work for a given problem, to be able to correctly reject its application.

The converse of the need to understand statistical methods in order to reject a particular research approach that employs them is, of course, that one clearly needs this understanding in order to be able to make the decision to employ them. This understanding is needed to develop a sound argument in support of a statistically-based approach and to reject the alternatives.

The other, and perhaps even more important, reason for at least an adequate knowledge of statistical research methods relates to the need to interpret statistics from previous research when reviewing the literature on the topic of the research. Researchers require this knowledge because they:

- need to judge the quality of the work;
- need to assess the content in order to help develop their own hypotheses;
- need to pass critical judgement and determine whether statistical methods have been correctly used;
- may find statements they agree with but which are not statistically supported by the research;
- want to ensure all supporting arguments for their own research are based on valid work;

- need to determine whether the particular method(s) used were appropriate to the data and the hypotheses;
- need to determine whether internal reliability of the samples was adequately verified;
- need to determine that the samples used were representative;
- need to understand the difference between purely statistical significance (which may almost always occur with large samples) and relevance. This point is often overlooked when using correlation measures such as R^2 which, while significant, may be meaningless for large sample sizes.

It is clear, therefore, that a reasonable understanding of statistical methods can assist in almost all stages of a research project. When studying the background literature it can assist in critically analysing previous research. It can help in choosing a particular research approach and for developing arguments in support of that approach. Conversely, it can help to support the arguments for the rejection of other research approaches not appropriate to the proposed research project. Statistical knowledge can help develop and refine hypotheses (where appropriate) and, finally, is of great utility in carrying out the research and analysing the results obtained.

11.3 TYPES OF DATA

The purpose of measurement is to translate the properties of empirical events into a form that can be analysed by the researcher. Measurement is concerned with the assignment of numbers to empirical events, defined as a set of observable characteristics of an object, individual or group, according to a set of rules. The goal is to assign numerals so that the properties of the numbers are paralleled by the properties of the events we are attempting to measure.

The device which is used for the assignment of numbers to aspects of objects and events is commonly referred to as a measurement scale and these scales can range from simple to complex. Simple scales are one item devices which are used to measure some characteristics. An example of a simple scale of a dichotomous nature is 1 for male and 2 for female. Complex scales are multi-item devices which are used to measure some characteristic. An example of a complex scale used to measure health consciousness of an individual is to ask a series of attitude questions on, say, a seven point scale.

While the complexity and variety of measurement devices vary tremendously, all scales possess the properties of at least one of four major levels of measurement:

(1) nominal;
(2) ordinal;
(3) interval;
(4) ratio.

11.3.1 Nominal measurement

In information systems research, nominal scales are used at least as widely as any others. When we use a nominal scale, we partition a set into subsets or categories that are mutually exclusive and collectively exhaustive. If numbers are used for classification, e.g. if male is classified as 1 and female classified as 2, the numerals are recognized as labels only and have no quantitative value. Nominal scales are the least powerful of the four types. They indicate no order or distance relationship and have no origin.

11.3.2 Ordinal measurement

This measurement includes the uniqueness characteristics of the nominal scale plus an indicator of order. The use of an ordinal scale implies a statement of 'greater than' or 'less than' without our being able to state how much greater or less. Examples of regularly used ordinal scales include opinion and preference scales, and because the numbers of this scale have only rank meanings the appropriate measure of central tendency is the median. Measures of statistical significance are technically restricted to that body of methods known as non-parametric methods.

It should be noted that ordinal measures have been used in three major ways in information systems research with varying degrees of acceptance/correctness. They include:

(1) *The ranking of items* This use is the least controversial of the three because it represents the use for which the scale was originally intended.
(2) *The rating of a characteristic* This use is the most controversial because it interprets ordinal measure with interval characteristics as well. Here the researcher assigns numbers to reflect the relative

ratings of a series of statements, then uses these numbers to interpret relative differences.

(3) *The creation of other complex scales and indices* Though this use has been widely criticised it is still widely used in information systems research. These scales usually involve the use of several items that are rated by respondents then manipulated (e.g. summed) to arrive at the measure of some complex phenomenon.

11.3.3 Interval measurement

The interval scale has the powers of nominal and ordinal scales plus the additional strength in that it incorporates the concept of equality of interval. The classic illustration is that of temperature gauges. The arbitrary nature of the origin, zero, restricts our use of ratio concepts with interval scales. For example, we cannot say that 60°C is twice as warm as 30°C. More powerful statistical tools can be used with interval scales. The arithmetic mean is the appropriate measure of central tendency, while the standard deviation is the most widely used measure of dispersion.

11.3.4 Ratio measurement

These scales incorporate all the powers of the previous ones, plus the concept of absolute zero origin. The ratio scale represents the absolute amounts of a variable. Examples of ratio measurement include sales, costs, inventory and number of customers. All statistical descriptive measures and inferential techniques are applicable.

11.3.5 Which measurement scale is appropriate?

It should be noted that the decision on which measurement scale to use is not necessarily determined by the data itself. In collecting a given piece of data, the researcher may sometimes be in a position to choose the scale he or she prefers. For example, suppose a researcher wishes to make some assessment of the usage of a particular software product by end users. The question could be phrased, 'Do you use this product (Yes or No)?', and the data collected would be nominal. Alternatively it could be, 'Is your usage of this product low, medium or high?' and the data collected would be ordinal. Finally, the question could be, 'How many hours per week do you use this product?' and the data collected would be ratio.

It has been shown that the significance tests available for interval and ratio data are more powerful than those for ordinal and nominal data. However, this does not mean we should always collect interval and ratio data where we have the choice. Of critical importance is the accuracy of the data collected. It is all very well to collect data (interval/ratio) which is more amenable to sophisticated statistical tests, but if its collection is by guesswork and not actual known values then the results may be less useful.

For instance, in the example above on the usage of a software product, an end user can accurately say Yes or No to the first question and can also be fairly accurate in indicating the level of usage (low/medium/high), though there may be dangers in the latter case as low, medium and high may mean different things to different people. On the other hand, if users are asked to state exactly how many hours they use the product each week, the likelihood is they will make a guess and it may often be a poor one. In summary, the researcher needs to balance the power of the measurement scale with the accuracy which is likely to be achieved in the data collection. It requires a 'judgement call' by the researcher, but it must be done.

11.3.6 Evaluation of measurement scales

Once the variables of interest have been identified and defined conceptually, a specific type of scale must be selected. To a large extent, selection depends on the underlying properties of the concept to be studied and the researcher's anticipated use of the variable in the data analysis stage of the research process. In other words, in order to select the proper type of scale, the researcher must choose a device that accurately and consistently measures and achieves the research objectives of the study. This process requires the evaluation of the adequacy of the measurement device.

Two issues need to be addressed when evaluating scales. The first deals with the issues of validity and reliability in measurement, and the second deals with the types of statistical analysis that can be used to analyse the data.

Validity

A measurement scale is valid if it does what it is supposed to do and measures what it is supposed to measure. Validity is concerned with one type of error commonly referred to as 'within error'. There are different kinds of validity, but there are three that need special mention:

(1) *content validity*, which is the degree to which the scale item represents the domain or universe of the concept under study;
(2) *construct validity*, which represents the degree to which the measurement scale represents and acts like the concept being measured;
(3) *criterion validity*, which is the degree to which the scale under study is able to predict a variable which is designated a criterion.

Reliability

Reliability refers to the consistency and stability of a score from a measurement scale. Where validity is concerned with consistency, reliability is concerned with accuracy. We cannot possess validity unless we demonstrate reliability.

While there are numerous techniques available to the researcher for assessing the reliability of a measurement scale, they can be summarized under the broad methods of test-retest, internal consistency and the alternative forms method. The three approaches to estimating reliability all attempt to determine how much systematic, or true, variance exists in various tests of the measurement scale.

The usual means of estimating the amount of systematic variance in a measure takes the form of a correlation exercise where the scores from your measurement scale are correlated with the scores from some variation or replication of that scale. The only real difference in the three approaches to estimating reliability is to what you are going to correlate the scores of your test. The coefficient of reliability can range from 0 to 1 and the closer to 1 the score is, the greater the reliability.

Good measurement cannot guarantee valuable results but it is an essential and necessary condition in ensuring that one obtains valuable information. The measurement scale one uses also sets limits on how the data can be analysed. Each of the techniques described below requires a measurement scale of a specific type and form.

11.4 STATISTICAL TECHNIQUES IN INFORMATION SYSTEMS RESEARCH

Statistical techniques used in information systems research can be classified into three categories: non-parametric, uni-variate and multi-variate. This section will look briefly at the first two categories and then give a brief synopsis of some of the more common multi-variate techniques.

11.4.1 Non-parametric methods

Researchers in information systems are often faced with the task of deciding testing procedures to use when the measurement attained on the data is only qualitative or in ranks. The researcher is more interested in such features as randomness, independence, symmetry or goodness-of-fit rather than the testing of hypotheses about particular population parameters. The techniques used in these circumstances are called non-parametric methods for hypothesis testing. Some of the more common tests are discussed below.

The popular Chi-squared test is used when data is arranged in a table (referred to as a contingency table) to determine whether or not two classifications of a population of nominal data (and/or ordinal data) are statistically independent. An example might be a situation where the researcher is interested in determining if there is a relationship between organizational type and the use or non-use of IT. In both instances the measurement type is nominal. When using the more complicated multi-variate models in research, there are certain assumptions that have to be met with respect to the distribution of the independent variables used in the model.

The Chi-squared is also a useful goodness-of-fit test used to determine whether it is reasonable to assume that a sample has been drawn from a hypothesized population. The Wilcoxon rank sum test is another useful test for comparing two populations where the data scale is ordinal and samples are independent. For example, in IS research we might be interested in testing to see if productivity within a job is a function of different technology configurations used. The Wald-Wolfowitz test for randomness and the Spearman rank correlation procedure are other useful techniques within this class of tests.

11.4.2 Uni-variate methods

As the name implies, uni-variate statistical methods refer to a range of descriptive and inferential techniques that have been developed to handle situations where analysis on a single variable is required. It is concerned with extracting useful information from a set of data that may be used in a descriptive sense, where the main interest is only in summarizing the data in order to present it in a more convenient or more easily interpreted form. Alternatively, it may be used in an inferential sense where the main aim is to use data from a sample to make estimates (or inferences) about the characteristics of a population.

For example, the average number of hours per week spent using a particular software package for a sample of 22 engineers was computed to be 17 hours. Using this sample result, an estimate of the average usage per week for the population of all the engineers in the firm would be made. This estimate would take into account the inherent uncertainties associated with sampling, and appropriate levels of statistical confidence (significance) would be attached to these estimates. The Z-test, t-test and estimator of the population mean, and the Chi-squared test and estimator of the population variance are some of the more common tests and estimations used in uni-variate analysis.

11.4.3 Multi-variate techniques

Multi-variate statistics refers to a range of descriptive and inferential techniques that have been developed to handle situations where sets of variables are involved, either as predictors or as measures of performance. If the researcher is interested in the association between two sets of variables, then the appropriate class of techniques would be those commonly referred to as dependence methods. Examples of these techniques include regression analysis and discriminate analysis.

If, on the other hand, the research is concerned with mutual association across all variables, with no distinction made among variable types, then the appropriate class is referred to as independence methods. Examples of these techniques include factor analysis and cluster analysis.

Multiple regression

This is one of the most commonly known and used dependence multi-variate methods. Multiple regression is a method of analysing the change in one variable (the dependent variable) by using a set of other known variables (the independent variables), in order to predict or estimate the mean value of the dependent variable on the basis of the known values of the other independent variables.

Regression techniques are useful in prediction or estimation studies. Predictive studies involve the use of current variables to identify a variable of interest at a future time. Estimation, on the other hand, involves the identification and estimation of a current variable from other current variables.

Discriminate analysis

Discriminate analysis is a dependence method multi-variate technique for which the usual end purpose is to provide a procedure for classifying individual observations into one of a set of groups or populations. The discriminate procedure involves starting with a set of observations with known group membership. The initial set of data is used to fit a relationship which can subsequently be used to classify other observations with unknown group membership. Thus, investigators must begin the procedure knowing which groups are relevant for their analysis. They must also begin with samples of observations from each of the relevant groups.

For each observation, investigators must have information on group membership and also on the values of one or more discriminator variables which can be used to establish a classification rule. The discriminate procedure fits such a rule. For subsequent observations, the investigator must know values of the discriminator variables only. They then use the results of the discriminate analysis to determine the probabilities of the group membership for those new observations.

Factor analysis

Factor analysis is a technique for analysing the internal structure of a set of variables. The basic idea is that the members of a set of variables, each of which has been measured or observed for a number of observations, have some, though not all, of their structure determined by certain underlying, unobservable common constructs or factors.

Cluster analysis

Cluster analysis involves the grouping of entities that are similar to one another. The entities may be observations. For example, we might collect information on the information usage habits of individuals, with one observation for each individual. We might then group or cluster the individuals into groups whose usage patterns are similar. In other cases the entities on which we perform cluster analysis may be variables rather than observations.

For example, in the early stages of our research project we might have a large number of questions that we are considering asking of a large sample of respondents. To reduce the number of questions needed we could administer a long questionnaire, with all of the questions, to a smaller sample of people. We could then cluster the questions or variables to find which ones are really redundant, in that their answers are very highly correlated with the answers to other questions from the list.

Several decisions must be made by users of cluster analysis. Users must decide how the similarity or dissimilarity between entities is to be measured. They must also select one of many possible procedures for selecting clusters of entities. In fact, cluster analysis might best be thought of as a collection of techniques for grouping entities. One of the challenges for the investigator is to select the specific technique to be used in a particular problem.

11.5 PITFALLS OR MISUSE OF SIGNIFICANCE TESTS

In the use of the techniques described above it is not uncommon to see researchers analysing their results using tests of significance (hypothesis testing). Many writers have attempted to explain and elaborate on what significance testing is, but relatively few users of multi-variate statistical techniques in their interpretation of statistical significance testing really understand what it is, or how to discriminate between what it is and what it is erroneously interpreted to be. Because of this lack of understanding, researchers in using the various statistical techniques for data analysis place too much emphasis on these tests of significance, to the neglect of getting a better feel for the data and its decision-making implications. We argue that it is important to understand clearly not only what a significance test does, but also to appreciate what it does not do.

To provide focus, an example of the t-test for a regression coefficient (b) will be used. The same general logic applies to other tests of statistical significance, such as the F-test and the Durbin-Watson (D-W) test.

Suppose the coefficient (b) for a regression equation was calculated based on a sample of size n. The hypothetical research question that would normally be addressed would be:

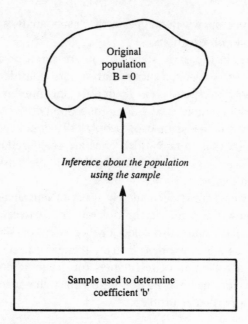

Fig. 11.1 The null hypothesis.

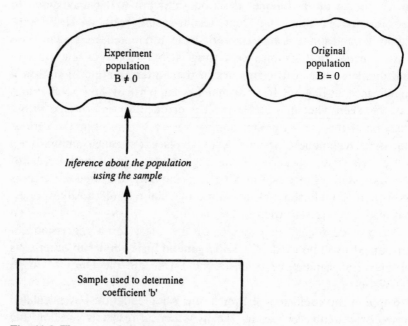

Fig. 11.2 The research hypothesis.

Is this independent variable (x) in the model contributing towards the dependent variable (y)?

If the independent variable is *not* contributing towards the dependent variable (the equivalent to that is saying B equals 0) then Fig. 11.1 can represent the situation. If the independent variable on the other hand *is* contributing towards the dependent variable (i.e. B does not equal 0), then Fig. 11.2 depicts the solution best.

From the above we can generalize and say that Fig. 11.2 can represent the research hypothesis or alternate hypothesis (H_1).

In research using regression we do not know if the sample represents a population with B = 0, but the null hypothesis says that we will assume that they do. The H_0 states that the non-zero value we get in our sample is due to sampling fluctuations (sampling error).

Statistical significance tests set up a dummy, the null hypothesis, and try to knock it down. Researchers usually want to reject H_0 and try to seek support for the research hypothesis H_1 (i.e. that the independent variable, through its coefficient, contributes to the value of the dependent variable).

When the H_0 is used in regression, the calculation for the t-test provides a p value (such as p = 0.04). It is a number which tells us the proportion of the time that we can expect to find coefficients as large as, or larger than, the particular value we get when we are sampling from a population assumed under the null hypothesis.

Correctly interpreted, statistical significance testing provides a p value, or the probability of obtaining coefficients of given sizes under the null hypothesis. Thus the p value may be used to make a decision about accepting or rejecting the idea that chance caused the results. This is what statistical significance testing is – nothing more, nothing less.

It is unfortunate that users of statistical tests tend to read more into the test, and this misuse can be grouped, as suggested by Carver (1978), into three major types.

First, researchers interpret the value of p as the probability that the research results were due to chance or caused by chance. As was pointed out earlier, the p value is the probability of getting the research results when it is first assumed that it is actually true that chance caused the results. Therefore it is impossible for the p value to be the probability that chance caused the value to be non-zero. Researchers still read the p value as the probability that the null hypothesis is true given the evidence, that is $P(H_0/E)$, when p is really the probability that this evidence would arise if the null hypothesis were true, which is represented by $P(E/H_0)$.

Second, researchers interpret statistical significance as the probability of obtaining the same results whenever a given experiment is replicated using a different sample. What this interpretation says is that the complement of p, i.e. $(1 - p)$, yields the probability that the results are replicable (R) or reliable. Hence they would say that $P(R/E) = 0.95$, which is incorrect. The problem with this is that too often researchers with statistically significant results will say that the value obtained was a 'reliable value' or the 'results were reliable'. Again we do not have $P(R/E)$; what we have is $P(E/H_0)$.

Finally, they believe that statistical significance directly reflects the probability that the research hypothesis is true. That is, the value of, say, 0.05 is interpreted to mean that its complement 0.95 is the probability that the research hypothesis is true. Since H_1 is commonly used as the symbol for the research hypothesis, what this interpretation says is:

$$P(H_1/E) = 1 - P(E/H_0).$$

The danger with this is that the size of the p value reflects the degree of validity of the research hypothesis and the lower the p value (i.e. say $p = 0.001$), the more highly significant or valid the research hypothesis. We stress that the p value has nothing directly to do with the inferences about the research hypothesis. All we get from the statistical significance test is $P(E/H_0)$.

The approach to information systems research using statistical methods should be much broader. It should be viewed as a set of data analytic techniques that are used to help understand the interrelationships among a given set of variables, and this understanding should be used as a basis for determining relationships. The emphasis should not be on formal statistical tests and probability computations. We feel that more information is obtained from an informal examination of the summary statistics and data plots from the different techniques used, rather than from an over-reliance on formal tests of statistical significance or some limited null hypothesis.

Many writers have argued against the use of statistical tests on the basis that statistical significance depends on sample size, and that trivial results are often interpreted as significant or important when they are simply results that would rarely happen when randomly sampling from the same population using large sample size.

The greater danger, we feel, is when non-significant results are conventionally interpreted as providing no support for the research hypothesis (H_1), even when the actual results support it. When small samples are used, as in many of our studies on information systems, large values can more often occur by chance and therefore lead to the rejection of the research hypothesis.

For example, if we only had a small sample we might get a relatively large value for the coefficient in, say, a regression model – large enough to have an important impact on the regression model and provide support for the initial belief that there was a contribution from that variable even though it might not be significant at the 0.05 level. The least we can do at this stage is to treat it as important enough to justify replication of the study with a large sample to see if the large coefficient could be found again.

We argue that information systems research should be guided by the principles and concepts of exploratory data analysis rather than being biased towards, or only reliant on, statistical significance tests.

Another common pitfall when developing multi-variate statistical models is in not ensuring that the conditions required and assumptions made about the variables used in the model are satisfied. For instance, when developing a discriminate model the assumption that has to be preserved is that the independent variables (or discriminators) have to be normally distributed and have equal variance. Most novice users fail to check for this requirement and hence the validity of the results and the usefulness of the model are compromised.

There are other pitfalls associated with statistical methods, but the above represent key dangers which are frequently ignored. The lesson to be learned is that researchers should make sure they understand the statistical methods they use and correctly interpret their output.

11.6 CHOOSING THE APPROPRIATE TEST

The decision concerning the appropriate test to use in a given set of circumstances depends on a number of factors, including the type of measurement scale, the number of variables involved, the size of the sample and the type of relationship between variables.

The following tables summarize some frequently used tests applied to uni-variate data and bi-variate data. Table 11.2 shows some examples of the case of uni-variate data of either nominal, ordinal or interval/

Table 11.2 Common uni-variate tests.

Type of data	Example null hypothesis	Test statistic	Name of test
Nominal	Observed frequency distribution fits some expected distribution	χ^2	Chi-square goodness-of-fit test
Ordinal	Same as for nominal	Kolmogorov-Smirnov D	Kolmogorov-Smirnov test
Interval or ratio	Mean $<=$ given value	t	t-test*
	Proportion $>=$ given value	z	Normal test
	$Mean_1 - Mean_2 = 0$ ($_{1,2}$ represent two populations)	t	t-test*
	$Prop'n_1 - Prop'n_2 = 0$	z	Normal test

* Normal test can be used when samples are large (over 30).

Table 11.3 Common bi-variate techniques.

Dependent variable	Independent variable	
	Nominal scale	Interval scale
Nominal scale	Contingency table	Discriminate analysis
Interval scale	Analysis of variance	Regression and correlation

ratio scale and cites the tests which are commonly used in those situations.

In the case of bi-variate data, one must consider the dependence relationship between the variables and the type of scale for each variable. Table 11.2 summarizes the techniques applicable to these alternative situations.

These two tables summarize a few of the alternatives available to the researcher in the case of uni-variate and bi-variate data. In Section

11.4 some information was also provided on the methods useful for multi-variate data.

Making the decision on which test(s) to apply in which circumstances, however, requires consideration of many hundreds of alternatives. The most sensible way to organize these is in a (very large) decision tree. Here we will explain the key questions to ask in the decision tree, but the reader who desires a 'complete' tree might consult *A Guide for Selecting Statistical Techniques for Analysing Social Science Data* produced by the Institute for Social Research, University of Michigan (see Section 11.7).

The starting question relates to the number of variables (Fig. 11.3).

How many variables does the problem involve?

One	Two	More than two
(Go to Fig. 11.4)	(Go to Fig. 11.6)	

Fig. 11.3 Number of variables.

The next major question the researcher should consider relates to the type of measurement scale used for the data. For example, in the case of *one* variable the tree continues as in Fig. 11.4.

Which measurement scale is being used for the variable?

Nominal	Ordinal	Interval or ratio
	(Go to Fig. 11.5)	

Fig. 11.4 Measurement scale – one variable.

In each case, the researcher must then ask about the distribution of the variable (Fig. 11.5).

What do we want to know about the distribution of the variable?

Central tendency	Dispersion	Frequencies
Median	Inter-quartile deviation	Relative or absolute frequencies

Fig. 11.5 Distribution – one variable (ordinal data).

The answers given in the boxes in Fig. 11.5 are for the case of ordinal data and provide a recommendation of the appropriate statistic to be used with that data. The researcher can then go ahead and apply those statistics for these data.

The decision making for the case of two variables (Fig. 11.3) is no more difficult than for the one variable case, but there are more permutations and so more branches in the decision tree. The measurement scale question would be as in Fig. 11.6.

Which measurement scale is being used for each variable?

Both	Both	Both	Interval	Interval	Ordinal
Interval	Ordinal	Nominal	Ordinal	Nominal	Nominal

Fig. 11.6 Measurement scale – two variables.

Where there are two or more variables the key question to be identified by the researcher relates to the dependence relationship(s) between the variables. These vary with the types of data and are very dependent on knowledge of co-variance and correlation.

From the few branches of the tree described in this section there are two points which should now be clear:

(1) There are many possible branches and numerous alternative statistics applicable to different problem situations. A certain amount of statistical skill must be needed to understand the implications of these alternatives.
(2) The decision making required to navigate the decision tree is not complicated. Any reasonable IS researcher should be able to answer questions relating to the number of variables, the type of data, the size of sample, which variable(s) depend on which others, what distributions, and so on.

In summary, this section has described some of the decision making necessary for IS researchers to be able to choose sensibly from the alternative methods and statistics available to them. A complete picture of this process has not been presented (because its size requires the space of a small book), but this is available in references such as the guide referred to in Section 11.6. Details are provided in Section 11.7.

11.7 FURTHER READING

There are many books that cover the various techniques and statistical methods discussed in this chapter. This section will give a brief synopsis of some useful references.

11.7.1 Non-parametric methods

Most introductory statistics texts contain a chapter on non-parametric tests. The two references under the section uni-variate methods (below) have such introductory sections. For a more comprehensive coverage, the reader should refer to Siegel S. (1956) *Non Parametric Statistics for the Behavioural Sciences*, McGraw Hill, New York. A wide range of tests are covered in this book and most are explained via worked examples that allow the user to follow through the logic and calculations easily. For a more recent text, reference should be made to Conover W.J. (1980) *Practical non-parametric statistics* 2nd edn, Wiley, New York.

11.7.2 Uni-variate methods

Harrison S.R. and Tamaschke H.U. (1984) *Applied Statistical Analysis*, Prentice-Hall, Australia.

This book covers a wide range of applied statistical methods commonly employed in business and economics and is useful to practitioners as well as researchers in IS. It provides a balance between the theoretical background and the 'how to' by way of examples. It covers all the regular uni-variate tests and has a chapter on a few basic non-parametric statistical methods.

Keller G., Warrack B. & Bartel H. (1990) *Statistics for Management and Economics – A Systemic Approach*, Wadsworth Publishing Company, California.

This book attempts to expose statistical methods by providing many meaningful practical examples and working through these examples systematically. It focusses on the interpretation of the results of these cases rather than emphasising the number-crunching aspect of statistics. It covers most of the uni-variate statistics and provides most of the worked examples in both Minitab and SAS (two popular statistical packages) output.

11.7.3 Multivariate techniques

Dillon W.R. & Goldstein M. (1984) *Multivariate Analysis – Methods and Applications*, John Wiley and Sons, New York.

These authors attempt to reach an audience that consists of users who want a sound understanding of the methods being employed without the burden of having to deal with mathematical concepts for which they are not prepared. Though the authors attempt to use verbal explanations in place of more direct mathematical arguments, readers with weak statistical/mathematical background might find this book a little heavy going. Most of the more common multivariate techniques are covered.

Brown F.E. (1980) *Marketing Research – structure for decision making*, Addison-Wesley, Reading, Mass.

Though this is a marketing research text it has a good section on multi-variate dependency techniques and is structured in a way that helps the reader to understand the similarities and differences particularly with respect to the scaling of variables.

11.7.4 Experimental design

Kirk R.E. (1968) *Experimental Design: Procedures for the Behavioural Sciences*. Wadsworth, California.

This book is intended for the behavioural researcher with a moderate statistics background and covers all the major experimental designs in a readable style.

11.7.5 General

Andrews F.M., Klein L., Davidson T.N., O'Malley P.M. & Rodgers W.L. (1981) *A Guide for Selecting Statistical Techniques for Analysing Social Science Data*, 2nd edn, University of Michigan, Ann Arbor.

This publication guides the researcher in the selection of the statistics or statistical methods appropriate to a particular analysis. It uses a decision tree, a simplified partial version of which is explained in Section 11.6 of this chapter. In addition to advice on appropriate statistics it also provides information on further references to the specific choice and the commands associated with this choice in the more common statistical software packages such as SPSS, SAS and others.

Chapter 12

An Individual and Group Strategy for Research in Information Systems

GORDON B. DAVIS

Carlson School of Management, University of Minnesota

(Shaw Professor, Information Systems and Computer Science
National University of Singapore
1986–87)

I am frequently asked by new academics what they should do to get promoted and establish themselves as scholars in the field. The academics have a way of stating the issue: 'Publish or perish'. Every academic has heard it, but what does this mean in terms of a research and publication strategy? At the same time that I get these questions from academics, I get inquiries from practitioners about which academics are experts on a certain topic, and practitioner comments about the lack of research on the 'real' problems.

This paper will describe a research and publication strategy that has a high probability of success in turning a young academic into a respected scholar and achieving promotion and tenure at a major institution. The strategy also provides insight for practitioners who wish to identify good scholars in a given subject area and who wish to encourage 'relevant' research.

The chapter was written as a tutorial for a new faculty member in information systems while Professor Davis was visiting the National University of Singapore, but it can provide 'reminder clues' for experienced researchers in the field as well, and has relevance throughout the world.

12.1 THE ACADEMIC ENVIRONMENT FOR A RESEARCH STRATEGY

The academic world can be divided into three types of institutions: those that emphasize research, those that emphasize teaching, and those that are ambivalent. The institutions may talk the same way about the need for teaching, research and service, but the reward

230

structure for the research institutions is based on research. Teaching is still valued in the research institution; poor teaching will be detrimental to promotion, but good teaching will bring praise rather than promotion.

The direction of change in the major universities of the world is to place an emphasis on research. Research implies publications. To do research without publishing the results is like giving a musical concert to an empty hall; it may be instructive and rewarding to give the performance, but no one else benefits and no one will appreciate or reward you for it.

Academics rank journals in terms of their scholarly reputation. An article appearing in a journal is thus assigned a scholarly value consisting of the merits of the article times the merits of the journal. The most valued scholarly journals are those which have a formal process for review of the merits of an article. This review is performed by about three scholars in the field. The acceptance rate for the best journals (after revisions) is about 15 to 25%. Very few articles are accepted without some revision. The style of the articles places emphasis on the research methodology rather than the value of the results for practice. The three top-rated academic journals in information systems are:

- *Communications of the ACM*;
- *Management Science*;
- *MIS Quarterly*.

There are other excellent, high quality journals, but these are the big three (at the moment).

Practitioner journals are generally accorded little academic merit in terms of promotion. This does not mean they have no value for an academic; it means they have a different purpose and different reward than the academic journals. Their purpose is to disseminate ideas (based on research when possible) on how to improve practice. They provide a method for linking academics and practitioners: identifying academic expertise for practitioners, identifying practitioner interest and expertise, establishing relevance of research, and surfacing ideas for research (based on practice).

The top-rated practitioner journal is the *Harvard Business Review*.

Type of course where used

	Standard	Advanced
Imitate	The market place gives you your reward	Doing it better may be given recognition by colleagues
Innovate	Combination of market place and colleague recognition	Major factor in colleague recognition

Content and presentation

Fig. 12.1 Reward structure for college textbooks.

Datamation presents an interesting case. It has a huge practitioner audience but its contents are a mixture of thoughtful articles and trivia. On balance, however, it is an excellent vehicle for communicating with practitioners.

Proceedings of conferences and seminars do not do much for academic promotion, but again they have a different kind of value. Their value is in exposing ideas and getting feed-back. Good ideas that are presented at conferences can be refined and published in the regular journals.

How do textbooks fit into a publication strategy? There are essentially two kinds of textbooks: those that innovate in some way and those that imitate. The content can be standard for elementary courses, or advanced content. These characteristics can be arranged into a 2 × 2 matrix, as shown in Fig. 12.1.

That which is innovative will change with the state-of-textbooks. For example, I would rank the first edition of every book I have written as an innovative book. The second edition for most of my textbooks cannot be classed as an innovation because the market has moved such that most textbooks have imitated my innovation. A significant exception is the MIS book *Management Information Systems: Conceptual Foundations, Structure, and Development*. The second edition remains an innovative book that straddles the standard and advanced markets.

A good standard textbook is a big undertaking and should probably be left until your basic reputation is established. If you want to write one, my opinion is that you should have a comparative advantage in terms of a better pedagogical presentation or a significant comparative advantage as a writer.

12.2 KNOWING YOUR RESEARCH STRENGTHS

Research is discussed as if it were of one type, but it comes in a number of varieties. Rather than focussing on the variety of research method such as experiments, I think a more fundamental issue is an individual discovering his own talents relative to four tasks that define four roles or four talents in the conduct and reporting of research. I characterize these as:

- theorize-synthesize;
- design;
- manage;
- report.

Everyone has some talent for performing each of these, but some are better at some tasks than others.

By theorize-synthesize, I mean the activity that takes existing ideas and formulates new ideas and frameworks. The person who is very good at this has a broad vision of the world and seeks ideas from many fields. He also has high ideaphoria (lots of ideas). Out of the disorder of many observations, experiments, articles and reports, the theorizer-synthesizer makes a framework or a theory that brings order and sets the direction for future research.

The designer of research thinks in terms of how to get the data and other evidence so that ideas and theories may be empirically accepted or rejected. Some people have the ability to visualize experiments or experimental systems and to provide the design so that they can be conducted.

There is a strong managerial aspect in research projects involving experiments or field study. Attention to detail and human relations skills in dealing with organizations and subjects are required for this task.

The report task is to clearly explain what has been done in a research project and clearly define its contribution. Clarity in exposition is the important skill for this task.

The reason for identifying these tasks and the related skills is to encourage group research in which complementary skills are brought together to achieve a result that is better than that done alone.

12.3 A LONG TERM PROFESSIONAL DEVELOPMENT STRATEGY

One of the issues in organizations is the development of personnel so that they become more and more valuable through the years of service. However, the basic competence for most jobs is found in new graduates of universities and other training institutions. A new engineer has as good or perhaps better knowledge of engineering than an engineer with many years on the job. The older employee has more experience, but the critical elements of experience can be gained fairly quickly.

How then can a person become more valuable with years of service? In a research programme involving engineers and other professionals, Dalton *et al.* (1977) identified factors that cause some employees to be more valuable than others. Their model can be usefully applied to many professionals including researchers. The model suggests there are four stages of professional development with the employee becoming more and more valuable as he or she progresses to higher stages:

(1) *Apprentice* At the apprentice stage, the person works competently but always under supervision. There is little initiative or risk taking in activities. Some people remain apprentices for their entire life; others develop very slowly in independence. Advancement to the next stage comes when an apprentice demonstrates independent, individual competence and initiative.

A researcher is an apprentice in the first job after schooling at a university or research institute. Technical competence is assumed, but independent competence as a person has yet to be demonstrated.

(2) *Colleague* To be in the colleague stage, the person has done some significant jobs very competently, so that others view him as having ability to do other jobs also. The jobs where competence was demonstrated may vary, but they are viewed as important by others in the organization.

For a researcher, being a major part of a research project and demonstrating individual responsibility and initiative in competently completing the research and publishing the results establish credentials as a colleague. Part of the process of becoming a colleague is establishing a network of colleagues who are engaged in the same type of research. This network of colleagues is limited and specialized, but if a person at the colleague stage has a need to contact someone who is an active researcher in the specialized area of research where competence has been demonstrated, he or she probably knows them.

(3) *Mentor* The person at this stage takes on the responsibility for helping others who are apprentices to develop. One of the ways a mentor can assist an apprentice is to help them meet people who can aid them in the problems they face. A mentor will tend to have many contacts and friends within the organization, and these facilitate the mentor role.

For a researcher, the mentor relationship means taking some responsibility for bringing young researchers into projects and aiding them by critiquing their work and introducing them to others in the organization or in the specialized research area.

(4) *Sponsor* The person who reaches this stage has developed a large network of professional contacts both inside and outside the organization. The person has also established an ability to deal with the problems of organizing and managing projects.

For a researcher, the network of contacts include many in other fields and disciplines, funding agencies, and those having responsibility for decisions regarding research projects.

The research indicates that an apprentice has the lowest value to the organization and the sponsor the highest. This suggests a development strategy for a researcher:

- Look for and take opportunities for independent work on projects of significant scope, so that others in the organization will recognize one's competence and status as a colleague (years 1–4).
- Actively build a network of contacts, first emphasizing the specific area of research (years 1–5), next expanding into the organization (years 4–8) and then emphasizing a larger sphere of influence (years 8 and beyond).
- Take on the role of mentoring and develop and use a network of professional colleagues to aid those being mentored (years 6 and beyond).
- Build competence in managing projects and expand the network

of contacts that aid in attracting funds and support for research projects (years 8 and beyond).

The stages have been presented as discrete periods, but in reality persons move directionally through the stages on the basis of periodic experiences and events. A person can manage progression to a great extent because many of the experiences and events that cause (and signal) movement are under the control of the individual in the sense that initiative and willingness to assume responsibility will often result in opportunities.

12.4 ESTABLISHING A PERSONAL NETWORK OF COLLEAGUES

The stage model and other parts of the strategy for becoming a good scholar emphasize the value of developing a personal network of contacts in the field. For someone in Singapore, this means:

- A network of faculty members in the same university but in different departments who share interests related to research topics in information systems. This network is developed by taking the initiative to search out faculty members who appear to have common interests with you.
- A network of nearby faculty members in the information systems field in Singapore and Malaysia. This network is developed by attending local meetings of professional societies dealing with information systems, and nearby meetings in locations such as Kuala Lumpur. Giving talks and presenting papers at professional meetings aids in making the contacts. Publishing in the local journals and newsletters is another approach. *Information Technology* is a valuable opportunity in this context.
- A network of information systems professionals in Singapore and nearby cities. These contacts are made in the same way as the nearby faculty contacts. Making visits to information systems groups in local companies (when one contact arranges the visit) also expands these contacts.
- A network of faculty members in information systems in the USA, Canada, Europe and Australia. These are the major concentrations of research at the moment. These networks can be developed by

taking study leaves in these locations and working to have many contacts. Another way is to deliver papers or attend without a paper the major conferences where academics and other researchers congregate. The best general conference for information systems academics is the International Conference on Information Systems. A third method is to become active in one of the working groups of IFIP. Technical Committee 8 (Information Systems) is the relevant committee for this purpose. It has four working groups.

- A network of faculty members in information systems in the region. This includes Thailand, Indonesia, Taiwan, People's Republic of China and Hong Kong. Regional conferences provide the opportunity for building this kind of network.

Singapore is an isolated location, and the natural tendency is to not interact with an international network because of the cost of doing so. However, my perception is that, for the person who will be a good researcher, the cost is well worth it.

In this connection, Bitnet is invaluable. It is rapidly emerging as the network of choice. All major researchers in the world are either on Bitnet or a related network or soon will be. There is evidence to support the fact that the dynamics of interaction are changed when an electronic mail system is readily available. There is an analogy with the telephone; when few people had telephones it did not change communications, but when many people had them the dynamics of interpersonal communications were altered.

Start communicating on Bitnet and slowly build up the use of that medium. There is an early cost of checking for mail when very little mail is arriving, but early adopters always pay a price.

12.5 ESTABLISHING A PERSONAL RESEARCH STRATEGY

A good personal research strategy rests on seven ideas or principles:

- research needs in the field;
- personal interests and preferences;
- personal competence;
- personal comparative advantage;
- personal research portfolio planning;
- cumulative effect of research;
- opportunistic action.

The personal strategy is to identify the needs in the field, match these with personal interests and preferences, and constrain the choices by considering personal competence and personal comparative advantage. The choices are made from those passing the screening, to reflect a balanced portfolio based on time required, risk, potential for real contribution, 'hot topic', and availability of resources and data access. The selections should also reflect a strategy to have several projects that have a cumulative effect and establish the researcher's competence.

The foregoing presents a rational, slow-moving process, but on many occasions really good research projects arise because there was an opportunity, even though it did not quite fit the plan.

12.5.1 Outlining research needs in the field

It is useful to develop a taxonomy for one's broad area of interest and to then define broad areas of research needs for the field. The research needs or research questions can come from articles, discussions with practitioners, consulting, prior research, and conference proceedings dealing with research questions. It may be helpful to use a research taxonomy as a generator of topics.

A taxonomy of the field of information systems is given in Section 12.11 at the end of this chapter. It may not include all possible topics but is a useful starting point for outlining the research needs of the field. (See also Chapter 6.)

Two examples of information system research taxonomies that are useful in generating ideas for research are:

- Mason & Mitroff (1953) definition of an information system: *a person* of a certain *psychological type* who faces a *problem* within some *organizational context* for which he needs *evidence* to arrive at a solution where the evidence is made available through some *mode of presentation*.
- Ives, Hamilton & Davis (1980) taxonomy of information systems research developed to classify dissertations and to generate ideas. (See also Chapter 8.)

12.5.2 Personal interests and competence

The survey of the research needs defines a large number of general areas and may have identified a number of research topics. Only some of these will fit the personal interests of the researcher. When competence is considered, only a few general areas will remain.

Basic competence can be obtained with little difficulty, so basic competence should not be a deterrent to most fields of endeavour. When the research requires significant experience, this may be a deterrent.

12.5.3 Comparative advantage

Each researcher has some skills or access to expertise or access to data that provide a comparative advantage compared to most other researchers. For example, a comparative advantage at Minnesota is our very good access to the information systems professionals in large organizations headquartered in Minnesota; another advantage is a very good psychology department to support behavioural, laboratory research. In Singapore, there are some natural advantages for cross cultural research; there is also the advantage of the national IT plan. For information systems research in the National University of Singapore, there is good equipment support.

12.5.4 Personal research portfolio planning

The concept of an investment portfolio can be applied to a set of research projects. There should be a balance between factors such as the following:

- *Completion risk* How likely is the project to be able to be completed?
- *Output risk* How long will the project take to produce a meaningful research result?
- *Performance risk* How likely is the researcher to be able to do a good job?
- *Contribution risk* How likely is the result to be considered as a scholarly contribution or a contribution to practice?
- *Publication risk* Are the results likely to be publishable?

A researcher may have two or three research projects in his portfolio at a given time, so there is no need for a sophisticated analysis. The main point is to consider these risks and balance the short term projects against longer term ones.

12.5.5 Cumulative effect of research

A researcher who wished to be recognized for good research in an area should plan to get a cumulative result from the research he performs. Research should not be a set of random projects that show no coherent thrust. They should build on one another and establish the researcher as an expert (a colleague). The cumulative research approach also supports the building of a mentor role and of extending one's influence.

12.5.6 Opportunistic action

The value of planning may be more in the planning process to get a sense of direction and to establish priorities. But the plan should not prevent opportunistic action. Opportunities for good research will come in unexpected ways at unexpected times. It is always a good idea to evaluate opportunities and not be convinced by the glitter of what appears to be a great or glamorous chance. Yet one should not put things off when a good opportunity arrives. Two personal examples illustrate what I mean:

- Service with an organization that serves mainly auditors was not in my plan, but when I was offered the opportunity I decided to take it. During the 15 months I spent in New York, I conducted a state-of-the-art study of auditing and computers; this established me as an authority in the field. This has opened many other opportunities.
- When I was offered the opportunity to go to Belgium for 18 months to help start up the European Institute for Advanced Study in Management, I first said I could not go because I had so many things to do. But in examining the constraints that existed at that time and comparing them with a similar list for a year later, I discovered they were essentially identical. The year was very productive: I revised *Computer Data Processing*; wrote a classic book, *Management Information Systems*; and wrote a monograph on *Writing the Doctoral Dissertation*. Yet I almost did not do it.

12.6 DEVELOPING RELEVANT RESEARCH IDEAS

In many parts of the university, academic life is almost a closed system. Scholars talk to scholars, do research on the same set of problems, and publish for each other. They develop a jargon and a way of doing things that excludes anyone who is not part of their field. There may be some fields in the university where this is appropriate; it is not good for information systems.

Information systems is an applied field. That does not mean that it does not have theory or have lots of very esoteric, academic research possibilities. However, the reason for its existence is to provide research and instruction for a field of societal endeavour. There is a relevant practitioner community. The problem is how to keep in touch with the problems of practitioners without losing out as an academic.

The value of keeping in touch with information systems practice is stated simply in two propositions:

(1) Consulting provides relevant
   - *teaching materials* which aid better teaching and can be used for
   - *writing practitioner articles*.

(2) Consulting provides relevant
   - *research ideas* and
   - *access to research data* and may aid in
   - *research funding* and leads to
   - *research articles*.

These two propositions support the idea of getting practical experience and keeping in touch with practitioners. Some ways are:

- consultation;
- directing student projects in industry;
- inviting practitioners to give lectures on selected topics for your classes;
- teaching courses for practitioners (and getting them to interact about their problems);
- attendance and participation in professional meetings having practitioner attendance;
- leaves in industry, both short term and long term.

My most recent experiences illustrate what I mean:

- I taught a course for DPMA (Data Processing Management Association) here in Singapore; some of the discussion and coffee break conversations suggested research ideas.

- For the first six months of 1986, I spent three days a week studying the information systems function of a large company. This was part of a plan to return to the practitioners and review in detail the management problems being encountered in planning and operating information systems. A large number of research projects were suggested by the experiences I had.

12.7 DECIDING ON A RESEARCH METHODOLOGY

The obvious answer is that the research methodology should fit the research question. However, in most cases research can be conducted in a variety of ways. For example, assume the research question is, 'Why do managers resist the use of decision support systems?' There are a variety of ways meaningful research might be conducted:

- *Unsupported speculation* Formulation of explanations of the decision support resistance based on a general knowledge of organizations and information systems and a general knowledge of the literature. Sometimes this activity can be very valuable; at other times it is worthless.
- *Library research* A comprehensive examination of existing research that bears on the topic and a building of arguments with supporting references for an explanation.
- *Case study* An in-depth examination of the behaviour of one (or a small number) of executives relative to their use of decision support systems.
- *Survey* A questionnaire or interview method is used to ask a number of executives about their experiences with decision support systems.
- *Field study* By questionnaires, interviews and observations, data on a number of variables expected to be important in determining behaviour relative to decision support systems are collected. Analysis is by standard statistical methods of correlation and determining significant differences.
- *Field experiment* A decision support system is proposed for an organization and is studied as it is implemented under experimental conditions.
- *Laboratory experiment* An experiment in the use of a decision

support system is developed and subjects are observed and data measurements are collected during the experiment.

- *Mathematical modelling* An abstract model of executive behaviour is proposed. Functional relationships are defined between organizational events and stimuli and organizational and executive responses. Assumptions are made and the consequences of these assumptions are examined.

These research methods are well known; that is not the issue. The point is that the entire range of research methods might be applied to the same problem area. The question is how to select a starting point. A reasonable starting point is always a survey of the literature. A next logical step is a case study in an organization to establish a reality for future research. After the case study, the other research methods may be selected based on funding, timing etc. In general, surveys are most useful in the early stages of research or to establish or re-establish the state of practice. The problem is that there are too many surveys and not enough experiments.

Field experiments are very difficult because the experimenter has little control over the organization; we have had some cases where the companies dropped out after much preparatory work had been done. Laboratory experiments have the advantage of control over variables but they usually lack the richness of the real world. Mathematical modelling has limited applicability in problems where behaviour cannot be modelled.

This discussion suggests a strategy for a new research area of the following research activities and papers that are produced.

(1) Literature review in order to write a survey paper for the field – primarily on the state of the art and the state of knowledge of practice.
(2) Case study in an organization or some period of observation of the phenomenon in its organizational setting. Case report for teaching or to illustrate research papers.
(3) Paper outlining the state of research with weakness and needs defined. A proposal for a stream of research is described.
(4) A field survey of practice if little is known; otherwise, begin with experiments. One of the first experiments may be to replicate in a different setting, a different culture, or for a different kind

of subject one or more well-known experiments reported in the literature. The results of the replication may be reported if they are meaningful.

(5) After a set of experiments, synthesize the concept, knowledge and research results in the area being researched. Explain the implications of research being summarized and define needs for further research. This can be a seminal paper for a topic.

12.8 A GROUP STRATEGY FOR RESEARCH

Faculty members tend to be individualistic; one of the reasons they like to be faculty members is the individual responsibility and freedom they feel. They do not like committees and a lot of structure. However, there is a need for some group effort in order to lever the work of the individual faculty and graduate students.

The approach is very simple. When there are two or more faculty members who have an interest in an area of investigation, do a short working paper together to define the area of interest and invite others to join in a research group. The group is informal with only a convener to handle simple announcements and housekeeping tasks and a discussion leader. The group should establish a regular meeting time (weekly, biweekly, or monthly). At each meeting, there is a discussion of items such as the following, all within the context of aiding each other in doing good research:

- a draft of a research proposal from one of the group;
- a draft of an article by one of the group;
- outstanding current articles on the topic of interest;
- 'classic' articles on the topic of interest;
- practitioner-led discussion of practitioner needs.

There should be more than one such research group in existence in a faculty group. An optimal number may depend on the general level of research activity. A low activity faculty might have one group for each six or seven faculty members; a high activity faculty group might have a group for each three or four faculty members.

If a group does not produce results, it is allowed to die and another group is formed. Under such a plan, each faculty member is actively part of at least one group at all times.

12.9 THE ROLE OF PRACTITIONERS IN PROMOTING GOOD INFORMATION SYSTEM RESEARCH

There are two reasons why a thoughtful information systems practitioner might take the initiative to promote good research at the university. The first is that a good department attracts good students who make good employees, and the way to make a good department is to get good people and encourage them to be active researchers. The second is that a good research department will attract good faculty who will be a resource for problem solving, consulting and in-house teaching.

A good approach for a practitioner who is interested in promoting excellence through research is to offer the following opportunities to faculty members:

- An opportunity to meet with staff to discuss the needs of practice and review the problems they encounter.
- An opportunity to collect research data in the organization. This might range from case studies to field tests. In all cases, the ground rules for this interaction can be your permission to start a project and your permission to identify the organization in a report. It is always possible to disguise the organization, but often the identity of the organization makes the results more meaningful. For example, a large world-wide study of organizational culture was published without identifying the organization as IBM; reading the report is much more meaningful if you know that the study used that organization.
- Provide opportunities for faculty members to take leaves in industry. One of the characteristics of a university is the idea that every so often, a faculty member should take a leave and go some other place. The other place is usually thought of as another university, but it can be a research organization or a position in the information systems function in an organization.

It is helpful for practitioners to have some expectations relative to acceptance of ideas. My experience is that about one out of four practitioner ideas for things that need to be studied can be profitably researched. Often, the actual research project is a small issue within the larger problem that was raised.

12.10 SUMMARY

To be a professor in a major research university, one must do research and publish research findings in major refereed journals. To develop practitioner contacts and maintain a free flow of ideas from the practitioner community, it is also necessary to publish in practitioner journals and participate in professional meetings.

The strategy for an individual is to think in terms of a strategy which increases one's worth to the organization. This strategy consists of searching out and accepting opportunities which develop experience, demonstrate individual competence early in one's career, develop ability to mentor, and result in an expanding circle of professional contacts and colleagues (expanding to related fields and administrative bodies).

The expanding circle of colleagues is achieved by regular attendance at conferences and giving papers at them. Bitnet and other electronic mail networks are now a method by which a professor in Singapore can maintain contact with colleagues around the world.

A researcher can be more effective by knowing his comparative strengths for the tasks that are required for research. These include theorize-synthesize, design, manage, and report.

A research and publications strategy requires some planning, although unplanned opportunistic choices are not excluded. The planning is based on considerations such as the following:

- research needs in the field;
- personal interests and preferences;
- personal competence;
- personal comparative advantage;
- personal research portfolio planning;
- cumulative effect of research.

There are many research methodologies from which to select. As part of the development of a new research area, it is useful to do library research to define what has been done and to do case research to gain practical insight. Survey research is valuable at certain times in the development of a research area, but is not generally as valuable as research involving experiments.

Developing research projects can come through academic interaction, but in information systems it is also vital to seek research ideas from the problems of the practitioners. Practitioners can aid in this interaction.

The individual research strategy is supplemented by a group research strategy to provide leverage and quality assurance for individual projects. The voluntary establishment and maintenance of research groups is the most desirable way of getting synergism within the faculty.

12.11 TOPICS THAT DEFINE THE FIELD OF INFORMATION SYSTEMS

The topics that follow define the field of information systems (also described by terms such as management information systems, organizational information systems, and computer-based information systems). These topics are not necessarily unique to information systems; they may be included in the field of computer science, management science, cognitive psychology etc. However, the topics are within the context of information systems in organizations, rather than being a topic of interest outside any specific context or primarily within the context of another discipline.

Hardware, software and communications technology for information systems represent underlying knowledge rather than topics of primary interest. Information systems professors and practitioners require a knowledge of the technology; however, their main interest is in the application of the technology rather than the development of new or improved technology.

12.11.1 Organization and management of the information systems function in an organization

(1) organization of the information systems function;
(2) management of the information systems function, including management of subfunctions such as computer operations, data administration, application development, information centres etc.;
(3) planning of informations systems, including alignment with strategy of the organization and planning for competitive advantage with information systems;
(4) diffusion of information technology in an organization;
(5) allocation of information systems resources;

(6) application development project management;
(7) economics of information systems and organizational value of information systems;
(8) evaluating information systems.

12.11.2 Specifications for and requirements of classes of systems common to organizations (or included in the general concept of management information systems)

(1) transaction processing systems for organizational transactions;
(2) applications for management of operations, management control and strategic planning;
(3) decision support systems;
(4) executive support systems;
(5) office automation systems;
(6) expert systems;
(7) electronic mail and messaging systems;
(8) inter-organizational information systems.

12.11.3 Information system application requirements

(1) human/machine interface requirements including human information processing limits and behaviours;
(2) social system requirements (socio-technical analysis);
(3) decision requirements considering human differences;
(4) procedural requirements considering human and organizational differences;
(5) methods for eliciting and validating information systems requirements;
(6) methods for measuring value of information to recipients.

12.11.4 Information systems development, implementation and maintenance

(1) systems theory and theory of artifacts applied to information systems, application design, development, etc.;
(2) methods for participation in application design;
(3) application development methods and methodologies including prototyping and use of packaged software;

(4) application software design and development (software engineering);

(5) application software testing and quality assurance;

(6) application software maintenance;

(7) programming languages for application programming;

(8) languages for retrieval and report generation;

(9) end-user computing software and applications;

(10) implementation of information systems;

(11) user information satisfaction;

(12) training in information system use.

12.11.5 Development and maintenance of databases for organizations and design of record structures for applications.

Emphasis of the information systems field is on logical design rather than physical design.

(1) data modelling;

(2) logical database design;

(3) data administration function;

(4) security and integrity controls for databases;

(5) data structures and relationship to applications.

12.11.6 Impact/interaction of information systems, information systems technology and applications on humans in various settings

(1) effect on individual users;

(2) effect on group performance and group behaviour;

(3) effect on organizations including management and supervision structures and behaviours;

(4) effect on society and societal interactions.

12.11.7 Information systems personnel

(1) recruitment and selection of information systems personnel;

(2) training of information systems personnel;

(3) motivation and job satisfaction of information systems personnel;

(4) performance evaluation;

(5) career management for information systems personnel.

12.11.8 Control, audit and security for information systems

(1) error control and quality assurance in operation of computer applications;
(2) human performance and errors in application use;
(3) forms of fraudulent use and security violations;
(4) security principles and security mechanisms for information processing installation, facilities, applications and data;
(5) audit procedures and use of audit tools and techniques in computer information systems environment.

CHESTER COLLEGE LIBRARY

Further Reading

Undertaking and managing research – background reading and helpful hints

Easterby-Smith M., Thorpe R. & Lowe A. (1991) *Management Research: An Introduction*. Sage Publications, London.

Howard K. & Sharp J.A. (1984) *The Management of a Student Research Project*. Gower Publishing, Aldershot.

Lawler III, E.E., Mohrman, A.M. Jr., Mohrman S.A., Ledford G.E. Jr., Thomas G. Cummings & Associates (1985) *Doing Research that is Useful for Theory and Practice*. Jossey-Bass Publishers, San Francisco.

Locke L.F., Spirduso W.W. & Silverman S.J. (1987) *Proposals that Work: A Guide for Planning Dissertations and Grant Proposals*, 2nd edn. Sage Publications, Newbury Park, Calif.

Phillips E.M. & Pugh D.S. (1987) *How to Get a PhD: Managing the Peaks and Troughs of Research*. Open University Press, Milton Keynes.

Business research methodology – alternative approaches and guidance

Buckley J.W., Buckley M.H. & Chiang H-F. (1976) *Research Methodology and Business Decisions*, National Association of Accountants and The Society of Industrial Accountants of Canada, New York and Hamilton, Ontario.

Gummesson E. (1988) *Qualitative Methods in Management Research*. Studentlitteratur, Lund, Sweden.

Information systems research – approaches

Benbasat I. (Ed.) (1989) *The Information Systems Research Challenge Volume 2: Experimental Research Methods*. Harvard Business School Press, Boston.

Cash J.I. Jr. & Lawrence P.R. (Eds.) (1989) *The Information Systems Research Challenge Volume 1: Qualitative Research Methods*. Harvard Business School Press, Boston.

Mumford E., Hirchheim R.A., Fitzgerald G. & Wood-Harper A.T. (Eds.) (1985) *Research Methods in Information Systems.* North-Holland, Amsterdam.

Nissen H-E., Klein H.K. & Hirschheim R.A. (Eds.) (1991) *Information Systems Research: Contemporary Approaches & Emergent Traditions.* North-Holland, Amsterdam.

Information systems – issues

McFarlan F.W. (Ed.) (1984) *The Information Systems Research Challenge.* Harvard Business School Press, Boston.

Boland R.J. & Hirschheim R.A. (Eds.) (1987) *Critical Issues in Information Systems Research.* Wiley, Chichester.

Writing a thesis – style and content

Albough R.M. (1968) *Thesis Writing: A Guide to Scholarly Style.* Littlefield, Adams & Co, Totowa, NJ.

References

Ackoff R.L. (1967) Management Misinformation Systems. *Management Science*, **14**, 4, December, pp. 147–156.

Aiken M.W., Liu Sheng O.R. & Vogel D.R. (1990) Integrating expert systems with group decision support systems. *ACM Transactions on Information Systems*, **8**, 4.

American Psychological Association (1974) *Publication Manual of the American Psychological Association*. American Psychological Association, Washington, D.C.

Albough R.M. (1968) *Thesis Writing: A Guide to Scholarly Style*. Littlefield, Adams & Co., Totowa, NJ.

Antill L. (1985) Selection of a Research Method. In Mumford *et al.* (1985), *op cit.*, pp. 203–215.

Appleton D.S. (1983) Data-driven prototyping. *Datamation*, **29**, 11.

Astley W.G. (1985) Administrative science as socially constructed truth. *Adm. Sect. Q.40*, **4**, December, pp. 497–513.

Astley W.G. & Van de Ven A.H. (1983) Central perspective and debates in organization theory. *Adm. Sect. Q.28*, **2**, June, pp. 245–273.

Audet M., Landry M. & Dèry R. (1986) Science et résolution de problème: liens, difficultés et voies de dépassement dans le champ des sciences de l'administration. *Philosophie des Sciences Sociales*, **16**, 4, December, pp. 409–440.

Avison D.E. (1991) The discipline of information systems and the role of practice. *Proceedings: ISTIP-91*, Fourth UK Conference on Information Systems Teaching: Improving the Practice, Sunningdale, 3–5 April, 1991.

Ball L. & Harris R. (1982) SMIS members: a membership analysis. *MIS Quarterly*, **6**, 1, pp. 19–38.

Banville C. & Landry M. (1989) Can the field of MIS be disciplined? *Communications of the ACM*, **32**, 1, January, pp. 48–60.

Baroudi J.J. & Orlikowski W.J. (1989) The Problem of Statistical Power in MIS Research. *MIS Quarterly*, **13**, 1, pp. 87–106.

Barton A.H. & Lazarsfeld P.H. (1969) Some Functions of Qualitative Analysis in Social Research. In *Issues in Participant Observation*. Ed. by G.J. McCall & J.L. Simmons, Addison Wesley, Reading, Mass., pp. 163–196.

Beer S. (1966) *Decision and Control.* Wiley, London.

Benbasat I. (1984) An Analysis of Research Methodologies. In McFarlan (1984), *op cit.*, pp. 47–85.

Benbasat I., Dexter A.S., Drury D.H. & Goldstein R.C. (1984) A Critique of the Stage Hypothesis: Theory and Empirical Evidence. *Communications of the ACM*, **27**(5), May, pp. 476–485.

Benbasat I. (Ed.) (1989) *The Information Systems Research Challenge Volume 2: Experimental Research Methods.* Harvard Business School Press, Boston.

Benjamin R.I., Dickinson C.J. & Rockart J.F. (1985) Changing role of the Corporate Information Systems Officer. *MIS Quarterly*, **9**, 3, pp. 177–188.

Benson J.K. (1983) Paradigm and Praxis in Organizational Analysis. In *Research in Organizational Behavior*, **5**. Ed. by L.L. Cummins & B.M. Shaw, JAI Press, Greenwich, Conn.

Berg P.O. (1979) *Emotional Structures in Organizations: A Study of the Process of Change in a Swedish Company.* Studentlitteratur, Lund, Sweden.

Bertalanffy L. Von (1968) *General Systems Theory – Foundations, Development, Applications.* George Braziller, New York.

Bjørn-Andersen N. (1983) Challenge to certainty. In *Proceedings IFIP W.G. 8.2 Conference*, Minnesota, August 22–24, 1983.

Bjørn-Andersen N. (1985) Conference Review: IS Research – A Doubtful Science. In E. Mumford, *et al.*, *op cit.*, pp. 273–277.

Bleicher J. (1982). *The Hermeneutic Imagination: Outline of a Positive Critique of Scientism and Sociology.* Routledge and Kegan Paul, London.

Bohme G. (1975) The social function of cognitive structures: A concept of the scientific community within a theory of action. In *Determinants and Controls of Scientific Development.* Ed. by K.D. Knorr, H. Strasser & H.G. Zilian, Reidel, Dordrecht, pp. 205–225.

Boisot M. (1987) *Information and Organizations – the Manager as Anthropologist.* Fontana Collins, London.

Boland R.J. (Jr.) (1984) Sense making of accounting data as a technique of organizational design. *Management Science*, **30**, 7.

Boland R.J. (Jr.) (1985) Phenomenology: A Preferred Approach to Research on Information Systems. In Mumford, *et al.* (1985) *op cit.*, pp. 193–201.

Boland R.J. (Jr.) (1987) The information in information systems. In R.J. Boland (Jr.) & R.A. Hirschheim (1987), *op cit.*

Boland R.J. (Jr.) & Hirschheim R.A. (1987) *Critical Issues in Information Systems Research*, Wiley, Chichester.

Bouchard T.J. (Jr.) (1976) Field research methods. In *Handbook of Industrial and Organizational Psychology.* Ed. by M.D. Dunnette (1976), Rand McNally, Chicago, pp. 363–413.

Boulding H.E. (1956) General systems theory – the skeleton of science. *Management Science*, **2**, 3.

Brancheau J.C. & Wetherbe J.C. (1987) Key issues in information systems management. *MIS Quarterly*, **11**, 1, pp. 23–45.

Brown F.E. (1980) *Marketing Research – Structure for Decision Making*. Addison-Wesley.

Brown S., Fauvel J. & Finnegan R. (Eds.) (1981) *Concepts of Inquiry*. Open University Press, London.

Buckingham R.A., Hirschheim R.A., Land F.F. & Tully C.J. (1987) *Information Systems Education: Recommendations and Implementation*. British Computer Society Monographs in Informatics, Cambridge University Press, Cambridge.

Buckley J.W., Buckley M.H. & Chiang H-F. (1976) *Research Methodology and Business Decisions*. National Association of Accountants, New York & The Society of Industrial Accountants of Canada, Hamilton, Ontario.

Bullen C. (1986) Do we need a new I.S. journal??? *MIS Interrupt*, **32**, July.

Burrell G. & Morgan G. (1979) *Sociological Paradigms and Organisational Analysis*. Heinemann, London.

Caldwell B. (1984) *Beyond Positivism: Economic Methodology in the Twentieth Century*, 2nd edition. George Allen & Unwin, London.

Callan C. (1989) A New Year's agenda. *CIO Journal*, January, pp. 10–11.

Campbell W.C. (1969) *Form and Style in Thesis Writing*, Houghton Mifflin.

Carver R.P. (1978) The case against statistical significance testing. *Harvard Educational Review*, **48**, 3, pp. 378–99.

Cash J.I. (Jr.) & Lawrence P.R. (Eds.) (1989) *The Information Systems Research Challenge Volume 1: Qualitative Research Methods*. Harvard Business School Press, Boston.

Chalmers A.F. (1982) *What Is This Thing Called Science?* 2nd edition. The Open University Press, Milton Keynes.

Chatfield C. (1984) *The Analysis of Time Series*, 3rd edition. Chapman & Hall, London.

Chatfield C. (1988) *Problem Solving: A Statistician's Guide*. Chapman & Hall, London.

Checkland P.B. (1981) *Systems Thinking, Systems Practice*. Wiley, Chichester.

Cherns A. (1969) Social research and its diffusion. *Human Relations*, **22**, pp. 209–218.

Chervany N.L. (1973) Discussion comments on empirical studies of management information systems. *Database*, **5**, pp. 180–181.

Clark P.A. (1972) *Action Research and Organizational Change*. Harper & Row, London.

Clegg S. & Dunkerley D. (1980) *Organisation, Class and Control*. Routledge and Kegan Paul, London.

Cook T.D. & Campbell D.T. (1976) The design and conduct of quasi-experiments and true experiments in field settings. In *Handbook of Indus-*

trial and Organizational Psychology. Ed. by M.D. Dunnette (1976), Rand McNally, Chicago, pp. 223–326.

Copeland R.M., Franca A.J. & Strawser R.H. (1973) Students as Subjects in Behavioral Business Research. *Accounting Review*, April.

Copeland R.M., Franca A.J. & Strawser R.H. (1974) Further Comments on Students as Subjects in Behavioral Business Research. *Journal of Business*, July.

Culnan M.J. (1986) The intellectual development of management information systems, 1972–1982: a co-citation analysis. *Management Science*, **32**, 2 February, pp. 156–172.

Culnan M.J. (1987) Mapping the intellectual structure of MIS, 1980–1985: a co-citation analysis. *MIS Quarterly*, **11**, 3, pp. 340–353.

Culnan M.J. & Swanson E.B. (1986) Research in management information systems, 1980–1984: points of work and reference. *MIS Quarterly*, **10**, 3, September, pp. 288–302.

Cyert R.M. & March J.G. (1963) *A Behavioural Theory of the Firm*. Prentice-Hall, Englewood Cliffs, NJ.

Dalton G.W., Thompson P.H. & Price R.L. (1977) The four stages of professional careers: A new look at performance by professionals. *Organizational Dynamics*, Summer.

Davenport R.A. & Boday R. (1988) *Critical Issues in Information Systems management in 1988*. Index Group, London.

Davis G. & Olson M. (1985) *Management Information Systems: Foundations, Structure and Development*. McGraw-Hill, New York.

Davitz J.R. & Davitz L.J. (1967) *A Guide for Evaluating Research Plans in Psychology and Education*. Teachers College Press, New York.

De Mey M. (1982) *The Cognitive Paradigm*. Reidel, Boston.

Dearden J. (1970) MIS is a Mirage. *Harvard Business Review*, **50**, 1, January–February, pp. 90–99.

Delbecq A.L., Van de Ven A.H. & Gustafson D.H. (1975) *Group Techniques for Program Planning*. Scott Foresman, Glenview, Il.

Dickson G.W. (1981) Management Information Systems: Evolution and Status. In *Advances in Computers*, **20**, Academic Press, New York, pp. 1–37.

Dickson G.W., Leitheiser R.C., Wetherbe J.C. & Nechis M. (1984) Key Information Systems Issues for the 1980's. *MIS Quarterly*, **8**, 3, September, pp. 135–159.

Dickson G.W., Benbasat I. & King M.R. (1980) The management information systems arena: problems, challenges and opportunities. *Proceedings of the First International Conference on Information Systems*, Philadelphia, pp. 1–8. Reproduced in *Data Base*, **14**, 1, Fall 1982, pp. 1–8.

Dickson G.W., Senn J.A. & Chervany N.L. (1977) Research in management information systems: The Minnesota experiments. *Management Science*, **23**, pp. 913–925.

Dillon W.R. & Goldstein M. (1984) *Multivariate Analysis – Methods and Applications*. Wiley, New York.

Draper N.R. & Smith H. (1981) *Applied Regression Analysis*, 2nd edition. Wiley, New York.

Durkheim E. (1938) *The Rules of Sociological Method*. Free Press, New York.

Earl M.J. & Hopwood A.G. (1980) From management information to information management. In *The Information Systems Environment*. Ed. by H. Lucas, F.F. Land and T. Lincoln (1980), North-Holland, Amsterdam.

Easterby-Smith M., Thorpe R. & Lowe A. (1991) *Management Research: An Introduction*. Sage, London.

Easton D. (1965) *A Framework for Political Analysis*. Prentice-Hall, Englewood Cliffs.

Ein-Dor P. & Segev E. (1981) *A Paradigm for Management Information Systems*. Praeger, New York.

Farhoomand A.F. (1986) The evolution of management information systems as an academic discipline. In *Proceedings of the 14th Annual Information Systems Conference*. Ed. by F. Bergeron, Administrative Sciences Association of Canada, Whistler, B.C.

Farhoomand A.F. (1987) Scientific progress of management information systems. *Data Base*, **18**, 4, Summer, pp. 48–56.

Fay B. (1975) *Social Theory and Political Practice*. George Allen and Unwin, London.

Forrester J.W. (1961) *Industrial Dynamics*. MIT Press, Cambridge, Mass.

Foster M. (1972) An introduction to the Theory and Practice of Action Research in Work Organizations. *Human Relations*, **25**, 6.

Fromkin H.L. & Streufert S. (1976) Laboratory Experimentation. In *Handbook of Industrial and Organizational Psychology*. Ed. by M.D. Dunnette Rand McNally, Chicago, pp. 415–466.

Gadamer H-G. (1981) *Reason in the Age of Science*. MIT Press, Cambridge, Mass.

Galliers R.D. (1985) In Search of a Paradigm for Information Systems Research. In Mumford, *et al.* (1985), *op cit.*, pp. 281–297.

Galliers R.D. (1987a) Educating Information Systems Managers into the 1990s: The WAIT Example. In R.A. Buckingham, *et al.* (1987), *op cit.*, pp. 166–178.

Galliers R.D. (Ed.) (1987b) *Information Analysis: Selected Readings*. Addison-Wesley, Maidenhead, Berks.

Galliers R.D. (1991) Choosing Appropriate Information Systems Research Approaches: A Revised Taxonomy. In H-E. Nissen, *et al.* (1991), *op cit.*, pp. 327–345.

Galliers R.D. & Land F.F. (1987) Choosing Appropriate Information Systems

Research Methodologies. *Communications of the ACM*, **30**, 11, November, pp. 900–902.

Galliers R.D. & Land F.F. (1988) The importance of Laboratory Experimentation in IS Research: A Response. *Communications of the ACM*, **31**, 12, December, pp. 1504–1505.

Galliers R.D., Smith D.R. & Palmer J. (Eds.) (1984) *Proceedings: International Microcomputer Conference*. WAIT, Perth, Western Australia, May.

Garfield E. (1972) Citation analysis as a tool in journal evaluation. *Science*, **178**, pp. 466–472.

Garratt R. (1987) *The Learning Organization*. Fontana Collins, London.

Gibson C.F. (1975) A methodology for implementation research. In *Implementing Operations Research/Management Science*. Ed. by R.L. Schultz & D.P. Slevin, American Elsevier, New York, pp. 53–76.

Giddens A. (1976) *New Rules of Sociological Method*. Hutchinson, London.

Giddens A. (1978) Positivism and its criticisms. In *A History of Sociological Analysis*. Ed. by T. Bottomore & R. Nisbet, Heinemann, London.

Ginzberg M.J. (1978) Steps towards more effective implementation of MS and MIS. *Interfaces*, **8**, 3.

Glaser B. & Strauss A.L. (1967) *The Discovery of Grounded Theory: Strategies for Qualitative Research*. Aldine, Chicago.

Gouldner A. (1962) Anti-minotaur: the myth of value free sociology. *Social Problems*, **9**, 3.

Greenacre M.J. (1984) *Theory and Applications of Correspondence Analysis*. Academic Press, London.

Gummesson E. (1988) *Qualitative Methods in Management Research*. Studentlitteratur, Lund, Sweden.

Gupta A. (1982) Emerging trends in office technology. In *Office Information Systems*. Ed. by N. Naffaf (1982), North-Holland, Amsterdam.

Hamilton S. & Ives B. (1982) Knowledge utilization among MIS researchers. *MIS Quarterly*, **7**, pp. 220–235.

Hamilton S. & Ives B. (1982) MIS Research Strategies. *Information and Management*, **5**, December, pp. 339–347.

Hamilton S. & Ives B. (1983) The Journal Communication System for MIS Research. *Data Base*, **15**, 2, Winter, pp. 3–14.

Hamilton S., Ives B. & Davis G.B. (1981) MIS doctoral dissertations: 1973–1980. *MIS Quarterly*, **5**, pp. 910–934.

Hammer M. (1981) Life cycle management. *Information Management*, **14**, 4.

Harrison S.R. & Tamaschke H.U. (1984) *Applied Statistical Analysis*. Prentice-Hall, Sydney, Australia.

Hartog C. & Herbert M. (1986) 1985 opinion survey of MIS managers: key issues. *MIS Quarterly*, **10**, 4, pp. 351–361.

Hartog C. & Rouse R.A. (1987) A blueprint for the new IS professional. *Datamation*, **33**, 20, 15th. October, pp. 65–69.

Hempel C. (1964) Explanation in Science and History. In *Frontiers of Science and Philosophy*. Ed. by R. Colodny, George Allen and Unwin, London.

Hesse M. (1978) Theory and value in the social sciences. In *Action and Interpretation: Studies in the Philosophy of Social Interpretation*. Ed. by C. Hookway & P. Pettit, Cambridge University Press, Cambridge.

Hesse M. (1980a) Theory and observation. In *Revolutions and Reconstructions in the Philosophy of Science*. Ed. by M. Hesse (1980b), *op cit.*

Hesse M. (1980b) *Revolutions and Reconstructions of Science*. The Harvester Press, Brighton.

Hirschheim R.A. (1985a) User experience with and assessment of participative systems design. *MIS Quarterly*, **9**, 4.

Hirschheim R.A. (1985b) Information systems epistomology – an historical perspective. In E. Mumford, *et al.* (1985), *op cit.*, pp. 13–36.

Hirschheim R.A. (1985c) *Office Automation – a Social and Organizational Perspective*. Wiley, Chichester.

Hirschheim R.A., Earl M., Feeny D. & Lockett M. (1988) An exploration into the management of the information systems function: key issues and an evolutionary model. In *Information Technology Management for Productivity and Competitive Advantage*. IFIP TC-8 Open Conference, Singapore, pp. 4.15–4.38.

Hirschheim R.A., Land F.F. & Smithson S. (1984) Implementing computer based information systems in organisations – issues and strategies. *Proceedings: Interact 84*. North-Holland, Amsterdam.

Hofstede G. (1980) *Culture's Consequences: International Difference in Work-related values*. Sage, Beverley Hills, CA.

Holton G. (1974) On Being Caught between Dionysians and Apollonians. *Daedalus*, **103**, Summer.

Horne N.W. (1991) Involving the User in IT Research and Development. *JWIT News*, DTI/SERC, May.

Horowitz E., Kemper A. & Narasimhan B. (1984) Application generators. *IEEE Software*, **12**, 1.

Howard K. & Sharp J.A. (1984) *The Management of a Student Research Project*. Gower, Aldershot.

Huber G.P. (1983) Cognitive style as a basis for MIS and DSS designs: much ado about nothing? *Management Science*, **29**, 5 May, pp. 367–379.

Husserl E. (1936) The Origin of Geometry. In *Phenomenology and Sociology*. Ed. by T. Luckman, Penguin, Harmondsworth.

Iivari J. (1983) *Contributions to the Theoretical Foundations of Systemeering Research and the PIOCO Model*. Institute of Data Processing, University of Oulu, Finland.

Information Systems Faculty Development Institute/Advanced Information Systems Faculty Development Institute (1986) *MIS Faculty Training Programs*. American Assembly of Collegiate School of Business, St. Louis.

Ivanov K. (1984) *Systemutveckling och adb-amets utveckling*. Dept. of Computer Science Report LIU-IDA-R-84-1, Linkoping University, Sweden, June.

Ives B., Hamilton S. & Davis G.B. (1980) A framework for research in computer-based management information systems. *Management Science*, **26**, 9, September, pp. 910–934.

Jarvenpaa S. (1988) The importance of Laboratory Experimentation in IS Research. *Communications of the ACM*, **31**(12), December, 1502–1504.

Jenkins A.M. (1977) *An Investigation of Some Management Information System Design Variables and Decision Making Performance: A Simulation Experiment*. Unpublished Ph.D. Dissertation, University of Minnesota.

Jenkins A.M. (1983) *Prototyping – a Methodology for the Design and Development of Application Systems*. Discussion paper 227, Indiana University Graduate School of Business, Bloomington, Indiana.

Keen P.G.W. (1974) *Towards a Behavioral Methodology for the Study of OR/MIS Implementation*. Working Paper 701–74, Sloan School of Management, Massachussetts Institute of Technology, Cambridge.

Keen P.G.W. (1980) MIS research: reference disciplines and a cumulative tradition. *Proceedings of the First International Conference on Information Systems*, Philadelphia, pp. 9–18.

Keen P.G.W. (1984) Building the Information Systems Research Community. *Information Technology Training*, November.

Keen P.G.W. & Scott-Morton M.S. (1978) *Decision Support Systems – an Organizational Perspective*. Addison-Wesley, Reading, Mass.

Keller G., Warrack B. & Bartel H. (1990) *Statistics for Management and Economics – A Systemic Approach*. Wadsworth, California.

Keys P. (1988) A Methodology for Methodology Choice. *Systems Research*, **5**, 1, pp. 65–76.

Khera I.P. & Benson J.D. (1970) Are Students Really Poor Substitutes for Businessmen in Behavioral Research? *Journal of Marketing Research*, November.

Kilman R.H. (1979) On integrating knowledge utilization with knowledge development. *Academy of Management Review*, **4**, pp. 417–426.

Kilman R.H. & Mitroff I.I. (1976) Quantitative versus qualitative analysis for management science: different forms for different psychological types. *TIMS Interfaces*, February.

King J.L. & Kraemer K.L. (1984) Evolution and Organizational Information Systems: An Assessment of Nolan's Stage Model. *Communications of the ACM*, **27**(5), May, pp. 466–475.

Kirk R.E. (1968) *Experimental Design: Procedures for the Behavioral Sciences*. Wadsworth, California.

Klein H.K. (1984) Quo Vadis information 'science'? *Proceedings: Fifth International Conference on Information Systems*, Tucson, November, pp. 28–30.

Klein H.K. & Hirschheim, R. (1987) *Legitimation and Information Systems Development*. RDP 87/4 Oxford Institute of Information Management, Templeton College, Oxford University.

Klein H.K. & Lyytinen K. (1985) The Poverty of Scientism in Information Systems. In Mumford, *et al.* (1985), *op cit.*, pp. 131–161.

Klein H.K. & Welke R.J. (1982) Information Systems as a Scientific Discipline. *Proceedings, ASAC*, University of Ottawa, June 1–3, pp. 106–116.

Kling R. (1980) Social Analyses of computing: theoretical perspectives in recent empirical research. *Computing Surveys*, **12**, 1, March, pp. 61–110.

Koch S. (1980) A possible psychology for a possible post-postitivist world. Paper presented at the 88th. Annual American Psychological Association Conference, Montreal, September.

Koestler A. (1964) *The Act of Creation*. Hutchinson, London. (Second edition: 1969).

Kolakowski L. (1972) *Positivist Science*. Penguin Books, Harmondsworth.

Knorr-Cetina K.D. (1981) *The Manufacture of Knowledge: An Essay on the Constructivist and Contextual Nature of Science*. Pergamon Press, Oxford.

Koontz H. (Ed.) (1964) *Toward a Unified Theory of Management*. McGraw-Hill, New York.

Krathwohl D.R. (1966) *How to Prepare a Research Proposal*. Syracuse University Bookstore, Syracuse, NY.

Kraemer K.L. & Cash J.I. (Jr.) (1991) *The Information Systems Research Challenge Volume 3: Survey Research Methods*. Harvard Business School Press, Boston.

Kroll W.P. & Peterson K.H. (1966) Cross Validation of the Booth Scale. *Research Quarterly*, **37**, pp. 66–70.

Kuhn T.S. (1961) *The Structure of Scientific Revolution*. University of Chicago Press, Chicago. (Second edition: 1970).

Kuhn T.S. (1974) Second Thoughts on Paradigms. In *The Structure of Scientific Theories*. University of Illinois Press, Chicago, Illinois.

Kuhn T.S. (1977) *The Essential Tension*. University of Chicago Press, Chicago.

Lakatos I. & Musgrave A. (Eds.) (1970) *Criticism and the Growth of Knowledge*. Cambridge University Press, Cambridge.

Land F.F. (1982) Adapting to Changing User Requirements. *Information & Management*, **5**. Reproduced in R.D. Galliers (1987) *op cit.*, pp. 203–229.

Land F.F. (1987) Social aspects of information systems. In *Management Information Systems: The Technology Challenge*. Ed. by N. Piercy (1987), Croom Helm, London.

Land F.F. (1988) Information systems and complexity. In *Systems Theory and Systems Engineering*, IEE Proceedings, **135**, Part A, 6.

Land F.F. & Kennedy-McGregor M. (1987) Information and information systems: concepts and perspectives. In Galliers R.D. (1987) *op cit.*, pp. 63–91.

Laudaen L. (1977) *Progress and Its Problems: Towards a Theory of Scientific Growth*. Routledge and Kegan Paul, London.

Lawler E.E., (III), Mohrman A.M. (Jr.), Mohrman S.A., Ledford G.E. (Jr.) & Thomas D. Cummins & Associates (1985) *Doing Research that is Useful for Theory and Practice*. Jossey-Bass, San Francisco, Ca.

Le Moigne J.L. (1985) Towards new epistemological foundations for information systems. *Systems Research*, **2**, 3, pp. 247–251.

Lee A.S. (1989) Scientific Methodology for MIS Case Studies. *MIS Quarterly*, **13**(1), March, pp. 33–50.

Lessnoff M. (1974) *The Structure of Social Science*. George Allen and Unwin, London.

Liebenau J. & Backhouse J. (1990) *Understanding Information: An Introduction*. Macmillan, London.

Lipset S.M., Trow M. & Coleman J.S. (1956) *Union Democracy*. The Free Press, New York.

Locke L.F. & Spirduso W.W. (1970) *Proposals that Work: A Guide for Planning Dissertations*. Teachers College Press, New York.

Locke L.F., Spirduso W.W. & Silverman S.J. (1987) *Proposals that Work: A Guide for Planning Dissertations and Grant Proposals* (2nd edition). Sage, Newbury Park, Calif.

Lucas H.C. (1981) *Implementation: the Key to Successful Information Systems*. Columbia University Press, New York.

Lyytinen K. (1987a) A taxonomic perspective of information systems development. In R.J. Boland & R. Hirschheim (1987), *op cit.*

Lyytinen K. (1987b) Different perspectives on information systems – problems and solutions. *ACM Surveys*, **19**, 1.

Macrae M. (1988) Education gap needs closing. *Computerworld Australia*, 12th August, p. 8.

Mason R.O. & Mitroff I.I. (1973) A program for research on management information systems. *Management Science*, **19**, 5, January, pp. 475–485.

Masterman M. (1970) The nature of a paradigm. In *Criticism and the Growth of Knowledge*. Ed. by I. Lakatos & A. Musgrave, Cambridge University Press, Cambridge, pp. 59–89.

McFarlan F.W. (Ed.) (1984) *The Information Systems Research Challenge*. Harvard Business School Press, Boston.

McLean E. (Ed.) (1980) *Proceedings: First International Conference on Information Systems*. Philadelphia, Pennsylvania, December, Association of Computing Machinery, Baltimore, Maryland.

Mill J.S. (1843) *A System of Logic.* Longmans, London.

Mintzberg H. (1979) *The Structuring of Organizations.* Prentice-Hall, Englewood Cliffs, NJ.

Mintzberg H. & Waters J.A. (1985) Of strategies, deliberate and emergent. *Strategic Management Journal,* **6**.

MISRC/McGraw-Hill (1986) *1986 Directory of Management Information Systems Faculty.* McGraw-Hill, New York.

Morgan B.J.T. (1984) *Elements of Simulation.* Chapman & Hall, London.

Morgan G. (1980) Paradigms, metaphors and puzzle solving in organization theory. *Administrative Science Quarterly,* **25**, December, pp. 605–622.

Morgan G. (1986) *Images of Organization.* Sage, Beverley Hills.

Mulkay M. (1979) *Science and the Sociology of Knowledge.* George Allen & Unwin, London.

Mumford E. (1983) *Designing Human Systems – the ETHICS Method.* Manchester Business School, Manchester.

Mumford E., Hirschheim R.A., Fitzgerald G. & Wood-Harper A.T. (Eds.) (1985) *Research Methods in Information Systems.* Proceedings of the IFIP WG 8.2 Colloquium, 1–3 September, 1984, Manchester Business School, Elsevier, Amsterdam.

Naisbitt J. (1982) *Megatrends.* Warner Books, New York.

Narin F. (1976) *Evaluative Bibliometrics: The use of publication and citation analysis in the evaluation of scientific activity.* National Science Foundation, NTIS PB#, pp. 252–339.

Nilles J. (1984) Microfutures. In R.D. Galliers, *et al.* (1984), *op cit.*

Nilles J., Mohrman A. (Jr.) & El Sawy O.A. (1983) *The Strategic Impact of Information Technologies on Managerial Work: Prospectus for a Study* (F-52), Center for Futures Research, University of Southern California, September.

Nissen H-E., Klein H.K. & Hirschheim R. (Eds.) (1991) *Information Systems Research: Contemporary Approaches & Emergent Traditions.* North-Holland, Amsterdam.

Nolan R.L. (1979) Managing the crises in data processing. *Harvard Business Review,* **57**, 2, pp. 115–126.

Nolan R.L. & Wetherbe J.C. (1980) Towards a comprehensive framework for MIS research. *MIS Quarterly,* **4**, 2, June, pp. 1–19.

Norman D.A. (1980) Twelve issues for cognitive science. *Cognitive Science,* **4**, 1.

Nunamaker J.F. (Ed.) (1990) *Decision Support Systems and Knowledge Based Systems.* Proceedings of the Twenty-Third Annual Hawaii International Conference on Systems Sciences, IEEE Computer Society Press.

Payne R. (1976) Truisms in organisations behaviour. In *Interpersonal Development.* Ed. by F. Massarik, Karger, Basel.

Perrow C. (1973) The short and glorious history of organisational theory. *Organisational Dynamics*, Summer.

Pettigrew A.M. (1983) Contextualist Research: A Natural Way to Link Theory and Practice, *Proceedings: Conference on Conducting Research with Theory and Practice in Mind*. Center for Effective Organizations, University of Southern California, November. Also in Mumford, *et al.* (1985), *op cit.*, pp. 53–78.

Pettigrew A.M. (1985) Contextualist research and the study of organisational change processes. In *Doing Research that is Useful for Theory and Practice*. Ed. by E. Lawler & S. Fransico, Jossey-Bass, San Francisco.

Peters T.J. & Waterman R.H. (1982) *In Search of Excellence*. Harper and Row, New York.

Phillips L. (1989) People-centred group decision support. In *Knowledge-Based Management Support Systems*. Ed. by G.I. Doukidis, F.F. Land & G. Miller, Ellis Horwood, London.

Phillips E.M. & Pugh D.S. (1987) *How to Get a PhD: Managing the Peaks and Troughs of Research*. Open University Press, Milton Keynes.

Piaget J. (1967) Les Mèthodes de l'épistémologie. In *Logique et Connaissance Scientifique*. Ed. by J. Piaget, Gallimard, Paris.

Pinch T. (1984) Book review of *The Intellectual and Social Organization of the Sciences* by R. Whitley. *Sociology*, **19**, 4, pp. 651–653.

Polanyi M. (1958) *Personal Knowledge: Toward a Post-Critical Philosophy*. University of Chicago Press, Chicago.

Polkinghorne D. (1983) *Methodology for the Human Sciences: Systems of Inquiry*. State University of New York, Albany.

Pondy L.R. & Mitroff I.I. (1979) Beyond open systems models of organisation. In *Research in Organisational Behaviour*, Vol. 1. Ed. by L. Cummings & B. Staw, JAI Press, Greenwich, Conn., pp. 3–39.

Popper K.R. (1959) *The Logic of Scientific Discovery*. Harper Torchbook, London.

Popper K.R. (1963) *Conjectures and Refutations*. Routledge and Kegan Paul, London.

Popper K.R. (1972) *Objective Knowledge: An Evolutionary Approach*. Clarendon Press, Oxford.

Porter M.E. (1980) *Competitive Strategy*. Free Press, New York.

Rao K.V., Huff F.P. & Davis G.B. (1987) Critical issues in the management of information systems: a comparison of Singapore and the USA. *Information Technology*, **1**, 3, pp. 11–19.

Reason P. & Rowan J. (Eds.) (1981) *Human Inquiry: A Sourcebook of New Paradigm Research*. Wiley, Chichester.

Ritzer G. (1975) *Sociology: A Multiple Paradigm Science*. Allyn and Bacon, Boston.

Robey D. (1983) Cognitive style and DSS designs: a comment on Huber's paper. *Management Science*, **29**, 5, May, pp. 580–582.

Rockart J.F., Ball L. & Bullen C.V. (1982) The Future role of the information systems executive. *MIS Quarterly*, **6** (special issue), pp. 1–14.

Schneiderman B. (1978) Improving the human factors aspect of database interactions. *ACM Transactions on Database Systems*, **3**, pp. 417–439.

Scruton R. (1984) *A Short History of Modern Philosophy: from Descartes to Wittgenstein*. ARK Paperbacks, Routledge and Kegan Paul, London.

Shannon C.E. & Weaver W. (1949) *The Mathematical Theory of Communications*. University of Illinois Press, Chicago.

Siegel S. (1956) *Nonparametric Statistics for Behavior Sciences*. McGraw-Hill, New York.

Simon H.A. (1960) *The New Science of Management Decision*. Harper and Row, New York.

Simon H.A. (1978) Rationality as Process and as Product of Thought. *American Economic Review*, **66**(2), pp. 1–16.

Snyder P. (1978) *Toward One Science: The Convergence of Traditions*. St. Martin's Press, New York.

Spencer L. & Dale A. (1979) Integration and Regulation in Organizations: A Contextual Approach. *Sociological Review*, **27**(4), pp. 479–702.

Stamper R. (1974) *Information in Business and Administrative Systems*. Wiley, Chichester.

Stegmüller W. (1976) *The Structure and Dynamics of Theories*. Springer-Verlag, New York.

Suppe F. (1974) The search for philosophical understanding of scientific theories. In *The Structure of Scientific Theories*. Ed. by F. Suppe. University of Illinois Press, Urbana. (2nd edition: 1977).

Swanson E.B. *One Hundred and One References for Information Systems Research*. Information Systems Working Paper #2-91, Anderson Graduate School of Management, UCLA, Los Angeles, Ca., May.

The Western Australian (1989) Dawkins' deregulation 'a farce', 24th May, p. 13.

Toulmin S. (1953) *The Philosophy of Science: An Introduction*. Hutchinson, London.

Toulmin S. (1972) *Human Understanding: The Collective Use and Evolution of Concepts*. Princeton University Press, Princeton, NJ.

Tricker R.I. (1969) *Management Information Systems – an Annotated Bibliography*. The Institute of Chartered Accountants in England and Wales, London.

Turner J.A. (1980) Improving the quality of information systems research.

Proceedings of the First International Conference on Information Systems. Philadelphia, pp. 91–97.

Van de Wall M. (1975) Utilization and methodology of applied social research. *Journal of Applied Behavioral Science*, 1, pp. 14–38.

Van Gigch J.P. & Pipino L.L. In search of a paradigm for the discipline of information systems. *Future Computer Systems*, 1, 1, 1986, pp. 71–97.

Van Horn R.L. (1973) Empirical studies on management information systems. *Database*, 5, pp. 172–180.

Vickers G. (1980) Education in Systems Thinking. *Journal of Applied Systems Analysis*, 7, pp. 3–10.

Vitalari N.P. (1985) The Need for Longitudinal Designs in the Study of Computing Environments. In Mumford, *et al.* (1985), *op cit.*, pp. 243–265.

Vogel D.R. & Wetherbe J. (1984) MIS Research: A Profile of Leading Journals and Universities. *Data Base*, 16, 1, Fall, pp. 3–14.

Wasserman A. (1980) Software tools and the user software engineering project. *Laboratory of Medical Information Science*, #46, University of California, San Fransisco.

Wasserman A. (1982) The user software engineering methodology – an overview. In *Information Systems Design Methodologies – a Comparative Review.* Ed. by T. Olle, H. Sol & A. Verreijn Stuart, North-Holland, Amsterdam.

Watson R.T. (1989) Key issues in information systems management: an Australian perspective – 1988. *Australian Computer Journal*, 21, 2, August 1989, pp. 118–29.

Weber R. (1985) *Toward a theory of artifacts: a paradigmatic base for information systems research.* Working Paper, University of Queensland, Australia.

Weick K.E. (1984) Theoretical assumptions and research methodology selection. In F.W. McFarlan (1984) *op cit.*, pp. 237–242.

Whisler T.L. (1967) The impact of information technology on organizational control. In *The Impact of Computers on Management.* Ed. by C.A. Meyers, MIT Press, Cambridge, Mass.

White K.B. (1985) Perceptions and Deceptions: Issues for Information Systems Research. In Mumford, *et al.* (1985), *op cit.* pp. 237–242.

Whitley R. (1974) Cognitive and social institutionalization of scientific specialities and research areas. In *Social Processes of Scientific Development.* Ed. by R. Whitley, Routledge and Kegan Paul, London.

Whitley R. (1975) Components of scientific activities, their characteristics and institutionalization in specialties and research areas: a framework for the comparative analysis of scientific developments. In *Determinants and Con-*

trols of Scientific Development (vol. 10). Ed. by K.D. Knorr, H. Strasser & H.G. Zilian, Reidel, Dordrecht, pp. 37–73.

Whitley R. (1982) The establishment and structure of the sciences as reputational organizations. In *Scientific Establishments and Hierarchies*. Ed. by N. Elias, H. Martins & R. Whitley, Reidel, Dordrecht, pp. 313–357.

Whitley R. (1984a) *The Intellectual and Social Organization of the Sciences*. Clarendon Press, Oxford.

Whitley R. (1984b) The development of management studies as a fragmented adhocracy. *Soc. Sci. Inf.*, **23**, 4/5, Sage, London, pp. 775–818.

Whitley R. (1985) The transformation of business finance into financial economics: the roles of academic expansion and changes in US capital markets. Working Paper, Manchester Business School, Manchester.

Whitley R. (1986) Knowledge production, vocational training and professional skills in the administrative sciences. In *Séminaire Alfred Houle*. Faculté des sciences de l'administration. Université Laval, Québec.

Whitley R. (1987) The management sciences and managerial skills, Working Paper, Manchester Business School, Manchester.

Wiener N. (1948) *Cybernetics*. MIT Press, Cambridge, Mass.

Wilensky H.L. (1967) *Organizational Intelligence – Knowledge and Policy in Government and Industry*. Basic Books, New York.

Winch P. (1958) *The Idea of a Social Science*. Routledge and Kegan Paul, London.

Winograd T. & Flores C. (1987) *Understanding Computers and Cognition*, Ablex, Addison-Wesley, Reading, Mass.

Wood-Harper A.T. (1985) Research Methods in Information Systems: Using Action Research. In Mumford, *et al.* (1985), *op cit.*, pp. 169–191.

Yearley, S. (1986) Book review of *The Intellectual and Social Organisation of the Sciences* by R. Whitley. *Sociology Review*, **34**, 3, August, pp. 724–726.

Name Index

Subject Index